IN THE REALM OF PLEASURE

IN THE
REALM
OF
PLEASURE

VON STERNBERG, DIETRICH, AND THE MASOCHISTIC AESTHETIC

Gaylyn Studlar

University of Illinois Press
Urbana and Chicago

Society for Cinema Studies annual dissertation
award winner.

Publication of this work was supported in part by a grant
from the Andrew W. Mellon Foundation.

This book is printed on acid-free paper.

Library of Congress Cataloging-in-Publication Data

Studlar, Gaylyn.
  In the realm of pleasure.

  Includes index.
  1. Masochism in motion pictures.   2. Motion
pictures—United States—Aesthetics. 3. Von Sternberg,
Josef, 1894–1969—Criticism and interpretation.
4. Dietrich, Marlene—Criticism and interpretation.
5. Paramount Pictures Corporation.   6. Women in motion
pictures.   7. Feminism and motion pictures.   8. Motion
picture audiences—Psychology.   9. Psychoanalysis and
culture.   I. Title.
PN1995.9.M38S78   1988   791.43'01   87-35738
ISBN 0-252-01536-3 (alk. paper)

For C.A.G.

"Venus in Furs!" I cried, pointing at the picture.
"That is how I saw her in my dream."
"I, too," said Severin, "but I was dreaming with my eyes open."
—Leopold von Sacher-Masoch, *Venus in Furs*

It is a strange picture, he said, and a strange sort of prisoner.
—Plato, *The Republic*

Contents

Acknowledgments

In the process of writing this book, I realized that inclusion in the Acknowledgments would be a woefully inadequate gesture to extend to those who gave their time and effort in helping me bring this work to fruition. Nevertheless, I hope that in doing so I in some measure demonstrate the appreciation I feel.

I am very much indebted to Beverle Houston, Peter Lehman, Linda Williams, John Belton, and John Fell, who read the manuscript at various stages of its development and provided suggestions that contributed immensely to the book's final form. I am grateful as well to Peter Manning, who taught me the necessity of tough criticism (against my will, I might add) and not only introduced me to the work of Margaret Mahler but saved me from many foolish errors. Thanks also to Joanna Hitchcock, whose early and enthusiastic support of the manuscript meant a great deal to me.

My gratitude extends to family, friends, and colleagues who gave personal and professional encouragement during the best and worst of times. To Elvern and Emil Barton, Grace and Frank Goodwin, Constance Goodwin, Richard Jewell, Don Studlar, Gerry Veeder, Karen and Mark Wall, and Mark Williams, I offer thanks. I must also acknowledge Ned Comstock of the University of Southern California Archives of the Performing Arts and Janet Lorenz for their help in obtaining photographic materials.

Finally, I am most indebted to Marsha Kinder, who changed the way I view film—and film theory. This book literally would not exist without her guidance, encouragement, and model of scholarly excellence.

Introduction

Why is film pleasurable? Within contemporary film studies, the question of why and how film produces pleasure for its audience has influenced much of the field's theoretical discussion. The production of spectatorial pleasure is a complex process, but the link between cinematic pleasure and sexuality is obvious. From its earliest beginnings, the pleasures of the moving picture show were never entirely respectable. Initially based on the privatized looking of the "peep show" Kinetoscope, cinematic spectating has always been a suspect pastime. Frequently unredeemed by even a veneer of high-art pretensions and, worst of all, hidden by darkness, film has always posed the threat of slipping from harmless, publicly sanctioned escapism into the realm of forbidden pleasure, of pure, unbridled sexual looking.

If the cinema's pleasures are sexually charged, they cannot be magically insulated from the power relations inscribed in patriarchal culture's definition of sexuality and sexual difference. It is logical, then, that issues of pleasure have been of particular interest to feminist film theory. In its initial phase in the 1970s, feminist film criticism was most often limited to an inquiry into Hollywood's representation of women. Moving beyond rather naive sociological approaches that characterized its earliest phase, feminist film theory has embraced psychoanalysis as a key methodological tool for examining the medium within a poststructuralist framework.[1] In her useful survey article, "The Problem of Sexual Difference and Identity," Janet Walker has remarked on the ways in which contemporary feminist film theory has appropriated psychoanalysis. She locates three fundamental uses: investigating women's patriarchal oppression in classical narrative cinema; exploring the meaning of femininity and its expression in cinema; and an application that "still has not been satisfactorily applied to the study of film. . . ." In this third approach, says Walker, psychoanalysis would be employed to critique "the limitations of psychoanalysis as used in the other two approaches" so that feminist film theory might formulate a model of female spectatorship beyond a purely negative field, ". . . as neither absent, nor totally repressed or punished."[2]

My own poststructuralist appropriation of psychoanalysis uses all three levels of analysis to explore questions of visual pleasure and sexual difference. However, it is the third level of which Walker speaks, the level of critique and reconceptualization of the spectating subject, that is most crucial to the overarching goals of this book. My primary objective is to offer a psychoanalytic-semiotic countertheory to psychoanalytic film theory that has conceptualized cinematic pleasure from the basis of Freudian and Lacanian psychoanalysis. I am concerned with redefining notions of feminine and masculine spectatorial pleasure in relation to both Hollywood cinema and a general level of cinematic experience. This is accomplished through a study of the pleasures afforded by a specific Hollywood textual system—that of the von Sternberg/Dietrich collaboration at Paramount.

My theory of cinematic pleasure constitutes a critique of the dominant modes of psychoanalytic film theory and an extended response to a line of feminist-psychoanalytic theory that rests, in large measure, on Laura Mulvey's "Visual Pleasure and Narrative Cinema."[3] Judith Mayne has written of this 1975 article: "It is only a slight exaggeration to say that most feminist film theory and criticism of the last decade has been a response, implicit or explicit, to the issues raised in Laura Mulvey's article: the centrality of the look, cinema as spectacle and narrative, psychoanalysis as a critical tool."[4] Building on Freud's castration theory and Lacan's account of the mirror phase, Mulvey asserts that desire is inscribed in the classical Hollywood cinema as an Oedipal, patriarchal desire which makes the woman the passive object of the male gaze. Pleasure is produced for a subject-spectator defined in terms of male psychic processes and psychological needs. Hollywood classical narrative norms are theorized as being sexually imbalanced between an active male protagonist who fuels the narrative and a passive female object who becomes the eroticized spectacle for the gaze of the male protagonist, the camera, and the spectator.[5]

Following Mulvey's lead, much of feminist film theory has accepted the premise that dominant narrative cinema's visual pleasures rest on male psychic mechanisms—fetishism, voyeurism, and scopophilia—which inscribe pleasurable (and power-laden) patterns of looking between spectator and screen.[6] This process reinforces patriarchal oppression in its representation of woman as sexual spectacle as it simultaneously excludes female spectators from a system of visual pleasures constructed to gratify the unconscious desire of one gender at the expense of the other.

Psychoanalytic theory following in the wake of Mulvey's article also regards the cinema as a privileged site of pleasures that are inextricably linked to the viewing subject's attainment of sexual and cultural identity within the patriarchy. In Lacanian theory, the mirror phase emergence of individual subjectivity is associated with pleasurable identificatory looking, while Freud's account of the castration complex also depends on a strategy of looking. In spite of the substantial contribution these theories have made to film scholarship, there has been a tendency in feminist work on film to accept these theories as "truth" and to ignore both their phallocentrism and the determinism that their prescriptive application often suggests.

Although I freely acknowledge my debt to psychoanalytic film theory, one of the key goals of this book is to analyze many of the psychoanalytic assumptions that have provided the foundation of feminist film theory's consideration of the role of sexual difference in spectatorial pleasure and to suggest new directions for understanding the interplay of spectatorship, gender, and identity formation. This book, then, is an overtly polemical intervention in contemporary film theory's approach to visual pleasure. The accepted theoretical boundaries of feminist film theory require scrutiny, less in terms of a negation than in the spirit of revisionism seeking to overcome impasses and oversights.

I believe a key oversight is the investigation of pleasures of male spectatorship that are beyond mastery and beyond the psychodynamics of the castration complex. In addition, a theoretical space must be created for a less deterministic account of women's response to classical narrative cinema. Although my primary project is to suggest answers to questions surrounding gender-differentiated spectatorship, I hope also to redress feminist theory's current neglect of sexually undifferentiated aspects of film reception.

I anchor my alternative theory of visual pleasure in a textual reading of the six films made by Josef von Sternberg and Marlene Dietrich at the Paramount studios during the 1930s: *Morocco, Blonde Venus, Dishonored, Shanghai Express, The Scarlet Empress,* and *The Devil Is a Woman.* I analyze multiple levels of textual operation in these films, including visual style and narrative structure, the construction of character, and the representation of sexual difference, to show how these films are informed by pleasures that cannot be accounted for in current theory. Out of an inductive approach to the films, a new psychoanalytic model emerges that is derived from Gilles Deleuze's *Masochism: An Interpretation of Coldness and Cruelty*.[7]

Originally condemned and later praised for their heady visual extremism, ironically inflated melodrama, and darkly exotic eroticism, the von Sternberg/Dietrich films have often been linked obliquely to masochism, though this connection has never been fully explored. I contend that masochism, redefined from Deleuze's revisionary psychoanalytic study, functions as the principal formal and psychoanalytic element in determining the multiple pleasures of the von Sternberg/ Dietrich texts—texts that can be said to exemplify a *masochistic aesthetic*. I further argue that the importance of masochism to psychoanalytic film theory extends beyond the close reading of a single film or a specific textual system and applies to cinematic pleasure in general.

My purpose in choosing the von Sternberg/Dietrich Paramount films for analysis is multivalent. Originally, the book's critical parameters were set by my goal of illuminating the films' visual style, which Bill Nichols has noted remains "poorly examined."[8] The von Sternberg/Dietrich films have by no means been critically neglected, but many approaches to von Sternberg have been limited to consideration of a single film, while studies of a broader scope seem to have addressed inadequately the films' relevance to feminist inquiry and their stylistic nuances. As this book evolved, it became clear that these films raised as many theoretical questions as critical/analytic ones. The revised thesis came to be, How would an understanding of these complex films alter our current notions of cinematic pleasure generally?

When first released, the von Sternberg/Dietrich Paramount films often garnered less than enthusiastic response. In 1934, B. G. Braver-Mann railed against von Sternberg as "a director who concentrates on surface effects, who emphasizes the externals of film mechanics in a most inarticulate manner and represents his own delirious fancies as real life."[9] In 1948, Richard Griffith confidently echoed the earlier critical consensus by dismissing von Sternberg's films as "trash dressed up as art."[10] However, with the advent of auteurist criticism, von Sternberg's foregrounding of style in a cinema of sublime visual beauty, dreamlike chiaroscuro, and stifling decorative excess could evoke but one response: Andrew Sarris placed von Sternberg in the rarefied atmosphere of his innermost circle of select auteurs who stamped their films with their own personal vision.[11]

In the context of the postmodernist critique of realism, the von Sternberg/Dietrich films have become the subject of yet another re-

evaluation, one less unified in opinion than either contemporary response to the films or the first wave of American auteurist criticism.
The films have been defined as everything from "emotional autobiography . . . in which eroticism . . . is a pretext for objectifying
pesonal fantasies" to *Cahiers du Cinéma*'s declaration that von Sternberg's *Morocco* stands as the very exemplification of "erotic fiction . . .
entirely determined by the ideology."[12] The films have drawn attention from critics employing myriad methodologies who use the films to
illustrate diverse theoretical vantage points. Consequently, the von
Sternberg/Dietrich Paramount films offer themselves as a prime case
study for a fusion of theoretical inquiry and critical analysis, as much
for the critical and theoretical discussion generated by the films as for
the films themselves.

The fact that I have chosen to analyze only the von Sternberg
American films that star Marlene Dietrich is also significant in light of
current feminist discourse.[13] No longer dismissed as the passive object
of von Sternberg's Svengali-like machinations, Dietrich is frequently
mentioned as an actress whose screen presence raises questions about
women's representation in Hollywood cinema.[14] She has also acquired
her own cult following of male and female, straight and gay admirers.
The diverse nature of this group suggests that many possible paths of
pleasure can be charted across Dietrich as a signifying star image and
across von Sternberg's films as star vehicles.

Throughout the book I simultaneously proceed on analytic and
theoretical levels in order to fully integrate textual considerations with
theoretical ones. In the first chapter I present an overview of theories
of masochism and explain the chief source of my model, Deleuze's
mother-centered theory of masochism. I discuss the difference between masochism and sadism as psychoanalytic entities and define the
masochistic aesthetic in comparative reference to the novels of the
Marquis de Sade and Leopold von Sacher-Masoch. I also discuss the interdependence of the formal structures of the masochistic text and
its psychodynamics in order to set the stage for later discussion of
spectatorial positioning. I then explore how the unique intersection of
masochism and fantasy raises questions concerning the relationship
of masochistic psychic structures to the cinematic process. I argue
that the psychic mechanisms that feminist film theory has associated
with the production of filmic pleasure must be reevaluated within the
context of the masochistic aesthetic's formal system and masochism's
pre-Oedipally influenced psychodynamics.

In chapter 2, I take up the issue of masochism's relevance to visual
pleasure. The question underlying this chapter is: How does film as

a spectatorial process resemble the mechanisms of perversion in general and masochism specifically? Here I establish my central premise, that the psychic processes and pleasures engaged by the cinema more closely resemble those of masochism than the sadistic, Oedipal pleasures commonly associated in psychoanalytic film theory with visual pleasure. I discuss cinematic pleasure's link to disavowal, fetishism, voyeurism, and scopophilia as I reconsider their etiology and function in light of the emphasis on pre-Oedipality by Deleuze and modern object relations theory. Applying the masochistic model, I show the ways in which the von Sternberg/Dietrich films articulate configurations of desire and identification that may encourage male subject-spectator positions that do not adhere to models of cinematic pleasure based on castration fear, Oedipal desire, and a sadistic voyeurism. I also consider the role of fetishism and scopophilia in the creation of an eroticized spectatorial position for women.

In chapter 3, I deal with the films' incorporation of masochistic fantasies and enunciation of masochistic desire. To ground a discussion of character function and masochistic performance within the larger context of shifting patterns of spectatorial identification and desire, I analyze how the structure of the gaze is inscribed within the von Sternberg/Dietrich Paramount films. I also examine the films' self-reflexive representation of woman and the relevance of masochistic masquerade to a consideration of female subjectivity.

Chapter 4 addresses the theoretical issues raised by the films' creation of a *masochistic heterocosm*. In this chapter I consider how the "illusion and delusion" of these self-consciously illusionistic texts can be used to reflect on classical theory's notion of iconicity and revise current theory's consideration of the iconic sign.[15] From a theoretical position informed by the work of Charles Sanders Peirce, I contend that the von Sternberg/Dietrich films present the spectator with a self-reflexive, anti-illusionary discourse. This iconic discourse reflects the formal requirements of masochism and challenges many current ideas regarding classical narrative's illusionary realism. I relate iconicity in filmic signification to other iconic systems, such as the iconic algorithms of dream, to show why the von Sternberg/Dietrich films cannot be understood from the perspective of a linguistically based (semiological) model of filmic signification.

Chapter 5 addresses questions of narrativity and spectacle. The argument dominating this chapter is that the von Sternberg/Dietrich films problematize the Oedipal family romance structure often assumed to be the norm for classical narrative cinema. Using a close textual analysis of *Blonde Venus* as my focal point, I discuss masochism's disruption of the conventions of classical narrative continuity to give voice to masochism's suspended desire. This leads to an examination of the ways in which a study of the formal strategies of the masochistic aesthetic may revise current narrative theory.

In chapter 6, I develop an extended analysis of metaphor and synesthesia as visual figures of cinematic organization in the von Sternberg/Dietrich films. I demonstrate the connection between these structuring devices and masochism's psychodynamics and then show how they relate to iconicity and narrative theory's considerations of the role of the image.

Chapter 7 is a continuation of the previous chapter's concerns. Here I approach the von Sternberg/Dietrich films' use of auditory and kinesthetic aspects of iconicity as defined in the work of Gregory Bateson.[16] In this chapter I also elaborate on the relationship between iconic communication and areas of concern that have emerged in recent discussions of filmic representation of sexual difference, including the treatment of space and performance signs.

Finally, chapter 8 addresses masochism's link to the pleasures of the cinematic apparatus, the technologically based aspect of film's appeal to the unconscious. The aim of this chapter is to show how a Deleuzian-based theory of masochism converges with other theorists' conceptualizations of cinema as a *dream screen* phenomenon to reveal a range of spectatorial pleasures that are not always sexually differentiated or informed by the pleasure of mastery. The psychoanalytic intricacies of the spectator's disavowing relationship to the cinema are discussed with close attention to the influence of the pre-Oedipal relationship with the mother on our desire for the cinema and its pleasures.

There is a certain amount of irony in writing a theoretically oriented study of film pleasure, for the "readerly" unpleasure of psychoanalytic theoretical discourse *on* film is frequently every bit as predictable as visual pleasure *in* film. Consequently, I have attempted to present my arguments in the clearest language possible to avoid the unpleasure often encountered in reading contemporary film theory. I also wish to make this book accessible to a wide number of readers who may not be schooled in feminist-psychoanalytic film theory but who are interested in von Sternberg's films, Dietrich's career, or in feminist criticism and practice outside the confines of film studies.

Although I challenge what can only be regarded as the dominant mode of feminist-psychoanalytic film theory, this book is, nevertheless, a reaffirmation of the theoretical knowledge and the methodological innovation that feminist approaches have brought to cinema studies. I also seek to reaffirm the power of film as a phenomenological experience, engaging us in pleasures that defy the limits of our most cherished assumptions and that may suggest possible avenues of resistance and rebellion to patriarchal imperatives binding women—and men—in their tenacious and repressive hold.

CHAPTER ONE

The Masochistic Aesthetic:
Form and Fantasy

> Fundamentally masochism is neither material nor moral,
> but essentially formal.
>
> —Gilles Deleuze

To study the relationship between masochism, film, and visual pleasure requires an initial examination of the definition of masochism as a perversion, the formal strategies of the literary prototype of the masochistic text, and the underlying psychoanalytic factors in its production. The purpose of considering a perversion such as masochism in relation to film texts is not to encourage biographical speculation regarding Josef von Sternberg; such a nosographic approach presents well-charted pitfalls.[1] Rather, my interest is in discovering the link between masochism and film in two related ways: (1) the creation of a *masochistic aesthetic* as a specific film style offering certain narrative and visual strategies as well as textual pleasures; and (2) masochism's relevance to spectatorial pleasures that extend beyond a single text or an aesthetic to embrace the psychic processes engaged by the cinematic experience in general. Central to this thesis is my argument that cinematic pleasure is much closer to masochistic pleasure than to the sadistic, controlling pleasure commonly associated with spectatorship in modern film theory.

Chapter 2 will concentrate on masochism's link to visual pleasure; however, the notion of a masochistic aesthetic requires preliminary explanation to clarify its meaning and provide a rationale for exploring its filmic manifestation. Although my model is derived primarily from Gilles Deleuze's *Masochism: An Interpretation of Coldness and Cruelty,* I also draw heavily upon contemporary psychoanalytic theory and clinical research to expand and enrich Deleuze's theory.[2] In support of my hypothesis, I emphasize the agreement between theories sometimes thought to be oppositional. For example, the Freudian drive/structure instinct model of development, in which the object is a function of instinct, is often regarded as irreconcilable with modern object relations theory, which focuses on developmental relations and the influence of the object on the psychoanalytic subject. My own model for using this dual approach is the work of Margaret Mahler, whose integration of drive theory with infantile object relations is referred to directly in chapter 8.[3] By emphasizing the shared similarities, not the differences, between theoretical and clinical approaches, I am consciously attempting a recognition of the multivalence rather than the singularity of psychoanalytic determinants. My methodology, therefore, is less eclectic than heuristic in intent.

Masochism: Defining the Perversion

The implications of perversion are much greater than the relationship of infantile sexuality to adult behavior might first seem to imply. Perversion relates to fantasy, to the dynamics of power in a patriarchy, and to pleasurable looking. Masochism's categorization as a perversion is important to a discussion of cinematic spectatorship that has been theorized as depending upon the same psychological mechanisms operative in actual pathological examples of perversion, such as fetishistic disavowal. Masochism's classification as a perversion is perhaps the single aspect of its structure that has not been disputed. Although Freud once succinctly defined masochism as the "lust of pain," the perversion has long been recognized as an extremely complex theoretical and clinical entity.[4]

The *vita sexualis* of masochism was named for German author Leopold von Sacher-Masoch by Richard von Krafft-Ebing in his famous 1886 study on sexual aberration, *Psychopathia Sexualis*.[5] Krafft-Ebing set the precedent of associating masochism with sadism in his definition of the former as "the opposite of sadism . . . the wish to suffer pain and be subjected to force." He concluded that masochism and sadism were so closely related that the analogy with sadism "alone is sufficient to establish the purely psychical character of masochism."[6] Krafft-Ebing's confident formulation of a unified sadomasochism depended upon two underlying assumptions: the simple reversal of active and passive positions as the distinguishing difference between the two perversions and masochism's status as a pathological exaggeration of natural feminine traits.[7] Many of his dubiously founded concepts would be perpetuated in Freud's earliest studies on the subject.

Like Krafft-Ebing, Freud affirmed the formulation of a sado-masochistic symptomatology. He supplemented the complementary association of sadism with masochism in his pairing of libidinal manifestations of the scopic drive: scopophilia and its opposite, exhibitionism. Scopophilia, like sadism, was directed toward another person; exhibitionism turned scopophilia toward the subject's own body. With its passive aim, exhibitionism required someone else to fill the active role of looking. Freud believed that the passive/active transitions of the scopophilic instinct were very much on the order of those turning sadism into masochism without a change in the content of the instinct.[8]

Freud dealt with the question of masochism's etiology and structure in several essays, including "Three Essays on the Theory of Sexuality" (1905), "Instincts and Their Vicissitudes" (1915), "A Child Is Being Beaten" (1919), and "The Economic Problem in Masochism" (1924).[9] He looked upon masochism, with its self-punishing ego activity, as a tremendous danger to humanity, much more so than sadism because the former paralyzed the normal functioning of the pleasure principle as "the watchman of our lives."[10] As Freud attempted to come to terms with the paradoxical ability of the masochist to enjoy pain in the pursuit of pleasure, his theory of masochism underwent considerable revision, but he never deviated from affirming Oedipal conflict as the perversion's impetus. Freud ultimately did admit that, in spite of what he felt was his solution for many of masochism's theoretical dilemmas, the perversion's genesis and the function of pain in its dynamic remained a mystery to him.[11]

It is significant that Freud originally interpreted masochism as a by-product of sadism, as a secondary phenomenon arising from a sadistic impulse brought to bear on the subject's ego. In "Three Essays on the Theory of Sexuality," Freud's early view on the sadomasochistic construct continued to affirm Krafft-Ebing's insistence on the active/passive reversal mechanism as the crucial difference between sadism and masochism. Freud assumed that the masochist was first a sadist, or at the very least experienced a sadistic fantasy. As the passive opposite of sadism, masochism reflected a change in aim (passive or active) and object (self or other) but not in the *content* of the instinct, as he had theorized for love/hate ambivalence.[12]

Freud reaffirmed the reversal of the primary sadistic instinct into masochism in "Instincts and Their Vicissitudes."[13] In this essay, he also approached masochism's most perplexing characteristic: the search for pleasure derived from pain. He concluded that the instinctual goal of pleasure could not change, only the aim and the object. The person's enjoyment depended upon a double identification with torturer and victim. Freud believed the masochist first experienced a sadistic fantasy; the sadist recognized pain as sexually pleasurable and then "masochistically" enjoyed the pain of his or her victim. Logically, this view would seem to suggest a primary masochism, but Freud was not yet ready to recognize the existence of such a phenomenon.[14]

In 1919, Freud published his first major clinical study of sadistic and masochistic fantasies, "A Child Is Being Beaten." With this essay he established the contextual importance of perverse childhood fantasies indicative of an infantile sexual fixation. The repression of fantasies was typical in a neurosis; but in a true perversion, conscious fantasies were not only tolerated but welcomed. Since these fantasies were acted out, perversion reflected a failure of defensive or repressive mechanisms.[15] Conversely, Freud defined neurosis as the "negative of perversion."[16] "Perversion," he said, was "an original and universal disposition of the human sexual instinct."[17] The normal mode of childhood sexuality was polymorphous perversity, which became pathological in adult life only when it replaced genital sexuality instead of coexisting with it.

In "A Child Is Being Beaten," Freud outlined the transformation of the "sadomasochistic" fantasies of a limited number of male and female subjects diagnosed as obsessional neurotics.[18] Guilt transformed the male subject's desire for the mother into an incestuous, homosexual wish for the father. Being beaten by the father substituted for castration by him (the punishment for desiring the mother). In acquiring "libidinal excitation," punishment also became "a regressive substitute" for Oedipal desire. In Freud's view, the curious connection between suffering and sexual excitement formed "the essence of masochism."[19] The mother as the punishing figure in the subject's conscious fantasy served to disguise the father and the fantasies' homosexual implications. The male subject's passive position and identification with the female (in coitus, in giving birth) were merely maneuvers to placate the father and gain his love.[20]

"The Economic Problem in Masochism" is notable because it demonstrates Freud's increasingly abstract approach to solving the clinical and theoretical problems of masochism. Here, he introduced the concept of *primary masochism* as a drive with its origin in Thanatos —the Death Instinct. Thanatos was an abstraction defined as the organism's tendency to return to stasis or nothingness. Like its opposite, Eros, it was never found in a pure form. Both sadism and masochism took their energy from Thanatos, but masochism was now defined as a separate, independent primary instinct. In primary masochism the Death Instinct was retained in the libido; in primary sadism it was projected outward.[21]

Although Freud had always maintained a distinction between

"masochism proper" and "sadism proper," he was continually drawn back into the supposition of the sadomasochistic duality.[22] Part of the force for affirming this theoretical convergence of the perversions is found in his hypothesis that sadism and masochism shared similar or identical superego/ego activity. In masochism, the ego became the victim of the "heightened sadism of the superego."[23]

In "The Economic Problem in Masochism," Freud also set about delineating three types of masochism: *erotogenic* (eliciting sexual excitement), *moral* (desexualized but still erotically gratifying to the libido), and *feminine*. He characterized feminine masochism as the most prevalent and easily distinguishable form. In feminine masochism the male subject evidenced a partial identification with the mother; he wished to assume a passive position in coitus and to give birth. As in "A Child Is Being Beaten," Freud continued his refusal to consider the mother's role in the formation of masochistic fantasies. He accounted for the male's identification with the mother and the denial of male genital sexuality through circuitous means: the apparent centrality of the mother was explained as the logical outcome of the child's relationship with the father.[24]

Deleuze and the Problem of Masochism

Deleuze boldly challenges Freud's father-centered construct of masochism as an expression of Oedipal conflicts. He engages in what he calls a "deductive" psychoanalysis based on an examination of the novels of masochism's namesake, Leopold von Sacher-Masoch.[25] Deleuze's primary goal in *Masochism* is to reintegrate the clinical/psychoanalytic concept of masochism with the literary texts that served as the original models for the psychoanalytic concepts. By attaching the Marquis de Sade's and Sacher-Masoch's names to distinct perversions, he says, psychoanalysis took "a major linguistic and semiological step" in that "*a proper name is made to connote signs.*"[26]

Deleuze's second major goal is to correct the misconceived notion of a sadomasochistic entity. He considers sadomasochism to be a semiological and clinical impossibility, a confusion of the two perversions' qualitative differences and formal characteristics: "As soon as we read Masoch we become aware that his universe has nothing to do with that of Sade. . . . We must take an entirely different approach, the *literary approach*, since it is from literature that stem the original definitions of sadism and masochism. . . . In place of a dialectic which all too readily perceives the link between opposites, we should aim for a critical and clinical appraisal able to reveal the truly differential mechanisms as well as the artistic originalities."[27] If qualitative differences are disregarded and only the pain-pleasure content considered, then sadism and masochism might well be regarded as complementary. Deleuze shows that to correctly define masochism as a distinct clinical syndrome or as an aesthetic, its formal patterns must be recognized as indicative of a unique underlying psychoanalytic structure.[28]

Deleuze considers masochism to be a phenomenology of experience that reaches far beyond the limited definition of a perverse sexuality. Similarly, the masochistic aesthetic extends beyond the purely clinical realm into the arena of language, artistic form, narrativity, and production of textual pleasure. Emerging as a distinct artistic discourse, the masochistic aesthetic structures unconscious infantile sexual conflicts, conscious fantasies, and adult experience into a form that is not only a measure of the influence of early developmental stages but also a register of the transformative power of the creative process.

To suggest that masochism governs Sacher-Masoch's novels or, as I assert, von Sternberg's films, is to maintain a thesis akin to the "regression-progression" idea advanced by Heinz Hartmann and Ernst Kris in *Organization and Pathology of Thought*.[29] Regression and progression should not be viewed as polarities but as a part of the dynamic, creative process of combining exploratory forms with archaic, unconscious psychic conflict. In this mediation, artistic creation serves to point backward toward the repetition of a childhood mode of thinking, yet the new construct does not repeat the old conflicts of the past without transforming them. In the masochistic aesthetic, the interplay of wishes from the past and a current, creative mode of consciousness produce something more than a wish-fulfilling expression of an unmediated infantile fantasy. Instead, a complex dialectic between the conscious and the unconscious, the present and the past is formalized. Like dream, the artistic solution may also point to new avenues for the progressive exploration of adult life.[30]

Deleuze's literary approach to masochism challenges the sadomasochistic linkage as well as Freud's Oedipally dominated, father-centered theory of masochism. His conclusions concerning the perversion's etiology and psychodynamics have much in common with revisionary psychoanalytic theory and the findings of modern clinical research which focus on the developmental significance of pre-Oedipal life. Deleuze's most radical divergence from Freud's theory is his redefinition of the mother's role and location of the perversion's etiology within the oral stage, an earlier period of development than the anal/sadistic and phallic phases emphasized in Freud's studies.[31] Consequently, Deleuze's theory can be used to call attention to Freud's neglect of prephallic stages of life and his preoccupation with the paternal function in shaping psychosexual development. As a result of this theoretical preoccupation, Freud failed to adequately acknowledge or investigate the role of the mother as an active, independent, powerful, and even threatening figure.[32] Deleuze, in accordance with researchers such as Robert Stoller, Roy Schafer, Nancy Chodorow, and Janine Chasseguet-Smirgel, regards the mother's influence and her authority as major factors in the child's psychosexual development.[33] As the child matures, the pre-Oedipal perception of the mother as a strong, nurturing figure continues to be a crucial influence, in spite of the increasing importance of the father.

Deleuze regards the female in the male's masochistic fantasy as the loving inflictor of punishment, not the substitute for a hidden father. The mother, simultaneously love object and controlling agent, is the object of the child's ambivalence.[34] Whether due to an experience of real trauma, as Bernhard Berliner asserts, or to the narcissistic oral infant's own insatiability of demand, masochistic desire merges the plenitude of the mother with the subject's need for suffering.[35] For the masochist, the maternal figure represents a femininity "posited as lacking nothing."[36] She assumes her authority because of her own importance to the child, not, as Freud asserted, because she hides the father figure. Noteworthy also is Victor Smirnoff's assertion that masochistic suffering per se may well be secondary to the need to be dominated, to occupy a position of passivity, dependence, and submission.[37]

In his analysis of the novels of Sacher-Masoch, Deleuze focuses on the male as the fantasizing masochistic subject, although he insists that the female can assume the same position as the male in relation to the *oral mother*, the nurturing mother imago associated with the critical oral stage.[38] In defining masochism as a "search for submission," Daniel Lagache helps to clarify Deleuze's theory in relation to gender difference and the dynamics of masochistic fantasy. Lagache believes that the masochistic subject takes the position of the child in an alliance modeled directly on a parent/child relationship, while in sadism the subject occupies the position of the controlling parent.[39] His statement finds a precedent in Freud's comments on the masochistic tendency of wanting "to be treated like a little, helpless, dependent child, but especially like a naughty child."[40] We are reminded, however, of Freud's essay, "A Child Is Being Beaten," and his account of

perverse fantasies which would seem to preclude the facile assumption
that males and females automatically produce equivalent or parallel
fantasies. In spite of the differences established along gender lines
between the fantasies of Freud's obsessional subjects, they all shared
one thing in common: the subject never took the position of the parent or authority figure who punished.[41] Additionally, the pre-Oedipal
beginnings of masochism in the oral, that is, pregenital, stage, may
mean that sexual difference is unimportant to the perversion's basic
dynamics. In subsequent chapters I will address the issue of sexual
difference in respect to masochistic fantasy, spectatorial positioning,
and textual representation.

In Deleuze's construct, the mother becomes the familiar dual
symbol of creation and death who crystallizes infantile ambivalence
in the masochistic ideal of "coldness, soliticitude and death."[42] She is
the figure of the cold oral mother who represents the good mother
from the infantile stage of imagined dual unity or symbiosis between
mother and child. Bad mother traits are projected on this imago and
are then idealized. In a process that eliminates the father from the
symbolic order, the good oral mother assumes and transforms the
bad mother functions of other maternal imagos, such as the Oedipal
mother who is associated with sadistic elements, and the seductive
uterine mother who is connected in fantasy with prostitution. The
father's punishing superego and phallic sexuality are then symbolically
punished in the child-subject, who must expiate likeness to the father
and reject his law.[43]

The contradictions in masochism's mixture of pain and pleasure
are not easily explained, but the symbolic nature of punishment is
essential to understanding the structure of masochistic pleasure. The
masochist does not actually lust after pain, as Freud asserted; but, as
Theodor Reik observes in *Masochism in Modern Man,* the masochist always seeks pleasure. There is no reversal of aim. Pleasure is arrived
at "by another road, by a detour," since the masochist "submits voluntarily to punishment, suffering and humiliation, and thus has defiantly
purchased the right to enjoy the gratification denied before."[44]

The masochist's disavowal of phallic power calls for the suspension of orgasmic gratification and the conditioning of its arrival with
pain. This is the price paid for a mature genital sexuality that is at
odds with infantile desire. The suspension of orgasmic gratification
symbolically expels the father's genital likeness. Deleuze adamantly
rejects Freud's account of the formative role of guilt in the perversion. The child is not guilty, maintains Deleuze; rather, guilt rests

with the father, who comes between mother and child and whose likeness is found in the child. Masochistic guilt becomes a trickster's device, a subversive masquerade in which the child repudiates the father, the superego, and Oedipal guilt. "When guilt is experienced *masochistically*," says Deleuze, "it is already distorted, artificial and ostentatious."[45] The child's phallic inheritance is disavowed because it symbolically obstructs the desired symbiosis with the mother. Deleuze stops short of affirming the subject's identification with the mother, but the logic of that identification is widely supported in modern research on masochism. The child identifies with and also desires the mother in an inverted parallel of Freud's theory of masochism in which the son identifies with and ultimately desires the father.[46]

Deleuze's account of the disavowal of the child's phallic inheritance (on symbolic and physical levels) permits a theoretical shift away from Freud's emphasis on castration fear in the perversion. Freud considered masochism's tortures less cruel than those he observed in sadism. Masochistic punishment was a "symbolic substitute, lesser punishment for desire" than castration by the father.[47] Clinical studies have proven that masochism's punishments are not watered-down versions of sadistic ones, nor is the perversion's relation to the castration complex as simple as Freud theorized. In "A Case of Masochistic Perversion and an Outline of a Theory," Michael de M'Uzan deduces from clinical observation that the masochist "fears nothing, not even castration . . . [and] desires everything including castration which is within his grasp."[48] In *Masochism in Modern Man*, Reik parallels de M'Uzan with his own assertion that castration anxiety is not of major significance in the perversion.[49]

Deleuze also differs from Freud in his theorization of the superego/ego/id structure of masochism. He borrows from Lagache's theory of ego/superego splitting in his description of how masochistic gratification is obtained through suffering.[50] Deleuze believes masochism and sadism have entirely different superego/ego structures. In sadism, the ego is expelled, rejected as the superego achieves exclusive power in the father. The sadist overinvests in the father. Turning outward, the superego is directed against "external victims who take on the quality of the rejected ego."[51] In masochism, the ego is split. Finding its ideal ego in the mother, the narcissistic ego seeks to mystify the superego's repressive demands for pain, which becomes an empty signifier, the masquerade for guilt. The active pursuit of pain by the so-called passive masochist guarantees a pleasure temporarily suspended. Rituals of suffering show the masochist's contempt for the superego's expectation that punishment could prevent forbidden pleasure.[52] Masochism as an expression of the Death Instinct liberates the child from genital sexuality even as it liberates the ego from the superego.

Sade, Sacher-Masoch, and the Literary Prototype for the Masochistic Aesthetic

If Sade's writing is "structurally linked to crime and sex," as Roland Barthes has stated, then the masochistic aesthetic exemplified in Sacher-Masoch's novels and von Sternberg's films demonstrates formal and narrative patterns structurally linked to self-abasement and suspended desire.[53] Masochism tells its story through very precisely delimited means: fantasy, disavowal, fetishism, and suspense are its formal and psychoanalytic foundations. From his comparative literary analysis of Sacher-Masoch's novels with those of Sade, Deleuze concludes that Sade's intentions and language are completely at odds with those of Sacher-Masoch. He argues that the psychoanalytic determinants of the two perversions and their representative texts are entirely different. His theoretical account of masochism stands in direct contrast with Freud, who believed that sadism and masochism, even in their primary forms, shared similar superego/ego structuring and a common etiology in which Oedipal rivalry and castration fear were the formative elements.[54]

Out of the paradoxes of masochism as a perversion emerge the dialectical structure of the aesthetic: imaginative excess balanced against the limitations of external reality, the tragedy of an obsessional desire disavowed through irony, ritualized torture contrasted with fetishizing romanticism. Sacher-Masoch's fictional heterocosm is mythical, persuasive, aesthetically oriented, and centered around the idealizing, mystical exaltation of love for the punishing woman. Sade's language—primarily demonstrative, imperative, and obscenely descriptive—creates a fantastic world based exclusively on the rule of reason. In this world, the mechanistic negation of Nature dominates in the routinely repeated destruction of female victims.

Short passages from Sacher-Masoch and Sade's novels illustrate the absurdity of equating sadism and masochism on a literary level and, as Deleuze shows, on a psychoanalytic level as well. Sacher-Masoch writes in a typical passage from his most famous novel, *Venus in Furs:*

> To love and be loved, what joy! And yet this splendour pales in comparison with the blissful torment of worshipping a woman who treats one as a plaything, of being the slave of a beautiful tyrant who mercilessly

tramples one underfoot. Even Samson, the hero, the giant, put himself
into the hands of Delilah who had already betrayed him once, only to
be betrayed yet again. And when he was captured and blinded by the
Philistines, he kept his brave and loving eyes fixed upon the fair traitress
until the very end.[55]

Compare this excerpt from Sade's *One Hundred Twenty Days of Sodom:*

> 32. He calls for four women; he fucks two of them orally, two cuntwardly,
> taking great care not to insert his prick in a mouth until after having
> first had it in a cunt. While all of this is going on, he is closely followed
> by a fifth woman, who throughout frigs his asshole with a dildo.
> 33. This libertine requires a dozen women, six young, six old and if 'tis
> possible, six of them should be mothers and the other six daughters. He
> pumps out their cunts, asses, and mouths; when applying his lips to the
> cunt, he wants copious urine; when at the mouth, much saliva; when at
> the ass abundant farts.[56]

The incompatibility of Sacher-Masoch's and Sade's attitudes toward
women is obvious even from these brief passages. Contrary to Sade,
Sacher-Masoch exalts the punishing female. Within a veiled sensuality,
tableaux vivants of suffering suspend action and freeze emotion. An
idealizing fetishization of the female replaces the Sadian world's frenzied communal destruction of nameless victims among hundreds. In
One Hundred Twenty Days of Sodom, the Duc comments: "I've not many
scruples over a girl's death."[57] Numbers, not individuals, count in the
experience of sadistic negation, and those numbers are counted primarily in female victims. Being victimized is synonymous with being
female.[58]

Even when Sade chooses a woman as the ostensible heroine of
his novel, she still acts out the criminally misogynistic impulse that
remains unsatisfied with objectifying women. Sade's murderous super-
women, such as Eugenie in *Philosophy in the Bedroom* or Juliette in the
novel of the same name, do possess a certain sexual freedom. Angela
Carter valorizes their freedom in *The Sadeian Woman and the Ideology
of Pornography* and argues that Sade's misogynistic fantasies have de-
mystified the most sanctified aspects of women to "put pornography
in the service of women, or perhaps, allowed it to be invaded by an
ideology not inimical to women."[59] But the freedom Sade's heroines
achieve is obtained at the price of destroying other women, most particularly the mother, who, as Carter admits, represents the daughter's
"own reproductive function."[60] In *Philosophy in the Bedroom,* Eugenie
"plays the husband" to her mother, Madame de Mistival. She tortures
her by injecting syphilitic poison into her mother's vagina and anus

and then sewing up her vagina so that she will "give me no more little brothers and sisters."[61]

The Sadian heroine exemplified by Eugenie gives credence to Pierre Klossowski's observation that Sade's novels reflect the fantasy of the Oedipal alliance formed by the father with the child.[62] In the sadistic Oedipal fantasy, the subject identifies with the controlling parent (father), not the child. The Sadian heroine may subvert the female's expected passive sexual role, but Carter, like Klossowski, recognizes the guiding hand of the father in the sadistic scenario that playacts at liberating women:

> Father must know all, authorise all, or else Eugenie might truly take possession of her autonomy. . . .
> She savages her mother in order to achieve sexual autonomy . . . to attack Father or his substitutes in order to achieve existential autonomy is against the rules. . . . Eugenie's rage is no different at source from her father's rage. The libertine frenzy of father and daughter in Sade's parable springs from greed, envy and jealousy, in helpless rage at the organs of generation—that bore us into a world of pain. . . .[63]

The child is the tool of the Sadian father who regards woman's reproductive capacity as an emblem of Nature, abhorred because it stands outside the control of sadistic reason and negation. What Carter does not acknowledge in her analysis is the possible subversive aspect of mothering which the sadist unconsciously fears. The woman's potential for motherhood paradoxically transforms her from a passive receptacle for the libertine's desires into a creating, controlling being.[64] Consequently, the mother/child alliance, core of the masochistic fantasy, is intolerable in the Sadian world. It must be defiled by incest, destroyed by abortion or infanticide so that the father can be exalted beyond all laws.[65]

Masochism's heterocosm is antithetical to Sade's myriad variations on sodomy, incest, matricide, infanticide, and meticulously orchestrated orgies of sexual torture. His impossibly active libertines challenge the limits of human endurance and evil in endlessly repeated cycles of sex and violence. In masochism, the excesses of Sadian debauchery and insatiability are replaced by the heightened emotionality of suspended vignettes of suffering. Violence is muted, sexuality diffused, suffering aestheticized into spectacles of disappointment. Intimacy between mutually chosen partners replaces the Sadian impersonality of masses of libertines and victims; idealized eroticism replaces the obscenity that strives for the Ideal of Evil. In contrast to the Sadian world of accelerated activity, the temporal core of masochism is the suspension of gratification manifested in games of waiting, surprise gestures of tenderness or cruelty, and masquerades that discreetly delay consummation.

In contrast to the Sadian text, the masochistic text is erotic but not pornographic. Sadian discourse is denotative, unblinkingly "scientific" in its obscene descriptions and cruel imperatives.[66] The masochistic text relies on suggestive description and narrative suspense enacted through games of disguise and tantalizing pursuit implying gratification forever postponed to the future. Deleuze remarks, "Of Masoch it can be said, as it cannot be of Sade, that no one has ever been so far with so little offence to decency."[67] Barthes suggests that the Sadian world might be called erotic, but in this instance eroticism does not, he says, subscribe to the usual meaning of the word, for the reader of Sade is not seduced through a strategy of "striptease" or "apologue," which Barthes identifies as the essence of Western eroticism. In Sade's novels, "there is no bodily secret to seek, but only a practice to achieve."[68] As an act of ordered negation, sadistic sexual activity has little in common with the disavowing eroticism of masochistic foreplay and fetishism.

Severin's description of Wanda in *Venus in Furs* illustrates the mystical, contemplative quality imposed on the erotic in masochism's *supersensual* world of spiritualized sexuality:

> At the sight of her lying on red velvet cushions, her precious body peeping out between the folds of sable, I realized how powerfully sensuality and lust are aroused by flesh that is only partly revealed. . . . Wanda, in one sweep, threw off her fur wrap and appeared to me like the goddess of Tribuna.
>
> At moment she seemed as saintly and chaste in her unveiled beauty as the statue of the goddess, and I fell on my knees before her. . . .[69]

This mythically evocative description of Wanda proclaims "partly revealed" flesh to be the ultimate source of arousal. Severin's declaration is strikingly similar to Barthes's definition of the erotic as the "intermittence of skin flashing between two articles of clothing . . . between two edges. . . . it is this flash itself which seduces or rather: the staging of an appearance-as-disappearance."[70] Masochism obsessively recreates the movement between concealment and revelation, disappearance and appearance, seduction and rejection, in emulation of the ambivalent response to the mother who may either abandon or overwhelm the child. In the masochistic fantasy, seduction offers the promise—and the danger—of symbiosis.

The masochistic aesthetic weaves a tapestry out of the mythical and the mystical to represent the female who is but a powerful figure, both dangerous and comforting. Unlike the sadist, the masochist does not seek to destroy the female or to fuck her, as one of a countless entourage of degraded, discarded objects, but to cling to her as an ideal and to make her the fantasy subject of an almost desexualized contemplation.

Deleuze insists that the female is not sadistic within the masochistic alliance but is called upon by the contract to play her role.[71] The masochistic agreement in the male fantasy reverses the normal patriarchal contract in which the woman is the submissive object. As Deleuze notes, the masochistic alliance paradoxically subverts the gender-defined, socially assigned positions of power/powerlessness, master/slave, with the ultimate paradox being the male's willingness to confer power on the female.[72] In *Venus in Furs,* Wanda is the archetypal Sacher-Masoch heroine. Severin begs Wanda to let him be her slave, but when Wanda plays the role of torturess too well, Severin responds as "surprised" victim. He disclaims any responsibility for the experiment, but his denial does not fool Wanda:

> "You are even more heartless than I thought," I replied, wounded.
> "Severin," began Wanda earnestly, "I have done nothing yet, not the slightest thing, and you already call me heartless. What will happen when I fully satisfy your wishes and lead a carefree life surrounded by a circle of admirers, when I fulfill your ideal and kick and whip you?"
> "You take my fantasies too seriously."
> "Too seriously? . . . Was it my idea or yours? Did I lead you into this or is it you who aroused my imagination? At any rate we are now in earnest."[73]

At first Wanda protests her role as Severin's dominatrix, but she soon seems to enjoy the arrangement. She is sensual yet cool. Severin's descriptions continually compare her to magnificent paintings, marble statues, icy goddesses. Without transition or explanation, these descriptions alternate with passages insisting on her great warmth and tenderness. Wanda's actions are either all cruelty or all compassion. The shifts register an ambivalence toward the female explained in the oral stage desire for and fear of symbiotic merging as they also reflect the projection of the subject's own split ego onto the object.[74]

The masochistic male protagonists often attempt to pass themselves off as the victims of the female; however, in *Venus in Furs,* Wanda emerges as the more complex and sympathetic character. Severin carefully establishes the rules of the masochistic contract, but Wanda fails to conform to his plans. She tires of Severin (as does the reader) and runs away to Paris in her own "search for submission." Wanda marries "The Greek," an androgynous male who represents the "sadistic" element in the narrative. Emulating Severin, she takes a masochistic role as "the anvil." Severin at least pretends to have turned into a sadist, "the hammer," convinced, he proclaims, that men must dominate women in any relationship until women are men's equals in rights and education.[75]

The turnabout between Wanda and Severin's roles should not be interpreted as an obvious confirmation of the sadomasochistic duality. There are dialectical shifts from inflicting to receiving pain in the masochistic scenario, but such an exchange of function between characters does not alter the fundamental psychic mechanisms grounding the fantasy. The masochistic exchange of position bears little resemblance to the Sadian narrative's inversions of action and subject. Unlike the Sadian text, the masochistic one has no place for the accelerated repetition of obscene sexual crimes. In the former, libertine and victim are rigidly locked into positions of mastery and involuntary submission. Barthes suggests that the Sadian education in vice never allows any change in a character's position as victim or master. "Justine," he says, "lectured to so often, never leaves her victim status."[76] The sadist would not want a truly masochistic partner who would enjoy pain. Sade hinted of the same incompatibility in Justine's declaration that anyone who came of their own free will to be tortured by the libertines would be rejected: "They would turn away any girl who was to come here voluntarily."[77] Just as the sadist does not wish to torture a masochist whose enjoyment of pain would undermine his/her status as true victim, so the masochist could not tolerate a sadistic partner who would undermine the masochistic scheme of mutual agreement. To control the masochistic performance, persuasion ensures mutual agreement between partners.

As Deleuze explains, persuasion and alliance are not part of the Sadian construct: "The libertine may put on an act of trying to convince and persuade. . . . But the intention to convince is merely apparent, for nothing is more alien to the sadist than the wish to convince, to persuade, in short to educate. He is interested in something quite different, namely to demonstrate that reasoning itself is a form of violence, and that he is on the side of violence, however calm and logical he may be."[78] The sadist attempts to disguise his or her real motive even as the masochist works to disguise complicity in the perverse arrangement. Sacher-Masoch's male narrator/subjects often bemoan their imposed fate and try to persuade the reader that they have been victimized by circumstance.

Where the Sadian's frenetic negation of all boundaries of con-

ventional morality makes for black comedy, ironic humor qualifies
the melodramatic absurdity of masochistic posturing. A passage from
Venus in Furs illustrates the irony in the characters' theatrical acting
out of masochistic fantasy:

> "Quiet, slave." She scowls and suddenly strikes me with the whip. The
> next moment she bends over me with compassion and tenderly strokes
> the back of my neck. "Did I hurt you?" she asks, torn between fear and
> shame. "No," I reply, "and even if you had, the pain you cause is pure
> delight. Whip me if it gives you pleasure." "But it does not give me
> pleasure."
>
> . . . . .
>
> "Tread on me!" I cry, throwing myself before her. "I dislike play-acting,"
> says Wanda impatiently. "Then hurt me in earnest."[79]

Sacher-Masoch's heroes are forever swooning before the blow hits
their backs or in anticipation of sexual union. The sadistic text refuses
emotion that would dispel the rule of reason and threaten the goal of
negation.

Masochistic pleasure does not reside exclusively in the whip or
the kiss but also in the suspenseful anticipation of bringing the fantasy to life. Fantasy, the cornerstone of the masochistic experience,
is denied its autonomous power by the sadistic subject. Sade's impossibly shocking fictional world obviously depends upon fantasy in its
creation, but *within* the Sadian scenario, fantasy is valued only as a
precursor to destructive action. Juliette advises: "For a whole fortnight
abstain from all lustful behavior. . . . Then lie down in the dark and
little by little imagine different wanton acts. One of these will affect
you more powerfully and become like an obsession, and you must then
note it down and promptly put it into action."[80] Dominated by the
paradoxical combination of apathy and perpetual motion, the Sadian
text relies upon the predictable immediacy of ejaculation. Sadian characters use fantasy for the specific aim of increasing their aggressive
power to act. The sadist wants to believe he is awake and acting even
when he is dreaming; the masochist, notes Deleuze, "needs to believe
he is dreaming even when he is not."[81]

Like the film spectator suspended in a kind of waking hypnosis,
characters in the masochistic text are often not quite sure if they are
awake or asleep, perceiving or fantasizing into dream. The seemingly
straightforward beginning of *Venus in Furs* exemplifies such a confusion when the narrator's supposed reality is unexpectedly revealed to
be a dream; waking reality and dream then move toward fusion when
the narrator recounts his dream to a friend. The friend, Severin, pro-

duces a portrait: "'Venus in Furs!' I cried, pointing at the picture. 'That is how I saw her in my dream.' 'I, too,' said Severin, 'but I was dreaming with my eyes open.'"[82] The masochist dreams with "eyes open" to live out the fantasy and fetishistically neutralize the real in the imaginative ideal. This use of fantasy has little in common with the grandiose sadistic projection of imagination that actively seeks to change the world. Through the masochistic alliance, conscious fantasies are enacted, but the original infantile fantasies remain unconscious, unremembered, impossible to recover consciously.[83] Masochism's emphasis on performance in the prolongation of desire means that the fantasy is aesthetically savored purely for itself.

Like dream, the masochistic text permits the expression of fantasies that arise from many different periods of life. Fantasies interplay, interlock, combine, and fragment in communicating the masochistic wish, its conflicts and contradictions. Instinctual conflict is to be expected in a perversion, but perhaps equally important for the male subject in a patriarchal society is the cultural conflict that informs the wish for symbiosis with the powerful mother figure. Focusing on the maternal role in masochism is not yet another psychoanalytic condemnation of bad mothering. Ambivalence toward the mother is exacerbated by the force the patriarchy exerts on the female as the primary parenting agent of early life.[84] Within the masochistic scenario, fantasies that have the structure of later developmental stages are brought into regressive adherence with the perversion's oral stage wish for symbiosis. Hence the presence of the primal scene and the Oedipal triangle of the family romance.

Jacob Arlow explains this rather confusing aspect of fantasy structuring as a process in which systematic groupings of unconscious fantasies cluster around certain instinctual wishes. A group represents a particular moment in the subject's development and the attempt to resolve intrapsychic conflicts surrounding these wishes.[85] Deleuze takes a similar stance when he discusses how the masochistic fantasy accounts for the aggressive return of the father within an Oedipal family construct. The father signifies the symbolic imposition of patriarchal reality and superego repression upon the masochistic fantasy world.[86] Although masochism disavows the presence of the father and separation from the mother, neither the father nor the reality of separation can be negated except in death's hallucinatory fulfillment of desire.

In regard to the masochistic text, there is no single masochistic fantasy, but there is a fantasy core—a governing infantile scenario—which creates an infrastructure of desire that relentlessly dominates the *form* of the fantasy. As Jean Laplanche and J.-B. Pontalis explain, fantasy functions as a mise-en-scène of desire "in which what was prohibited *(l'interdit)* is always present in the actual form of the wish."[87] The masochistic infantile fantasy cannot, by its very nature, fulfill the satisfaction of desire except in the imagination, for the fantasy goal of masochism is, as Gustav Bychowski explains, the "dual unity and complete symbiosis between child and mother."[88] Because symbiotic remerger is a physical impossibility, death becomes the fantasy fulfillment to desire. It does not signal the defeat of desire or the end of the masochist's anticipated final triumph; rather, it is the promise of a fantasmical parthenogenetic rebirth from the mother, which is the final mystical solution to the expiation of the father and the symbiotic reunion with an idealized maternal rule.[89]

The Masochistic Aesthetic, Fantasy, and Film

Masochism's relationship to fantasy is particularly important to cinematic spectatorship. Laplanche believes that masochism has a unique interdependence with fantasy not exhibited in other perversions. Although Reik and Deleuze agree that fantasy plays a vital function in masochism, Laplanche goes so far as *to place masochism at the origins of fantasy:* "Fantasy . . . is thus intimately related, in its origin, to the emergence of the masochistic sexual drive."[90] He also places masochistic fantasy within the context of the primal scene, the child's helplessness and emerging sexuality. While Christian Metz has suggested that the voyeurism of cinematic spectatorship is an "unauthorized scopophilia" that is not only in "direct line from the primal gaze" but sadistic to one degree or another, Laplanche's work leads to a possible alternative view of the primal scene as a guiding metaphor for cinematic looking.[91] He states:

> To fantasize aggression is to turn it round upon oneself, to aggress oneself; such is the moment of autoeroticism in which the indissoluble bond between fantasy as such, sexuality, and the unconscious is confirmed.
>
> If we press that idea to its necessary conclusion, we are led to emphasize the privileged character of masochism in human sexuality. The analysis, in its very content, of an essential fantasy—the "primal scene"—would illustrate it as well: the child, impotent in his crib, is Ulysses tied to the mast or Tantalus, on whom is imposed the spectacle of parental intercourse. Corresponding to the perturbation of pain is the "sympathetic excitation" which can only be translated regressively through the emission of feces: the passive position of the child in relation to the adult is not simply a passivity in relation to adult activity, but passivity in relation to the adult fantasy intruding within him.[92]

Like Freud, Laplanche believes sadism implies an identification with the suffering position, but Laplanche takes this view to its logical conclusion: "the masochistic fantasy is fundamental. . . . it is within the suffering position that enjoyment lies."[93]

Even though Laplanche helps to define the unrealized theoretical relevance of masochism to spectatorial pleasure, he does not consider the qualitative difference in this turning of aggression against the self or, as Deleuze carefully establishes, the impossibility of a simple, straightforward reversal of the sadistic impulse.[94] Deleuze's remarks are supported by reference to the work of David Rapaport, who also has suggested that aim reversal implies a qualitative change in experience that complicates the notion of instinctual drives to the point of requiring an alternative theorization of the relationship of instinctual discharge and organ systems.[95]

Deleuze's theory, taken in connection with Rapaport and, more crucially, with Laplanche, can be used to challenge current views on the power relations in cinematic spectatorship as a primal scene scopophilia. The voyeuristic separation of subject/screen object does not automatically align the spectator with sadism, as Metz implies in *The Imaginary Signifier:* "If it is true of all desire that it depends on the infantile pursuit of its absent object, voyeuristic desire, along with certain forms of sadism, is the only desire whose principle of distance symbolically and spatially evokes this fundamental rent."[96] Contrary to Metz, sadism is the one perversion in which the separation of object and subject is neither required nor maintained. Sade's work, judged as the prototype of sadistic object relations, demonstrates that sadists are driven to maim, to penetrate, to destroy, in order to bring about the directly experienced pleasure of orgasm and to *negate* their objects in a way that is not possible through the sadistic look emphasized in theories of spectatorship.[97]

Masochistic desire, by contrast, depends upon separation to guarantee a pain/pleasure structure. As Sylvan Keiser has noted, closing the gap between the desiring subject and the object actually threatens masochistic gratification because the masochist's ego boundaries are not well established; the increased boundary loss of orgasm is intolerable.[98] Hence the need to control desire and suspend consummation. Like the masochist, but unlike the sadist, the spectator must avoid the orgasmic release that destroys the boundaries of disavowal, takes him/her outside the limits of normal spectatorship and into the realm of the true voyeur, and disrupts the magical thinking that defines the infantile use of the cinematic object.[99]

Is spectatorship experientially and structurally closer to masoch-

istic pleasure than the sadistic, controlling pleasure generally associated with film? If, in von Sternberg's films, we discover an equivalent
to Sacher-Masoch's literary prototype of the masochistic aesthetic, the
value of a Deleuzean-based model should not be assumed to be limited
to analyzing texts that might be considered "masochistic." Rather, as
the interrelationship of masochism and primal scene fantasy implies,
the ultimate importance of a revisionary theory of masochism lies in
its potential for changing our view of all of spectatorship and the pleasures available through the cinematic experience. In the next chapter
I will consider how, like Severin in *Venus in Furs,* we too are led into
dreaming with our eyes open.

CHAPTER TWO

Masochism and Visual Pleasure: The Link to Pre-Oedipal Development

> But it is life which crystallizes the first objects to which desire
> attaches itself, before even thought can cling to them.
> —Jean Laplanche

The masochistic aesthetic in film appears to be a major focus for the development of a critique of theories of visual pleasure that hinge on castration fear and a polarized account of sexual difference. Masochism subverts traditional psychoanalytic notions, accepted all too uncritically in film studies, regarding the fundamental impetus for human desire and the mother's and father's roles in the child's psychic development. It underscores the need to consider spectatorial responses that pleasurably meet goals that conflict with conscious cultural assumptions about sexual difference, gender identity, identification, and object cathexis. Can visual pleasure be explained other than by a theory that focuses on sexual difference defined as castration threat? Are disavowal and fetishism, widely regarded as fundamental to visual pleasure, necessarily based on castration fear and indicative of an exclusively male paradigm of psychic structure? Is the female spectator always excluded from these "male" psychoanalytic manifestations and the cinematic-scopic pleasure based on them? This chapter will approach these questions and others from current theoretical discourse to begin a discussion of visual pleasure within the framework of the masochistic aesthetic and the von Sternberg/Dietrich Paramount films.

In returning to fantasies that have their origin in the prephallic, prelinguistic, pregenital stage of development, the masochistic aesthetic suggests that all of film may be capable of forming spectatorial pleasures divorced from castration fear and sexual difference defined exclusively as feminine lack. In masochism, as in the infantile stage of dependence, pleasure does not involve mastery of the female but

submission to her body and her gaze. This pleasure applies to the
infant, the masochist, and the film spectator. In the pre-Oedipal period of development, the mother is the object of the child's fantasized
oral introjection, a narcissistic taking in of the object. She is also a
figure of identification, of nondifferentiated ego, the mother of plenitude whose gaze meets the infant's in the oneness of the pleasurable
subjugation of the child's oral world. Film theory must recognize the
possibility of a powerful *maternal imago*, the unconscious image of the
maternal agent viewed as a complex, pleasurable *screen memory* by both
male and female spectators even in a patriarchal society. As Janine
Chasseguet-Smirgel asserts:

> *Now the woman as she is depicted in Freudian theory is exactly the opposite of the*
> *primal maternal imago* as she is revealed in the clinical material of both
> sexes. . . . the contradictions . . . throughout Freud's work on the problem
> of sexual phallic monism and its consequences, force us to take closer
> notice of this *opposition between the woman, as she is described by Freud, and*
> *the mother as she is known to the Unconscious. . . .* If we underestimate the
> importance of our earliest relations and our cathexis of the maternal
> imago, this means we allow paternal law to predominate and are in flight
> from our infantile dependence.[1]

By suggesting that the oral mother could be the primary figure in a
construct that centralizes scopic pleasure and fetishism, a theory of
visual pleasure derived from Deleuze's analysis of masochism brings
into focus many of the problems that have emerged within recent theories of sexually differentiated film spectatorship. The primacy of the
mother within the masochistic dynamic may be used to call attention to
blind spots, contradictions, and patriarchal assumptions in Freudian-
and Lacanian-based psychoanalytic film theory. Masochism's psychoanalytic structure shows that psychoanalytically oriented film theory
must reintegrate the actuality of maternal influence and authority into
its consideration of spectatorship.

Masochism, Identity Formation, and Phallic Monism

Masochistic desire calls into question Freud's preoccupation with
the castration complex and male genital supremacy in forming subjectivity. Within masochism, the mother is not defined as lack nor as phallic in respect to a simple transfer of the male's symbol of power; rather
she is defined as powerful in her own right. Although it might be argued that in the pre-Oedipal period the child defines male/female difference primarily in nonbreast/breast terms, the plenitude and power

of the mother must also be approached as the totality of mothering, a combination of socializing and nurturing functions. The male's identification with the mother does not end with the onset of the phallic phase, but the female defined as Otherness or lack evidences the patriarchy's need to consolidate its own power. In *Anti-Oedipus,* Gilles Deleuze and Felix Guattari comment on the refusal to consider the female as an authoritative figure who might derive her power from something other than an anthropomorphic anatomical part: "For if the woman is defined as lack in relation to the man, the man in his turn lacks what is lacking in the woman, simply in another fashion: the idea of a single sex (as Freud posed—only genital = penis) necessarily leads to the erection of a phallus as an object on high, which distributes lack as two nonsuperimposable sides and makes the two sexes communicate in a common absence—castration."[2]

Even if many of Freud's critics (and interpreters) distort his view of male superiority and female inferiority, his own writings, taken over a span of his life's work, inevitably define the male as the absolute norm —as social being and as completely developed psychic entity.[3] In 1947, Viola Klein commented on the basic contradiction in Freud's writings concerning sexual difference and psychic development: "It seems plausible to Freud and his school that one half of humanity should have *biological* reasons to feel at a disadvantage for not having what the other half possess (but not vice versa)."[4] Klein's accusation, that Freudian theory not only describes but actually encourages patriarchal oppression of women, is still relevant, in spite of many contemporary feminist theorists' efforts to reclaim Freud through reinterpretation.[5] Is psychoanalytic film theory inadvertently perpetuating the oppressive strategies that it seeks to uncover and change? In discussing the essentialism of French writer Luce Irigaray, Monique Plaza alerts us to certain dangers in psychoanalytic approaches:

> To found a field of study on this belief in the inevitability of natural sex differences can only compound patriarchal logic and not subvert it. . . . Far from taking the Difference as the basis of our project, we should demolish it and denounce its falsity. . . .
>
> Now it is not because of its intrinsic qualities that the penis is valued to the detriment of the vulva or the breasts which are themselves also *visible.* It is to the extent that culture is androgynous, patriarchal that the phallus is raised to the level of a symbol. The "phallic superiority" of man is nothing other than the interpretation, in terms of nature and hierarchy, of women's oppression by men. . . . Men are not aggressive by nature. *Nor are they masters of their existence.* Their dominant social position does not imply that they do not need to seek domination.[6]

Although Lacan avoids the biologicalism of Freud by emphasizing the role of language in the formation of subjectivity and the
symbolic significance of the phallus, his influential theory still rests on
the anatomical prop of the penis and woman still is inevitably symbol-
ized as castrated and inferior within the patriarchy.[7] Lacan's theory of
the mirror phase and the structuring of male subjectivity through a
méconnaissance of vision has been central to many psychoanalytic theories of cinematic spectatorship. Whether as a guiding metapsychology
or as a loosely drawn metaphor for cinema, Lacan's theory of the mirror phase and the transition from the Imaginary to the Symbolic raises
many questions about film and spectatorship. Not the least of these
concern the female's relationship to the mirror and looking, her attainment of subjectivity, or even her theoretically "impossible" acquisition
of language within a system in which she is unable to represent lack
and, therefore, is excluded from the fundamental access to language.[8]

The emphasis on the mirror phase moment of misrecognition
also overvalues a very narrow theoretical range of factors, a problem
shared with Freud's theory of the castration complex and Oedipal
desire. While Lacan considers the prelinguistic stage of infancy in his
theory of the mirror phase, he tends to regard the child's prephallic,
pre-Symbolic existence as a fleeting one. The child cannot linger in
the realm of the Imaginary. Lacan fails to fully consider the residual,
memorial, organizational importance of the pre-Oedipal stages in the
formation of gender identity or in the pleasure of looking.[9] Although
the analogy of the mirror and cinema may be a useful one, Lacan's
theory proves particularly problematic in providing the foundation for
a less deterministic and narrowly defined approach to the pleasures of
spectatorship.

The Bisexual Response

Masochism violates patriarchal society's dictum against polymorphous desire based on infantile, incestuous wishes. More important,
it emphasizes the male's identification with the powerful mother and
his concurrent disavowal of the father's patriarchal function. In the
masochistic ideal, gender identity is transmutative and triumphantly
bisexual. As Deleuze remarks, the masochist believes it is possible to
become both sexes.[10] Polymorphous, nonprocreative, nongenital sexuality undermines the fixed polarities of male and female as defined by
patriarchy's obsession with presence/lack, active/passive, and phallic
genitality.[11] Because masochism foregrounds the issues of bisexuality
and the transmutative nature of gender identity and socially defined,

sex-determined social roles, a theory of masochism leads to a reconsideration of many Freudian and Lacanian theoretical assumptions that have dominated psychoanalytic film theory.

Freud continually returned to an emphasis on the polarity between masculine and feminine, although he recognized the bisexuality of every human being (i.e., that everyone has in his/her biology the potential to be the other gender). His concept of bisexuality was sometimes vague, inconsistent, and misguided in its biological specificities, but the fundamental theory has not been disproved and the psychological implications of the theory surpass the anatomical or physiological aspects of sexual dimorphism.[12] Psychological bisexuality more directly emphasizes the social construction of gender identity and the subject's choice of sexual object. If we are concerned with a gender-differentiated spectatorship, we must be sensitive to the commonalities as well as the differences between the sexes in the search for filmic pleasure.

In his study "The Drive to Become Both Sexes," Lawrence Kubie details two psychosexual manifestations that express a psychological imperative toward bisexuality: (1) the reverse of penis envy; and (2) the urge to become both sexes. Kubie writes:

> . . . overlooked is the importance of the reverse and complementary envy of the male for the woman's breast, for nursing as well as his envy for the woman's ability to conceive and to bring forth babies. . . . from childhood, and throughout life, on conscious, preconscious, and unconscious levels, in varying proportions or emphases, the human goal seems almost invariably to be *both* sexes, with the inescapable consequence that we are always attempting in every moment and every act both to affirm and deny our gender identities.[13]

Janine Chasseguet-Smirgel, Ernest Becker, Eva Feder Kittay, and others confirm these same or similar goals and stress the inability of orthodox Freudian theory to explain male envy of the female except in terms of male sexuality (homoerotic or autoerotic desires).[14] The ability to simultaneously desire the opposite sex and also identify with it, as well as the desire to overcome sexual difference, complicates current notions of spectatorial identification and its relationship to gender.

Many feminist film scholars, including Laura Mulvey, B. Ruby Rich, Mary Ann Doane, and Judith Mayne, have theorized that women are forced to identify with a male spectatorial position defined by the relay of "male" gazes created by the camera, male characters controlling the action in the film, and sexual representation produced for an audience defined as male.[15] In "Afterthoughts on 'Visual Pleasure and

Narrative Cinema' Inspired by *Duel in the Sun*," Mulvey suggests that
the cinematic structures that force the female into a *masculinization*
of vision reactivate a memory of the woman spectator's active, phallic phase and allow her to "rediscover the lost aspect of her sexual
identity, the never fully repressed bed-rock of feminine neurosis."[16]
According to Doane, the female spectator's compliance with the structuring identification of male looks inscribed in and through the film
oscillates with a negatively defined masochistic overidentification with
the represented females, or with "the narcissism entailed in becoming
one's own object of desire, in assuming the image in the most radical
way."[17] Kaja Silverman writes that the classical narrative cinema offers
women a subjectivity limited to "a masochistic misrecognition" that
occurs when women spectators confront the "ideal representations"
of women stars (such as Katharine Hepburn and Rosalind Russell).
Viewing these impossibly noble (and self-sacrificing) representations,
women are plunged into "a negative narcissism" that encourages "an
intense self-loathing."[18] Because the uncompromising patriarchal nature of narrative film makes it impossible to achieve a positive feminine
spectatorial position, women, it is theorized, must assume a dialectical
stance between a masculinization of looking and a negative feminine
identification.[19] Female spectatorship emerges as a colonized, dialectical undertaking.

By contrast, psychoanalytic film theory has operated on the assumption that the cinema as apparatus and the classical narrative
structurally close off the male's possible identification with the represented female or the kind of dialectical viewing experience attributed
to women. Male spectatorship has frequently been reduced to a predictable reaction determined by the workings of the castration complex, Oedipal desire, and identification with the masculine ideal ego.[20]
The fantasy of being both sexes described by Kubie has not been considered as a motivating pleasure to either female or male spectatorship.
Freud suggested that identity change, the repetition of rediscovering
identity, in and of itself was a source of pleasure.[21] While Freud related
how characters in a fantasy shift identities, as does the subject in relation to his/her fantasy, Laplanche has stated that fantasy is one means
of achieving the goal of reintegrating opposite-sex identification.[22] In
film studies, Nick Browne, Raymond Bellour, and Janet Bergstrom
have all discussed the fluidity of the spectator's identificatory positioning.[23] Bergstrom asserts that the spectator can "take up multiple
identificatory positions, whether successively or simultaneously." She
calls for "greater attention to the movement of identifications" as the
"next logical step in attempting more accurately to account for the

quality of our involvement as spectators."[24] The freedom and pleasure of shifting identification relates directly to the use of masochism to develop a theory of bisexual response. Such a theory necessarily confronts some of the assumptions grounding the theories that polarize male and female spectatorial experience.

Like the wish and counterwish for fusion with and separation from the mother, the wish to become the opposite sex is an ambivalent one. The desire to cross the anatomical boundaries of gender identity may be interpreted as a primitive, literal representation of the wish to subvert the polarized gender-role stereotypes fostered by a patriarchal society. Envy of the opposite sex in terms described by Kubie may be exacerbated by patriarchal socialization which encourages the division of male/female psychological traits and discourages androgyny.[25] Through the mobility of multiple, fluid identifications, the cinematic apparatus allows the spectator to experience the pleasure of satisfying the "drive to be both sexes" and of reintegrating opposite-sex identification repressed in everyday life dominated by secondary process. The cinema provides an enunciative apparatus like fantasy or dream which acts as a protective guise permitting the temporary fulfillment of what Kubie regards as "one of the deepest tendencies in human nature."[26]

The Paradox of Masochism and the Problem of Polarities

Masochism's psychoanalytic complexity and its intricate formal expression reveal the shortcomings in psychoanalytic film theory's reliance on polarities. Exchanges of position are part of the dynamic of pleasure in the masochistic play of pursuit and disappointment. Subject/object, male/female, active/passive, control/acquiescence, rebellion/submission, suspension/anticipation, voyeurism/exhibitionism, pain/pleasure—all vital components of masochism's scheme of desire and its dynamic of perverse pleasure—become paradoxical "oppositions" because masochistic desire, in finding pleasure *through* pain, is the most paradoxical of desires. Its structure confronts the very applicability of a construct dependent on polarities.[27]

Unfortunately, polarization was a prominent feature of Freudian theory. As a result, many psychoanalytic approaches to cinematic pleasure have reflected this same polarization and its limitations. In *Goals and Desires in Man*, Paul Schilder comments: ". . . to think in polarities . . . is merely a habit without regard for the real structure of things, and excusable only as a preliminary step in the explanation of the world. . . . There is no polarity between activity and passivity, between aggression and submission. . . . masculinity is not the opposite of femininity."[28]

Mulvey's influential article on "Visual Pleasure and Narrative Cinema" employs Freudian polarities of masculine/feminine, active/passive, and voyeurism/fetishistic scopophilia to formulate a theory of visual pleasure. The female has a single determined fate within patriarchal representation since she cannot escape her passive, exhibitionistic role as the "bearer of the bleeding wound."[29] Mulvey's insistence on the visible difference of the presence or absence of the penis demonstrates how the biological and the symbolic easily slide into each other in a Lacanian approach and seems to preclude a conceptualization of femininity (or masculinity) that might subvert patriarchal oppression. Claiming that all of classical narrative cinema divides the function of the look into pleasures based on biological difference, Mulvey's theory emphasizes the fundamental polarity of the sexes: ". . . the female figure poses a deeper problem. She also connotes something that the look continually circles around but disavows: her lack of a penis, implying a threat of castration and hence unpleasure. Ultimately, the meaning of woman is sexual difference, the absence of a penis as visually ascertainable. . . . Thus the woman as icon, displayed for the gaze and enjoyment of men, the active controllers of the look, always threatens to evoke the anxiety it originally signified."[30]

According to Mulvey, narrative film is made for the pleasure of the male spectator who, in identifying with the male protagonist and the gaze of the camera, experiences the pleasure of "indirectly" possessing the female. However, the female's image also provokes castration anxiety in the male spectator, which he has two means of escaping. The first, a sadistic voyeurism, involves investigating and demystifying the woman: she is guilty, castrated, devalued, and must be punished or saved. The alternative is an unconscious disavowal of castration through fetishizing the woman so that she "becomes reassuring rather than dangerous."[31] The latter, called *fetishistic scopophilia,* is not as overtly sadistic as voyeurism, but it too oppresses women for the sake of patriarchal needs. Mulvey illustrates the style that evokes fetishistic scopophilia with examples from the films of von Sternberg. As a film style, fetishistic scopophilia deemphasizes narrative to focus on the eroticized figure of the female who is constructed as a "perfect product" to assuage castration fear.[32]

Mulvey's deterministic view of the female representation in narrative cinema and the male pleasure derived from it leads to a critical "blind spot" in her theory. As D. N. Rodowick explains, the neglected area of her construct is the role of masochism in the structure of the look: ". . . Mulvey defines fetishistic scopophilia as an overvaluation of the object . . . but he [Freud] would also add that this phenomenon is one of the fundamental sources of *authority* defined as passive submission to the object: in sum, *masochism*. . . . The concept of masochism is deferred by the political nature of her argument. How could the masculine look signify both the exercise of power and submission to power?"[33] The logical conclusion of Mulvey's theory should pair masochism with fetishistic scopophilia, but she is forced to limit the spectatorial gaze to that of the controlling, masterful, masculine look, which views the female as an object for possession, not for identification—and never as a source of authority.[34] Spectatorship is determined solely by the workings of the castration complex which constructs the female into an image of threatening lack, a passive, fetishized object in a theoretical construct of immutable polarities.

The structure of the look has been considered one of the most important elements in defining visual pleasure. Although Rodowick declines to offer an alternative theoretical model to Mulvey that would include masochism in the structure of cinematic vision, he does make the important distinction that visual pleasure is not automatically an action of control and mastery. As Freud maintained in "Three Essays on the Theory of Sexuality" (1905), looking contains passive and active elements; this duality is maintained, asserts Rodowick, in "the *act* of the look, but also in the *return* of the look" which verifies vision.[35] Mulvey's theoretical position, however, does not associate the male spectator or the film's relay of looks with any form of the gaze other than an active, sadistic one.

Masochism points to the need to reexamine the psychological sources of fascination underlying male and female spectatorship as well as the need to interrogate the terms that have been applied. As a clinical entity and as an aesthetic, masochism undermines a Freudian-based theory of scopic pleasure that reduces the female to an indicator of lack/phallic-fetish in a pattern of castration fear and assuagement such as that advanced by Mulvey. Because masochism develops from an oral stage, infantile fixation centered on the mother, the developmental dilemmas of symbiosis and separation are fundamental to its etiology and psychodynamic; castration fear is a secondary consideration.[36] Nevertheless, it is important to note that masochism has very consistently been aligned in theoretical and clinical studies with fetishism.[37] Consequently, masochism's oral stage beginnings and its focus on the mother may be used to critique the unquestioning adherence to narrow Freudian explanations of the genesis and meaning of disavowal, fetishism, and sexual looking that many psychoanalytic approaches to cinematic pleasure have relied upon. Current theory ignores the pregenital origins and multivalent nature of these perversions as it also often assumes that the castration complex always transforms all previous losses (and desires) into paternal signifiers.[38] As a result, the dominance of Freudian accounts of disavowal and fetishism in psychoanalytically oriented film studies necessitates a thorough examination to show why these tenets cannot adequately account for male spectatorial pleasure derived from the representation of the female.

Defining Disavowal and Fetishism

Disavowal, or *Verleugnung*, was defined by Freud as the "denial of reality through word or act."[39] The original disavowal was identified as the male child's denial of the female's lack of a penis. From his viewing of female genitalia, the male child interprets the perceived difference between the sexes as a castration of the female (by the father) and fears for the safety of his own penis. Two possible reactions ensue, either "horror of the mutilated creature or triumphant contempt of her."[40] Freud later modified this conclusion to lessen the implication that every woman was then forever despised by every male child. In the revised theory, the child adopts these devaluing attitudes toward selectively chosen females who "probably have been guilty of the same forbidden impulses." Freud concluded: "Women who are regarded with respect, such as the mother, retain the penis long after this date."[41]

If the glimpse of female "castration" arouses an even more extreme reaction, the child may resort to fetishism, to freezing the last moment when belief in the female phallus was still possible. The fetish, either an object, body part, or, as interpreted in film theory, the entire "phallicized" body serves as a talisman, reassuring the child that the mother does, after all, still possess a penis: she has a phallus in this fetish. From that moment, the fetish and the female are treated with a mixture of hostility and affection. The fetish is only a partially successful mechanism for patching over the overwhelming fear of castration. It continues to evoke castration fear as it works to abate that same fear.[42]

The structure of fetishistic disavowal as a formulation of "I know but nevertheless" is critical to any theory of cinematic pleasure. In balancing belief and disbelief, the spectator participates in a disavowal, but is fetishism's denial of loss necessarily directed toward the mother's loss of the phallus and reflective of the child/spectator's castration fear? Current psychoanalytic research dealing with the pregenital period suggests that the mechanisms of disavowal and fetishism exist much earlier than the phallic stage identified by Freud as their site of origin.[43] However, disavowal and phallic fetishism are not being disputed here. This study does take exception to the assumptions that: (1) castration fear is the single impetus for disavowal and fetishism; and (2) this phallocentric interpretation of the etiology of disavowal and fetishism is the only available or meaningful one even within the context of a patriarchal society and classic narrative cinema as its product.

Feminist-psychoanalytic criticism following in the wake of Mulvey's milestone article has continued to formulate its basic stance regarding the pleasures of the controlling male gaze and function of the female's cinematic representation on these Freudian concepts. While feminist discourse has spent much time reconceptualizing female spectatorship, this discourse most often continues to account for the fetishistic nature of cinema through the requirements of a male spectatorship defined by castration complex anxiety.[44] The basic assumptions underlying the Freudian view of disavowal and fetishism that Mulvey adopts have only occasionally been questioned in film theory.

In "On Pornography," John Ellis argues that the "massive dissemination of images of female genitals that characterizes . . . the pornographic sector" at once leads us to dispute Freud's belief that the sight of female genitalia (the terrifying cause of disavowal) evokes what Freud called "the fright of castration which probably no male human being is spared."[45] Ellis is convinced that Freud overstated the male child's horror at discovering the female's lack of a penis and grossly overestimated the child's ability to understand what Freud insisted was the child's literal viewing.[46] From another perspective, the conservative Erik Erikson, renowned for his identity studies, suggests that "from an adaptive point of view . . . it does not seem reasonable to assume that observation and empathy . . . would so exclusively focus on what is not there."[47]

Even if we consider that the male child retroactively considers what he has seen and emotionally reinvests in that moment because of patriarchal influence, the pleasures of pornography obviously create a problem in linking male spectatorial pleasure to the castration complex. Ellis believes that Mulvey's adaptation of Freudian theories of disavowal and fetishism precludes any explanation of the prolific vaginal imagery in the pornographic sector as well as the pleasure evoked by this imagery. Griselda Pollock voices a similar skepticism in "What's Wrong with Images of Women": the "directness [of vaginal imagery] radically questions the psychoanalytically based analyses of images of women undertaken by Claire Johnston and Laura Mulvey and the no-

tions of castration fears and the phallic woman."[48] In spite of what
would appear to be a major theoretical impasse in Mulvey's theory of
male spectatorship, Ellis and Pollock are clearly the exceptions among
film scholars; the general trend has been to show little skepticism concerning Freud's interpretation of fetishism and, consequently, to be
content with theories of visual pleasure in which castration becomes a
central governing factor in the libidinal pleasures of looking.

In contradistinction to psychoanalytically oriented film theory,
clinical research and modern psychoanalytic theory have not left intact
Freud's theory on these issues. In "Fetishistic Behavior: A Contribution to Its Complex Development and Significance," Robert Dickes
summarizes the various revisionary findings and compares this recent research to Freud's. According to Dickes, much of the research
into both childhood and adult fetishism shares a common conclusion:
". . . the fetish represents more than the female phallus."[49] Like masochism, fetishism is believed to demonstrate a prolonged need for
primary identification with the powerful pre-Oedipal mother. Dickes
concludes that the traditional Freudian view of the fetish as "a talisman for relieving phallic castration anxiety is a . . . late stage of the
development of a fetish. Ordinarily . . . *never reached.*"[50] M. Wulff's
research into childhood fetishism also leads to a startling revision of
Freud: ". . . the fetish represents a substitute for the mother's breast
and the mother's body; we have come into complete opposition to the
content of the letter of Freud with Friedjung . . . in which there occurs
the following . . . 'the fetish is a penis substitute for the missing penis of
the mother, and hence a means of defense against castration anxiety
—and nothing else.'"[51]

In a reversal of Freudian theory, researchers into fetishism such
as Wulff, Charles Socarides, and Joseph Solomon generally agree that
fetishism originates as a pre-Oedipal, not an Oedipal, phenomenon,
with its source in a crisis of primary identification with "the almighty
preOedipal mother."[52] Most children, regardless of sex, use *transitional objects* to ease the separation from the mother. If the separation
has been too early or too extreme, the transitional object may be de-
fensively retained to restore the mother's body through representation
and to protect the primary identification with her. Socarides suggests
that fetishism "may have no etiological connection with phallic or genital sexuality" and that, although the fetish may represent a maternal
phallus, it also represents other parts of her body "from which he [the
infant] did not wish to be separated."[53] Socarides considers the phallic fetish, the mother's fantasy penis, as the child's attempt to create
the mother as the ideal hermaphroditic parent. She becomes the fantasy projection of the child's own wish to become both sexes, to have

female genitalia, be able to bear a child, and "undo separation from the mother and be like mother in every way." Socarides believes that oral fantasies play a prominent role in identification with the mother and that fetishization depends, in part, on the child's wish for re-incorporation into the mother's womb as a fantasy of symbiosis.[54] That wish may arise, says Solomon, because fetishism originates from the "threatened loss of the mother."[55] The original fetishistic disavowal attempts to erase separation from the mother and repudiate the child's lack in relation to her.

If, as Socarides, Eva Feder Kittay, Gregory Zilboorg, and others theorize, the male child wants to be reunited with the first object of oral gratification and erotic stimulation as well as have the breast (and, perhaps, the womb) himself, then fetishization of the female reflects the child's disavowal of lack in relation to the mother and the attempt to create a physically observable bisexuality, of having both male and female sexual characteristics.[56] In "Some Dynamics of Fetishism," M. E. Romm details the same beliefs evident in the fantasies of an adult fetishist who dreams that he becomes a hermaphrodite with the breasts of a woman and male genitalia.[57] The fetishistic denial of sexual difference in masochism appears related to the wish for symbolic fusion, to a denial of separation and sexual difference that protects identification with the mother and union with her. Dickes connects the earlier forms of fetishism with the adult perversion: "Numerous factors including preoedipal experiences play a vital role in the production of this symptom complex. The fetish does not arise *de novo* in the adult, nor does it appear only in the phallic phase. . . . Thus there exists a continuum from the earliest objects through transitional objects to childhood and adult fetishes."[58]

Robert Bak maintains that the normal male child confidently assumes it is possible to emulate the mother's positive power (i.e., bear a child) and to repair separation from her (through fetishism) without endangering his phallic integrity.[59] Freud encountered a similar disavowal of sexual difference in the case of Little Hans, which he recorded in "An Analysis of a Phobia in a Five-Year-Old Boy" (1909).[60] Little Hans persistently refused the idea that he could not have a baby and informed his disbelieving father that he too would have one sometime in the future:

> "You know quite well that boys can't have children."
> "Well, yes. But I believe they can, all the same."[61]

Kittay notes that such a belief is quite common in boys, who "may even be willing to sacrifice the actual penis" to achieve the goal of being like the mother. She also suggests that the fantasy of the phallic mother reflects the male child's projection of his own wish for bisexuality onto the mother.[62]

The child's pre-Oedipal view of the female as a powerful, controlling, creative, and yet potentially destructive figure is not automatically obliterated by later stages including the castration complex, but societal pressures may complicate the male child's desire to be both sexes. Kittay argues that the male's identification with the mother actually increases later envy of the female. Society's devaluation of women "renders this identification, along with the desire to bear children, far more problematic than the bare biological, procreative difference would warrant."[63]

The male's sense of body intactness, usually spoken of exclusively in terms of castration fear, also finds its genesis in the child's sense of completeness with the body of the mother. Fear of castration may, in fact, be derived from the original ambivalence concerning union/separation from the mother.[64] According to Margaret Mahler's influential theory of object relations, ambivalence first arises out of the child's difficult struggle from this symbiotic stage into separateness and individuation. This struggle imprints the structure formation of the psyche. Pre-Oedipal, mother-centered ambivalence sets the pattern for all later ambivalent object relations and creates the persistent and essentially unresolvable conflict between the wish for separation/individuation and the conflicting wish for symbiosis.[65]

The male's ambivalent attitude toward the female may lead to disavowal and fetishism; however, these two common matrices of masochism and cinematic spectatorial pleasure do not always have their sole origin in castration fear and sexual difference defined as female lack. Nor do they exclusively signify the presence of Oedipal anxieties and wishes. The tension between attraction and fear is an ambivalence underlying much of cinema's depiction of the female, but it is reductive to collapse the entire signification of woman to phallic meaning. In criticizing what she regards as an "oversimplification" in film theory's discussion of cinema and female representation, Claire Pajaczkowska remarks: "The women I look at in films are not simply either castrated men nor fetishes, they are necessarily multiple, because the maternal imagos in infantile subjectivity are multiple."[66]

The representation of women through the cinema also cannot be limited to their representation of the maternal imagos of infancy. Although I stress the importance of reintegrating the notion of a powerful pre-Oedipal mother and pre-Oedipal object relations into psychoanalytic film theory, it would be a mistake to assume that the only level of spectatorial reaction to the female involves the uncon-

scious revival of the earliest mothering imagos. Redressing the neglect
of the mothering influence should not serve to replace one reductive
stance with another. Nevertheless, the original primary identification
with the mother and the symbiotic relationship with her are compelling unconscious influences on adult sexuality that require attention
in psychoanalytic film theory.

Within masochism, disavowal through fetishism is, as Deleuze
explains, a "protest of the ideal against the real."[67] Fetishism is a protective, idealizing neutralization of time and separation. The disavowal
of the mother's separation from the child served as a step backward
to total symbiosis with the ideal oral mother before the concepts of "I"
and "not-I" divided the narcissistic ego of the child from the mother
as ideal ego.[68] While fetishism dependent on castration fear no doubt
does occur, masochism, as a product of oral stage ambivalence, logically associates the fetish as a *screen memory* with the oral stage impetus
of masochistic desire—the mother. The masochistic fetish signifies the
attempt to reconstruct the mother as inseparable plenitude and returns the subject to the eroticized transitional object marking the point
of departure from her.[69]

Although Deleuze continues to link fetishistic disavowal to castration, he does not define fetishism as an inevitable indicator of feminine
lack. Rather, masochistic fetishism abolishes the father's functions; it
accords power to the female through a disavowal with a completely
different aim than expected. The disavowal of sexual difference abolishes the father to position the female as ideal ego. She completes
the child's identity and makes possible the fantasy of parthenogenetic
rebirth, restoring their symbiotic union. For Deleuze, the masochist's
disavowal endows the mother with a "phallus" that "does not have a
sexual character" but is "the ideal organ of neutral energy" that symbolically permits the mother to give birth to the subject without the
father.[70]

Masochistic disavowal transcends castration fear. Rather than
relegating the woman to a position of lack, it exalts her to an idealized
wholeness imitated in the son's fetishistic wish to restore identification and oneness with her and be reborn into a "new man devoid of
sexual love" who represents the denial of sexual difference and rejection of the father's sexuality.[71] In a reversal of patriarchal norms, the
masochistic male defines himself in relation to the female.

The identifications offered by fetishistic representations of the
female and the masochistic scenario/fantasy can be simultaneously
pleasurable and threatening. While the masochistic fantasy allows the
male to act out a submissive, "feminine" position, it may evoke other

conflicts. Identification with the female, normally denied or repressed in a patriarchy, may be difficult to integrate. Chasseguet-Smirgel believes that male contempt for women is not, as Freud wrote, the inevitable result of the Oedipus complex but evidence of the male's pathological and defensive reaction to maternal power.[72] The intrapsychic conflict caused by this repression of the original identification with the feminine is often projected onto the female. Chodorow comments:

> A boy, in his attempt to gain an elusive masculine identification, often comes to define his masculinity largely in negative terms, as that which is not feminine or involved with women. . . . Internally, the boy tries to reject his mother and deny his attachment to her and the strong dependence on her that he still feels. He also tries to deny the deep personal identification with her that has developed during his early years. He does this by repressing whatever he takes to be feminine inside himself, and importantly, by denigrating whatever he considers to be feminine in the outside world.[73]

The "norms" of the male, according to Chasseguet-Smirgel, Chodorow, and Ralph Greenson, rest on a tenuous gender identity that finds its origin in the problem of disidentifying from the mother. Although the girl also shares this developmental dilemma, the patriarchal sanctions against the male's retention of his "feminine" identification intensify his crisis of identity.[74]

In her article "Masochism and Subjectivity," Kaja Silverman discusses masochism's relation to the male spectator's identification with the female from the viewpoint of Freud's theory of instinct ambivalence.[75] Her consideration of masochism is highly problematic in its definition of masochism as a vague amalgamation of passivity, negation, and instinctual unpleasure, but she does make a cogent observation that has ample precedent in the work of Chasseguet-Smirgel and many others: "what provokes the crisis [of fetishism]," Silverman argues, is "not so much horror at the mother's 'lack' as an *identification* with her."[76] For the male spectator who participates in the disavowing, fetishistic pleasure of viewing the female, identification with her is a fragile, dangerous, but pleasurable enterprise that threatens society's view of what should differentiate male from female. If the male spectator identifies with the masochistic male character, he aligns himself with a position usually assigned to the female. If he rejects this position, one alternative is to identify with the female who inflicts pain; or, he may identify with the feminized "new man," the equivalent to Sacher-Masoch's "The Greek." In any case, the male spectator assumes a position in some way associated with the female. He identifies with culturally assigned feminine characteristics exhibited by the male within the masochistic scenario or with the powerful female who represents the pre-Oedipal mother of primary identification.

Female Fetishism and Spectatorship

Disavowal and fetishism are not exclusively male psychoanalytic manifestations originating from the castration complex. Females are capable of both mechanisms, but psychoanalysis has often been theoretically closed to an analysis of female fetishism. Additionally, the extreme pathological forms of fetishism are less "visible" in females because women can (and are encouraged to) hide impaired sexual function.[77] The male may be more likely to sustain fetishism because of problems with resolutions of gender identity, but this predominance of clinical studies on adult male fetishism does not appear to be related to any sexually differentiated scopic drive.[78] While it is naive to assume that the identification of pre-Oedipal (or female) scopophilia or fetishism would open a gap for the female spectator within dominant cinema, a reconsideration of fetishism challenges the dominant theoretical views that exclude the female from the structures of cinematic pleasure or even libidinalized looking. To assume, as Mulvey has implied, that the female does not take the male star as an object of sexual looking, or is encouraged to do so by the male star's glamourized (or *fetishized*) presence, inadvertently seems to promote the general cultural sanction against women's public right to sexual looking.[79]

The complex development and variations on disavowal and fetishistic activity suggest that females need not be totally excluded from the structures of cinematic pleasure because of these mechanisms. Mary Ann Doane makes such a claim in "Misrecognition and Identity" and "Film and the Masquerade: Theorising the Female Spectator."[80] Her work is worth considering in detail because it represents many of the dominant opinions on sexual difference and spectatorship in current feminist-psychoanalytic film theory. Her insistence on the monolithic structure of classical narrative cinema, her view of the privileged masculine viewing position as one defined by control and same-sex identification, and her dependence on a strict Freudian view of the perversions that are manifested in the scopic drive are all typical of current theoretical discourse.

Doane states in "Film and the Masquerade" that the female cannot separate herself from the "over-presence of the female body"; therefore, she cannot assume a reflective position on sexual difference:

The boy, unlike the girl in Freud's description, is capable of a re-vision of earlier events, a retrospective understanding which invests the events with a significance which is in no way linked to the immediacy of sight. This gap between the visible and the knowable, the very possibility of disowning what is seen, prepares the ground for fetishism. In a sense, the male spectator is destined to be fetishist, balancing knowledge and belief.

The female, on the other hand, must find it extremely difficult, if not impossible, to assume the position of fetishist.[81]

Yet, Freud's essay on "Female Sexuality" describes the female as also having the capacity for a disavowal of the visible and, we may conclude, the same fundamental capacity for fetishism as the male: "When the little girl discovers her own deficiency, from seeing a male genital, it is only with hesitation and reluctance that she accepts the unwelcome knowledge. As we have seen, she clings obstinately to the expectation of one day having a genital of the same kind too."[82]

Although Freud too eagerly confirmed the logic (and desperation) of the little girl succumbing to penis envy, Doane's exclusion of the female from fetishistic mechanisms and the structures of sight surpasses Freud's theoretical model. She quotes Luce Irigaray to confirm her view that the female is more comfortable with the tactile because of inherent structural problems with sight and form. Somehow, in spite of her "problematic relation to the visible," the female spectator manages to display an amazingly resourceful and flexible ability to use her "deficient" capacity for seeing.[83] She overcomes her limitations to move across gender boundaries and identify with the masculine gaze, the only nonmasochistic position offered to her by classical narrative cinema. She assumes "the position of transvestite" to understand a cinema structured for male fantasy. Thus, by taking up the theory of the female spectator's "masculinisation" of vision advanced by Mulvey, Doane denies the female a spectatorial position of her own other than a negative identification with the passive exhibitionism of masochistic female characters.[84]

In "The 'Woman's Film': Possession and Address," Doane compares the female spectator's masochistic position to that detailed by Freud as the third-phase conscious fantasy of his obsessional women patients in "A Child Is Being Beaten."[85] Unlike Freud's male subjects, the women took a position totally outside the structure of the fantasy, as de-eroticized spectators to the action. Doane uses Freud's delineation of this crucial difference between the fantasies of the male and female subjects to conclude that the third-phase fantasy may serve as a model for women's position at the cinema and the functioning of the woman's film as "masochistic fantasy *instead* of sexuality."[86] Yet, the very definition of masochism precludes its exclusion from erotic gratification.[87] Most important, Freud noted that his women patients observed *sadistic* actions in this third-phase fantasy but still derived masochistic gratification from the spectacle.

The fact that his male patients were never "spectators" placed outside the action of their fantasies makes Freud's essay of interest to a theory of masochism and visual pleasure. Instead of suggesting a direct parallel between female patients and female spectators, the situation of Freud's female subjects more exactly duplicates the cinema's positioning of *all* spectators. All film spectators can be said to watch a "fantasmatic gone awry," a fantasy disengaged from the body and no longer serviceable as a purely masturbatory object.[88] It would seem that the supposed visual "transvestism" of female spectators is matched by that of male spectators who are drawn into a position that resembles Freud's description of the positioning afforded by the third-phase *female* fantasy, a fantasy that evoked masochistic gratification from "sadistic" events.[89]

The Female Gaze: Erotic Rapport and Authority

Doane does not consider that the psychic structures of disavowal, fetishism, or a fetishistic scopophilia might operate beyond sexual difference and allow for the pleasures of opposite-sex identification for male as well as female spectators, nor does she consider whether these very same structures might make such identifications inevitable in the cinema. Scopophilia, like fetishism, originates in precastration complex development and predates Oedipal conflict and genital sexuality. In "Face-Breast Equation," Renato Almansi traces the origins of scopophilia to the oral phase and the relationship of the child to the mother: ". . . scopophilia was indissolubly linked with early visual sensitization due to feelings of oral deprivation and object loss."[90] Although Almansi calls for further research into the genesis of scopophilia in early object loss, his conclusions are compatible with the location of fetishism's etiology in the child's separation from the earliest source of gratification. In the scopophilia of this early period, pleasure in looking involves both identification and projection. The child sees itself mirrored in the face of the mother. Almansi proposes that the face and breast of the mother are equated—even fused—in the imagination, a perceptual confusion also associated with the dream screen phenomenon to be examined in detail in chapter 8.[91]

Through scopophilia of the oral period, pleasure is achieved in looking at the omnipotent mother. If the mother/child relationship is disturbed, fetishism may develop as a defensive maneuver to permit passive infant satisfaction, restore the mother's body, and protect identification with her.[92] Pleasurable looking is not only an active pleasure with the child as subject, as Lacan's theory of mirror-misrecognition emphasizes. It also entails the passive submission to the object-mother, an object who is also a subject and whose actions are beyond the child's control. Masochism and the spectatorial experience of the cinema duplicate the situation of passive submission to the object, which has not been fully recognized in Lacan's mirror theory.

The von Sternberg/Dietrich heroine is the object of male desire, but she is not the passive object of a controlling look. Dietrich looks back or initiates the look. She seems to question her objectification in defiance of the implicit cinematic rule against an illusion-breaking confrontation of gazes. This act is akin to the powerful oral mother's return of the child's gaze; her gaze asserts presence and power. The male's gaze often leads to his submission to the female, not his control of her; even in this, polarized notions will not suffice: male passivity is informed by the masochist's theatrical attempt to hide his activity, his pursuit of submission. Likewise, the female's authority contains passive elements.

The female is not developmentally excluded from scopophilia, disavowal, or fetishism, nor is she excluded from the enunciative mechanisms or an apparatus dependent on these. In Mulvey's discussion of von Sternberg's films, she observes that Dietrich is fetishized to the extreme so that ". . . the powerful look of the male protagonist (characteristic of traditional narrative film) . . . is broken in favor of the image of direct erotic rapport with the spectator. . . . there is little or no mediation of the look through the eyes of the main male protagonist. . . . the most important absence is that of the controlling male."[93] The direct "erotic rapport" created between Dietrich and the film spectator also complicates the distinction between identification and sexual looking as they apply to a female spectator. Unmediated by a controlling male gaze, the direct eroticization of the image, this imaginary closing of the gap between spectator and image, allows the female spectator to step beyond identification with the represented female. It may encourage a libidinalized position, a position of desire that subversively crosses the boundaries of heterosexual desire as it challenges current accounts of the pleasure available through fetishistic scopophilia.[94]

Mulvey asserts that von Sternberg's films turn Dietrich into a fetish to assuage male castration fear, but Dietrich's presence in the films articulates not an "excess femininity," as Doane argues, but an androgynous eroticism highly charged by sexual ambiguity.[95] Julia Lesage has commented on Dietrich's appeal to women, on her "underground reputation": "She seems to represent for some women a kind of subculture icon. She has a certain power in Von Sternberg's films. If her portrayal doesn't escape completely from the totality of Von Sternberg's male fantasy, the effect of her role is not totally explained in an analysis that sees women's desire primarily in terms of castration and lack. . . . Dietrich fascinates women as a lesbian figure with whom they identify."[96]

Dietrich's irony and detachment are much commented upon aspects of her persona. Described by Kathryn Weibel as "highly charged, self-confident, and strangely self-sufficient," Dietrich has also been labeled "subversive" by Molly Haskell, who explains that Dietrich "parodies conventional notions of male authority and sexual role playing."[86] Her persona in these films cannot be separated from von Sternberg's construction of her, but her distanciation from her own image, her sexual detachment, and her androgynous eroticism have not sparked the kind of "radical overidentification" with the image described as the masochistic norm for female spectatorship. Nor does Dietrich fit the image of the de-eroticized woman's film heroine or the conventionally passive object of male fantasy. Her overt eroticism seems to elicit sexual feelings from straight and lesbian women, gay and straight males.[98]

"Perversion," says Irving Buchen in *The Perverse Imagination*, literally means "turning across."[99] A consideration of masochism's role in visual pleasure "turns across" the argument that pleasure for the male spectator must be achieved exclusively through a controlling, essentially sadistic gaze. Control is turned across to the female; pleasure is found in the renunciation of domination. For the female spectator, the masochistic aesthetic's complex dynamic spectacle of "passive" female exhibitionism may evoke spectatorial pleasures equally complex and unaccounted for within current theory. If pleasure in looking at the cinema involves pre-Oedipal ambivalence and pleasure for both male and female spectators, then the role and reaction of the sexually differentiated spectator must be approached in a completely different light. Masochism forces us to reconsider the power of a desire not "born with language" and the castration complex, as Mulvey asserts, but born out of infantile helplessness and the dangerous bliss of symbiosis.[100]

CHAPTER THREE

Masochistic Masquerade in the Performance of Identity

Sight . . . is the most exquisite form of pursuit.

—Henry James

In von Sternberg's films, the masochistic mode of desire constitutes a unique interplay of pain and pleasure that determines the texts' psychodynamics. The masochistic dynamic of desire depends upon the transmutation of sexual identity and multiple character function. As a result, it reflects on issues of bisexuality, identification, and a pre-Oedipal locus of desire that relate to the vicissitudes of cinematic spectatorship. Through a twofold strategy, this chapter explores the enunciation of masochistic desire in the von Sternberg/Dietrich Paramount films. Of primary interest is the formation of character identity and the strategy of masochistic performance that self-referentially centralizes the representation of woman in film and the structure of the gaze. First, an analysis of character identity reveals how the masochistic psychodynamic is expressed in the six films. Then, I analyze how the films transform various interlocking levels of masochistic fantasy into a coherent structure. Using *Blonde Venus* and *The Scarlet Empress* as a springboard for discussion, the fantasy-governed psychoanalytic substructure of masochism is discussed with regard to the representation of the female.

Masochism as a Subversive Desire

The issue of identity with the von Sternberg/Dietrich films and their construction of character relate directly to the dynamic of masochistic pleasure and the identificatory process of spectatorship. The etiology of masochism during the oral period is concurrent with the first tentative process of identity formation in the individual. Heinz

Lichtenstein has suggested that psychosexual identity is imprinted by the sensory interaction of the infant with the mother, which prefigures and sets the stage for other socially imposed patterns of identity construction. Lichtenstein believes the extreme symbiotic nature of the mother child unit is not only "the primary condition for identity" but "becomes the very source of the emergence of human identity."[1] Ethel Spector Person has gone so far as to link power relations in adult sexuality to "the universal condition of infantile dependence" which overrides social conditioning into sexual differentiation.[2] Rather than regarding Lichtenstein's or Person's comments as contributions to an essentialist position of subjectivity, the extremeness of the mother/child dyad can be seen as reflecting the force exerted by the patriarchy in maintaining the mother as the sole parenting agent of early infancy.[3]

The realities of existence within a patriarchal society contribute to the complex signification of sexual and social identity within von Sternberg's films. These films evidence a thematic preoccupation with the interaction of pre-Oedipally determined identity with the socially constructed identity imposed through patriarchal norms. The characters' oscillation between stability and metamorphosis is a response to the predominantly unconscious demands of masochistic fixation, but it also reflects the contradictory demands of society. The individual's survival hinges upon her/his adaptation to society's demand for a single, recognizable, and permanent sociosexual identity. Masochism presents psychosexual identity transformation as a pleasurable enterprise that subverts normal genital sexuality and established gender-differentiated dominance/submission patterns. Characters realize their "true" identity within the locus of masochistic desire. Although Foucault argued that polymorphous perversity is recuperable within patriarchy and loses its subversive value, nongenital sexuality is culturally inadmissible and *inassimilable* in the sense that only genital sexuality, sanctioned by its procreative function within marriage, can be placed in the service of civilization.[4]

The masochistic mode of desire, as a desire that finds pleasure in polymorphous sexuality and "the pleasure of unpleasure," defies the arbitrary norms of society.[5] Deleuze and Guattari persuasively argue in *Anti-Oedipus* that desire can threaten the rule of the patriarchy. Masochism fulfills Deleuze and Guattari's requirements as a potentially subversive desire that threatens Oedipal imperialism and patriarchal domination: "If desire is repressed, it is because every position of desire, no matter how small, is capable of calling into question the established order of a society, not that desire is asocial; on the con-

trary. But it is explosive."[6] In finding pleasure through pain and in
violating the taboo against the regressive pleasures of infantile, nongenital sexuality, masochism positions itself against the very baseline
structure of society's patriarchal family unity—the psychic progress
to genital, monogamous heterosexuality. The destruction of superego
control makes the perversion doubly subversive since Freud regarded
the male's superior superego development as the mainstay of civilization. Female superego development was limited by women's inability to
participate in the castration complex: they were left with a less soundly
developed sense of ethical norms. As a result, said Freud, men had to
assume the burden of maintaining social conscience.[7]

Masochistic pleasure also undermines the patriarchal notion that
pleasure must depend on control as opposed to submission. By par-
taking in polymorphous perversity, masochism demonstrates the easy
exchange of power roles that are rigidly defined within the patriarchal sexual hegemony. In masochism, the power plays of sexuality are
made explicitly theatrical and ritualized so that their naturalness is
exposed as a construct.[8]

Character Identity and the Psychic Requirements of Masochism

The powerful pre-Oedipal mother may be the one element of
absolute continuity in masochism, but characteristic of the masochistic
scenario of desire is the participant-players' assumption of various ego
or superego functions, their shift in power positions from inflicting to
receiving pain, and their representation of partial psychic identities.
Leo Bersani has remarked that a text that creates characters with fragmented and transformational psychic identities generates the pleasure
of a "liberating participation in the dissolving of fixed identities" and
offers "the delight of returning to the multiple identities among which
those desires allow us to move."[9] If the cinematic apparatus is particularly adept at providing us with fragmented and multiple possibilities
for identification, as some film theorists have suggested, then the masochistic text may be the most cinematic of all texts in refusing the rigid
regulation of identification along lines of sexual difference and privileging the pleasures, not of a coherent self emphasized in the Lacanian
paradigm, but of the fragmented ego, bisexual identity, and a multiplicity of sites of pleasures that defy phallic unity and domination.

The instability of characters in the masochistic scenario in terms
of their lack of behavioral consistency may initially appear to be unmotivated and perplexing, but it is fully explainable within the dialectical framework of masochistic desire. Rooted in the demands of

infantile fixation, masochism paradoxically depends upon a theatrical exchange of roles to prolong the painful *play* of desire. Deleuze explains that these exchanges do not alter the masochistic nature of the situation. Instead, the shifting character identities can be traced to the dialectical spirit of masochism and the interplay of fantasies from different developmental periods.[10] The reasons and result of this flux of psychic character identity and narrative function are explained by Deleuze in reference to Sacher-Masoch:

> Masoch is animated by a dialectical spirit . . . by the whole technique of dialectical reversal, disguise, and reduplication. In the adventures with Ludwig II Masoch does not know at first whether his correspondent is a man or a woman; he is not sure at the end whether he is one or two people. . . . Dialectic does not simply mean the free interchange of discourse, but implies transpositions and displacements of this kind resulting in a scene being enacted simultaneously on several levels with reversals and reduplication in the allocation of roles and discourse.[11]

Masochism's acting out of fantasy also explains the presence of shifting or sliding identities with their implication of sexual transmutation. Characters in fantasies are subject to dreamwork processes such as condensation, displacement, overdetermination, and concrete representability. Laplanche and Pontalis note that "fantasies are scripts (scenarios) in which the subject has his own part to play and in which permutations of roles and attributes are possible." [12] In masochism, the play of partial psychic impulses is exemplified in the father/son figure, who represents the punishment of the father in the son and in the multiple maternal imagos. These are represented through characters who defy the notion of a stable sexual or social identity established within culturally approved modes of normative sexual role playing and gender identity.

Although the theatrical play of masochistic desire creates a complex range of possibilities in the expression of its dynamic, the films under consideration reveal a striking pattern of psychodynamic continuity that points to the clearly delimited infrastructure of the masochistic aesthetic. The barest summary of their plot lines illustrates a repeated pattern in which a woman is caught between the desire of two males (*Morocco, Blonde Venus, The Devil Is a Woman, Shanghai Express*) and/or between one man and a social system that condemns and represses mobile desire (*The Scarlet Empress, Dishonored*). *Morocco* (1930), the first film in the von Sternberg/Dietrich Paramount cycle, and *The Devil Is a Woman* (1935), the last film, are extremely different in tone but rest on the same configuration of emotional relationships.

In the former, the three principals, Amy Jolly, a cabaret singer (Marlene Dietrich), La Bessiere, a rich painter (Adolphe Menjou), and Tom Brown, a rough and tumble private in the French Foreign Legion (Gary Cooper), act with civilized restraint as their desires crisscross in disappointment. Amy meets La Bessiere aboard ship enroute to Morocco. In spite of his attention, she prefers Private Brown, who callously abandons her on the night of their planned rendezvous to leave Morocco together. Amy decides to marry La Bessiere, but at the dinner party marking their engagement, she leaves to locate Brown, who is rumored to have been wounded in a skirmish. Accompanied by La Bessiere, she finds Brown unharmed in a small desert town and bids him good-bye when his patrol leaves. Suddenly, she decides to follow him into the desert.

The last film of the von Sternberg/Dietrich collaboration, *The Devil Is a Woman,* is a bitterly humorous account of yet another cabaret singer caught in a love triangle. Concha Perez (Dietrich) oscillates between the attentions of a middle-aged army officer, Capt. Don Pasquale Castellan (Lionel Atwill), and a handsome young political exile, Antonio Galvan (Cesar Romero). Antonio meets Concha during a pre-Lenten carnival celebration and is smitten with her, but his old friend, Don Pasquale, warns him about her. Years before, Don Pasquale met Concha on a train. Their brief flirtation ended quickly, but when Don Pasquale met Concha again, he could not resist her charms. Concha, a Carmenesque seductress, greedily accepted Don Pasquale's money, humiliated him with her brazen infidelities, and callously left him as she called out: "If I'm not back in a week don't wait for me, Pasqualito!" Antonio does not heed his friend's advice, and when he and Concha are caught in an embrace by Don Pasquale, who has once again declared his love for Concha, the two men agree to duel. Don Pasquale is shot. Antonio and Concha start out for Paris, but Concha changes her mind, leaves Antonio at the border, and returns to Spain.

Shanghai Express (1932) uses a similar, if more obliquely drawn love triangle. Madeleine, alias Shanghai Lily (Dietrich), is a notorious "coaster" (i.e., prostitute on the Chinese coast). On a train journey she meets her former fiancé, an English army surgeon, Dr. Donald ("Doc") Harvey (Clive Brook). When the train is stopped by rebels, a passenger reveals that he is General Chang, the Chinese rebel army leader (Warner Oland), and threatens to blind Doc Harvey. Lily promises to become the general's mistress in order to save Doc from torture. The general is killed by Lily's companion, Hui Fei (Anna May Wong); Lily and Doc are reconciled.

"If I'm not back in a week don't wait for me." The femme fatale may appear to be sadistic, but as Deleuze insists, it is the pseudosadism necessitated by the woman's incarnation of the "element of inflicting pain in an exclusively masochistic situation." Marlene Dietrich in *The Devil Is a Woman* (1935). Publicity still.

In *Blonde Venus* (1932), the triangle between the female and two rival males is complicated by the demands of mother love. Helen Faraday (Dietrich) becomes the mistress of a local politician, Nick Townsend (Cary Grant), to finance her husband's experimental treatments for radium poisoning. When Ned Faraday (Herbert Marshall) returns from Europe, he learns of his wife's infidelity and demands custody of their young son, Johnny (Dickie Moore). Helen takes Johnny and flees. After being forced into prostitution, Helen finally decides to give up her son, although she has successfully eluded private detectives and police. She then rises to fame and fortune as a café chanteuse in Paris, where she again meets Nick Townsend. In the final reel, Helen returns to New York to be reunited with her child and reconciled with her husband.

The female's struggle against society is articulated as an important theme in several of the von Sternberg/Dietrich films, but the variation on the basic female/male/society pattern is most prominently displayed in *Dishonored* and *The Scarlet Empress*. In *Dishonored* (1931), Magda (Dietrich) is a prostitute in World War I Vienna. As agent X-27, she sacrifices herself to a firing squad from her own country rather than allow her lover, a Russian army officer (Victor McLaglen), to be executed. *The Scarlet Empress* (1934) traces the rise of Catherine the Great (Dietrich) as she is sexually exploited by a political system that forces her into an arranged marriage with the heir to the Russian throne, the Grand Duke Peter (Sam Jaffe). Catherine falls in love with Count Alexei (John Lodge), the ambassador who delivers her to her new husband, but ultimately rejects him and learns to use her sexuality to exploit the Russian oligarchy for her own purposes.

The synopses of these von Sternberg/Dietrich collaborations may invite ridicule: the radium-poisoned husband in *Blonde Venus*, the cynical prostitutes sacrificing themselves for true love in *Dishonored* and *Shanghai Express*, the older man humiliating himself because of his desire for a woman who is barely above the level of prostitute (*Morocco*, *The Devil Is a Woman*). The films appear to be absurd remnants of outworn melodrama, but in these scenarios of misplaced desire, betrayal, and sacrifice lie a psychological complexity, a sophisticated dynamic of pleasure, and an aesthetic intensity that transforms the potentially trivial into a tragic conflict between the contradictory demands of psychological obsession and social identity.

The films' view of woman's place in society also suggests an ambivalent reaction to the female that contains radically subversive elements yet is also romantically antiquated. The subversive quality of von Sternberg's films seems crucially dependent on the masochistic structures embedded in them, although it is impossible to separate unconscious from conscious (or auteurist) intent.[13] Whether the complex portrait of women offered in the films is the result of masochism's subversive desire to replace the father as the supreme symbol of authority with the mother or of von Sternberg's conscious insights into the relationship of the sexes under patriarchy is difficult to ascertain. Within the von Sternberg/Dietrich films, a dialectical relation is established between the compulsive repetition and transformation of different levels of masochistic fantasy and the films' clearly articulated recognition of the oppression of women.

Masochistic fantasies often assume the form of the primal scene fantasy of the excluded child, oral stage fantasies suggesting incorporation, destruction or abandonment, or the exaggerated rivalry of the Oedipal triangle. Within the masochistic psychodynamic, fantasies of post-oral phases do not function independently but are dominated by the masochistic wish with its oral stage etiology. The revival of fantasies from the infantile stage or any developmental period should not be regarded as a recapitulation of static entities from an archaic past. Their transformations demonstrate that adult experience and fantasy rework and reinterpret infantile wishes and conflict.

In von Sternberg's films, as in Sacher-Masoch's novels, the masochistic male character often assumes the same position as the fantasizing infant described in Laplanche's account of the primal scene as a scenario of exclusion that leads to masochistic fantasy.[14] The paternal superego as negative parental control is signified by the rejected father. The oral source fantasy is imposed on an Oedipal structure: the desiring child and mother as ideal paternal control expiate the father, who embodies the superego's repression of the incestuous, infantile, polymorphous sexuality of masochism. In the animistic omnipotence of imagination, the child controls the fantasy—the mise-en-scène of masochistic desire—that exalts loss of control and helplessness.

Male Identity and Masochistic Passion

Within the masochistic scheme, von Sternberg's male characters often play out the conflict between identity and desire, superego and ego, repression and perversion. Robin Wood has suggested that the behavior of these characters "confirms one's sense of Sternberg's personal involvement" in their humiliation and masochism.[15] Yet self-sacrifice and self-destruction are not limited to von Sternberg's male characters, nor is the implication of the director's "personal involvement" in their display of suffering (as interesting as it may be) a viable key to solving textual problems in the films. If it were, von Sternberg's notoriously bombastic declaration, "I am Miss Dietrich and Miss Dietrich is me," would be the simplest and quickest way to validate a theory of masochistic gender transmutation, identity reversal, and even the identification of the son with the oral mother.[16] Unfortunately, as provocative as his remark might be, the psychodynamics of the films and the characters' actions require a more involved explanation.

In von Sternberg's films, as in Sacher-Masoch's novels, the fantasizing masochistic subject is represented by a male character. In the aesthetic expression of the masochistic wish, the son must first iconically imitate the father so that the son's genital likeness to the father can be humiliated and expiated. This leads to an intricate masquerade. The son's psychic identity is *clothed* in the physical guise of the older man who unites the paternal self (superego/genital sexuality) with the filial self. La Bessiere in *Morocco* and Don Pasquale in *The Devil Is a Woman* are two such composite figures. Their worldliness, respectability, and social status signify the paternal superego to be disavowed. They also embody those aspects of the superego that Freud associated with the maintenance of social stability. The identity of the father in the son depends upon the superego's repressive control over instinct. In "An Outline of Psychoanalysis," Freud declared the superego's "chief function" to be "the limitation of satisfactions."[17] Superego control is destroyed in masochism's humiliation of the father figure and symbolic expiation of phallic sexuality, an expiation efficiently accomplished by the exquisite torturess—the femme fatale.

In *Morocco,* the destruction of the paternal superego begins in the film's very first scene. La Bessiere observes Amy Jolly as she steps past him on the deck of a night ship bound for Morocco. He initiates the look with Amy as his object, but his gaze of fascination leads to masochistic self-abnegation in the face of her desire for Private Brown. After picking up the contents of her spilled suitcase, he offers her his card and a promise of future assistance. "I won't need any help," she replies, then walks over to a solitary spot on the deck railing. With the calculating theatricality of one who knows she is being watched, Amy tears up his card and insolently flicks the pieces overboard. In borrowing a phrase from Lacan, it might be said that she literally destroys the "name-of-the-father." Her rejection of La Bessiere as father-protector-rescuer continues upon their arrival in port. At the nightclub where she sings, she refuses to meet him after the show. La Bessiere is undeterred by Amy's lack of interest or her questionable social and sexual status. He continues his genteel pursuit, offering her flowers, diamonds, then marriage. In the meantime, Amy is quite public in her interest in Private Brown, whose youth and attractiveness function as signifiers of his right to her. La Bessiere's position is analogous to the impotent child witnessing the mother's relations with the father: he cannot obtain the woman forbidden to him by society's taboos. For the child, the incest taboo is operative; in *Morocco*, the taboo of class substitutes.[18]

When Amy's legionnaire deserts her, she agrees to marry La Bessiere, but she abruptly leaves their engagement dinner when she learns that Private Brown's patrol is entering the city. After frantically searching for Brown, she returns to the dinner party and announces that she must go to Brown, who was wounded and left behind. La Bessiere does not appear to be jealous or angry; instead, he volunteers to take her to his rival. *Cahiers du Cinéma's* analysis of the film explains La Bessiere's action as a "devaluation" of Amy in that he "does nothing to restrain Amy Jolly and even drives her."[19] La Bessiere is a man who admits he has been too "exacting" and had never found a woman good enough for him until he met dive singer Amy Jolly. However, his insistent pursuit of her cannot be so readily assimilated under *Cahiers du Cinéma's* account of the film's devaluation of the female based exclusively on the ideology of patriarchal bourgeois capitalism.[20] La Bessiere's actions constitute a masochistic devaluation of self, a self associated with the father and fixed social identity. Consequently, his true psychic identity is that of the son whose masquerade as the father determines his punishment.

The dinner party scene climaxes La Bessiere's required and relished public moment of masochistic exhibitionism. With a derisory laugh he tells his guests, "You see, I love her. I'd do anything to make her happy." Masochistic desire validates male submission. La Bessiere's public humiliation serves two purposes. In the male's submission to the female's own desire, the superego is repudiated. La Bessiere's passive acceptance of Amy's desire for Brown also undercuts the notion of what constitutes male identity in the patriarchal society: the male is expected to control the female, especially female sexuality.[21] On still another level, La Bessiere's humiliation before his guests demonstrates masochistic triumph. His desire is resilient, unchanged by Amy's desire for another or by her absence. La Bessiere shows that masochistic desire thrives on pain. His announcement and self-mocking laugh present a telltale confirmation of the masochistic need to display suffering. Theodor Reik has observed: "We know that it is a psychological necessity for masochism to have witnesses, spectators or confidants to the discomfort and suffering. . . . the masochist does not hide his misery; he shows it to everybody, he propagates it. . . . He does not cover his defeat as best he can. With its assistance he shows off as best he can." [22] La Bessiere could end his attachment to Amy, but he chooses not to. Pretending to abolish his own will, he hides masochistic activity behind a masquerade of passivity.

The Tragedy of Pleasurable Suffering

Masochism's playacting, masquerades of defeat, and ironic self-awareness cannot mask the rigidity—the tragedy—of the perversion. Alain Robbe-Grillet identifies perpetual motion and the enjoyment of suffering as characteristic of tragedy: "Wherever there is distance, separation, doubling, cleavage there is the possibility of experiencing them as suffering, then raising this suffering to the height of sublime necessity. A path toward a metaphysical Beyond. . . . Under the appearance of perpetual motion, it actually petrifies the universe in a sonorous malediction. There can no longer be any question of seeking some remedy for our misfortune, once tragedy convinces us to love it." [23] Masochism's tragedy is the tragedy of infantile fixation and the exaltation of suffering. Reik notes that human beings could not avoid suffering but that "as long as there is suffering, masochistic tendencies are bound to gain prevalence. . . . there will exist the pleasure of suffering." [24] Suffering does not deter or confuse masochistic desire but inflames it. The pleasure of masochism is inseparable from the pain of suspense. Masochism's dynamic of pleasure does not depend on resolution or the recreation of the original plenitude; pleasure is found in the obsessive repetition of desire. Unlike a neurosis, the perversion cannot be cured by acting out to release the individual from repression because masochism does not have its source in repression. Theatricality does not cure masochism; on the contrary, it is essential to its expression. Masochism, like tragedy, convinces the audience to love the characters' misfortune.

Of masochism, Reik asks, "What else but a demonstration of absurdity is aimed at, when the punishment for forbidden pleasure brings about this very same pleasure?" [25] To receive punishment before experiencing the forbidden pleasurable act is absurd. Equally absurd is receiving the punishment at the hands of a woman who assumes the superego's punishing function as a disguise in a scheme seeking to disavow and deflect the superego. At the level of superego/ego functioning, masochism shows the absurd humor in this psychic masquerade. Masochistic humor reflects the ego's triumph at the expense of the superego. [26]

Masochistic guilt also plays an important part in the ironic tone that infuses von Sternberg's films. Traditionally, guilt in masochism has been defined as Oedipal in origin. Deleuze explains that the masochist "stands guilt on its head" in using punishment to make pleasure permissible and in inverting the order of sinner/sinned against. Guilt "is at its deepest and most absurd" because it is not the masochist but the father who is guilty.[27]

The composite figure of father/son has no psychological future. These characters move between the entrapment of the repressive patriarchy and the radical liberation of a desire that inevitably ends in disappointment or death. Masochistic freedom *is* death. The masochist longs for and dreads the mystical symbiotic union with the mother in an apotheosis analogous to orgasmic release—*une petite mort*. Symbiosis as ultimate pleasure cannot be represented except in the imaginary space of death. It is that tragic yet absurd solution, that place of transcendence where death and desire merge, that is the essence of masochism's and von Sternberg's paradoxical stance.

Guilt, Humor, and Passivity: The Masochistic Male in The Devil Is a Woman

Von Sternberg's films come very close to Robbe-Grillet's description of tragedy, but the ironic and excessive nature of masochistic suffering often pushes the films over the edge into the black comedy of the preposterous. By the end of the von Sternberg/Dietrich Paramount cycle, the masochistic male's voluntary submission to the female becomes so extreme that only a tenuous balance is maintained between absurdity and tragedy. Nowhere in von Sternberg's oeuvre is that paradox so clearly articulated than in *The Devil Is a Woman*. With the possible exception of Professor Rath in *The Blue Angel*, Don Pasquale Castellan is the most extreme masochistic type of any of the males who inhabit von Sternberg's universe.[28] Don Pasquale does retain some of the dignity of bearing that La Bessiere exhibited in *Morocco*, but his pursuit of Concha takes masochism to its most blatantly absurd conclusion.

Don Pasquale's actions parallel those of Severin in Sacher-Masoch's *Venus in Furs*. Like Severin, he is introduced as the disillusioned, even "dephantasized" narrator of his own incredible story. He relates a tale of fleeting, unresolved encounters with Concha Perez, the obscure object of his masochistic desire. After Concha leaves him for the last time, Don Pasquale's military career is ruined by the public scandal caused by their affair. Left an aged, broken man, he claims he has "not looked at a woman in three years."

Don Pasquale recounts his story of folly to dissuade his young friend Antonio from seeing Concha, "the savage, the toast of Spain." He demands that Antonio swear an oath not to see the devilish female, but his bitter denunciation of Concha is merely a feeble disavowal. In recounting his tale of woe, Don Pasquale protests that he "gain[s] no pleasure" in telling his story, yet it becomes obvious that he not only enjoys telling Antonio about his road to ruin but in the retelling finds the impetus for a new round of masochistic pursuit. Masochistic desire compels Don Pasquale to pursue Concha once again, in absurd defiance of his own suffering. His attempt to dissuade Antonio is not a cynical attempt to deter a rival, as Andrew Sarris has stated, but the prelude to a humorous and pathetic reversal.[29] Don Pasquale admits: "If I were to live my life again, I'd probably do the same foolish things over again." His career ruined, his health broken by "the most dangerous woman alive," he suddenly sends Concha a letter, which she reads aloud to Antonio: "I am at your feet. I love you more than ever. . . ." Don Pasquale's action is preposterous by rational standards but fully accountable and predictable within the logic of a desire that ends only in complete defantasization or death.

The humor in this absurd pursuit is not lost on von Sternberg. His characters, like Sacher-Masoch's, usually recognize the humor in their self-imposed misery. In *Venus in Furs,* Severin declares: "The comic side of my situation is that I could escape, but do not want to."[30] Don Pasquale repeats La Bessiere's "caricature of passivity" in which the masochist pretends to submit totally to the partner but actually retains a degree of control over punishment.[31] Don Pasquale could easily avoid suffering. He blames Concha for his ruin but admits that he had at least two options, "to leave her or to kill her." He adds, "I chose a third." In the masochistic third option, Don Pasquale returns to Concha to tell her that life without her means nothing. His misogynistic railings cannot disguise his need to suffer at the hands of a beautiful woman.

When Don Pasquale finds Antonio and Concha together, he challenges Antonio to a duel. Antonio refuses to fight, but Don Pasquale presses for the encounter. Don Pasquale's exhibitionary maneuvers provoke punishment. A crack shot, he submits to Concha's pouting demand that he not harm Antonio and allows himself to be shot to satisfy her desire for his rival. Thus he actively seeks out the pleasure of self-orchestrated victimization, a goal that is culturally inadmissible for the male because, as Kaja Silverman has observed, it "disputes the inevitable desirability of the active, masculine position, privileging instead what has been marked in the patriarchal culture as the inferior, feminine position."[32] The male assumes the traits associated

with the patriarchy's definition of the feminine: submissiveness, passivity—masochism.

Don Pasquale finds masochistic success in ruin. On his deathbed,
he attains what he desires most, Concha and Death, one and the same,
both still suspended, promised, but withheld. The eternal masochistic
attitude of waiting and suspended suffering is maintained in all its
tragedy and comic absurdity to the very end of this film, which marked
the conclusion of the von Sternberg/Dietrich collaboration.

The Greek: The Androgynous Male in the Masochistic Scheme

In the masochistic heterocosm, desire is given mirror reflection,
turned across. Desire's iconic repetition creates predicaments in which
characters experience the pain of sexual humiliation or abandonment.
The humiliation of the masochistic father/son figure is most frequently
increased by the entry of a second male whose prototype in Sacher-
Masoch's *Venus in Furs* is called The Greek.[33] The Greek also functions as a composite figure who incorporates several aspects of the
masochistic fantasy core. Like the father/son figure, he takes on ego
functions but also assumes superego (punishing) functions. Within the
framework of an Oedipal fantasy structure, The Greek represents
the aggressive return of the father in the primal scene, the imposition
of the *reality principle* on the child's fantasy. The child's masochistic
primal scene fantasy is made complete by this figure, who forms the
third side of the familial triangle and causes "the interruption of love"
necessary to suspend gratification.[34] The presence of The Greek ensures the repetition of a desire that is inseparable from the pain of
suspense.

The Greek also represents an idealized aspect of the son, the
"new man" as Deleuze calls him, who emerges in the son's fantasy
rebirth from the oral mother alone. In this rebirth, masochistic passion
is desexualized, then resexualized into the "new man" who emerges as
both virile and feminine, dephallicized into polymorphous, nonphallic
sexuality. Rebirth is equated with castration, which is not an obstacle
but rather a "precondition of its success with the mother."[35]

In *Venus in Furs*, Severin calls The Greek "a proud, handsome
despot" and fears that he "will capture and enslave" Wanda.[36] While
the jealous infant fears the mother's love will be usurped by the father
or a sibling, the masochist fears his rival will subjugate the female who
subjugates him. "Confronted with such fierce virility," says Severin,
"I feel ashamed and envious," but he also recognizes the effeminate

aspects of The Greek who, "like a woman . . . knows he is beautiful and behaves accordingly."[37] The Greek was said to have dressed as a woman and been courted by other men; his ambiguous sexual identity speaks to the "new man" whose rebirth from the mother cancels his allegiance to the paternal model of genital sexuality.

Within the masochistic scenario, the sexual repression and strict gender boundaries imposed by the patriarchal superego are rejected, and the erotic display of the androgyne is offered. Desire is repeated, doubled, given mirror reflection in the masochistic dialectic that confuses sex roles and gender identities. In *Morocco*, La Bessiere is the top-hatted, tuxedoed suitor to Amy; Amy becomes the top-hatted, tuxedoed suitor to Private Brown. In *The Devil Is a Woman*, Don Pasquale gives flowers and money to Concha, who passes them on to a new lover as Don Pasquale watches. Dietrich's trademark of cross-dressing is counterpointed by the effeminized masculine beauty of Count Alexei in *The Scarlet Empress*, Antonio in *The Devil Is a Woman*, and Tom Brown in *Morocco*.

In *Morocco*, when Private Brown first sees Amy Jolly at her debut in a rowdy Moroccan nightclub, he attempts to quiet the audience. Attired in tails and top hat, she looks him over with an appraising, steady gaze from her position above him on stage. Brown is placed in the passive, feminine position and becomes a fetishized object glamorized in two-dimensional close-ups. Amy throws him a flower, which he wears behind his ear. Sarris remarked of Cooper's portrayal of Brown: "As for Cooper, it is difficult to believe that this natural American landmark ever planted a rose behind his ear or flourished a fan behind which he stole a discreet kiss from Dietrich. . . . there is a genuine interplay between male and female, but even more, there is a perverse interchange of masculine and feminine characteristics."[38] The "perverse interchange" might be regarded as a liberation from the masculine/feminine polarities dominating notions of sexual identity in a patriarchal structure.

The nightclub scene also demonstrates how von Sternberg's films emphasize the active aspect of the female's gaze and the passive element in the male's look. If Amy's desire for Brown is set by her first glimpse of him, the ending of *Morocco* also confirms the association of the female with the active gaze. She watches the legionnaire prepare to set out across the desert with his patrol. Suddenly, an unexpected reverse close-up shows Private Brown, the object of the gaze, turning around to smile at Amy. The third shot reveals the source of that highly eroticized close-up of Brown—Amy, who smiles back, mockingly salutes him, then decides to follow him into the Sahara. In *The*

Wearing a flower behind his ear and languidly playing with a paper fan, Private Brown assumes the passive, feminine position as the fetishized object of Amy Jolly's gaze. Gary Cooper and Marlene Dietrich in *Morocco* (1930).

Scarlet Empress, when the young Sophia Frederica (later Catherine) first sees Count Alexei, she turns to stare at him until the door between them slowly closes. The matching of gazes determines mutual attraction with almost equal attention given to the male's "to-be-looked-at-ness."[39] In *The Devil Is a Woman,* Concha insists that Antonio remove his mask. He is reluctant because he is wanted by the police. When he unmasks, Concha responds with open delight.

If the gaze in these films is frequently linked to feminine desire, films such as *Morocco* and *The Scarlet Empress* compromise the integrity of the male's three-dimensional spatial domain, which Mulvey identifies as the necessary backdrop for male action in classical Hollywood cinema.[40] Von Sternberg's insistence on two-dimensional space and male inactivity contributes to the "feminization" of the male. The wedding sequence in *The Scarlet Empress,* discussed at length in chapter 5, addresses the full range of possible implications this phenomenon holds.

Dietrich's initiation of the look or her active looking back undermines the notion that the male gaze is always one of control. Not only does the female assume her particular powers within the masochistic dynamic, but she rejects her audience's attempts at tactile possession. *Morocco* and *Blonde Venus* offer a self-referential examination of the relationship of the spectatorial gaze to the image of the performer. Possession through the gaze is actually nonpossession, just as Amy cannot hold onto Tom or La Bessiere cannot keep Amy. Amy wanders through the nightclub audience; a man attempts to hold her by her clothing. She stops, stares at him, then pulls away. A similar sequence occurs in the Paris nightclub sequence in *Blonde Venus.* The gaze determines but cannot control the object of desire. Although the spectator (and the masochist) may assume that the gaze equals actual possession, Dietrich subverts this idea. Concha asks Don Pasquale in *The Devil Is a Woman,* "How can you lose what you never possessed?" Within the masochistic scheme, the object of desire is as elusive as it is for the film spectator who glimpses the cinema's shadow representation of the absent object.

Although the rival male is feminized in these films, the cruelly narcissistic aspect of The Greek is also evident in many of von Sternberg's male characters. At the beginning of their involvement with the female, the narcissism and aggressiveness of Tom Brown, Alexei, Antonio, and Nick Townsend are pronounced. During the course of the drama, these traits either defer to masochistic desire or are partially retained to increase the suffering of the masochistic father/son figure. When Tom meets Amy in her apartment, it is clear he has been there many times before with other women. He casually explains: "I've been stationed in this town a long time." Later, when Amy goes to bid him farewell, he has a girl tucked under each arm. "Anyone who has faith in me is a sucker," he tells Amy, and "the ladykiller" is true to his warning. Agreeing to leave Morocco with her, he waits in her backstage dressing room; but then, with a lazy, relaxed, even playful deliberateness, he writes out a message on her dressing room mirror: "Good luck, I changed my mind."[41]

In *The Devil Is a Woman*, Tom's attitude and words are not echoed by Antonio, as might be expected, but by Concha after she deserts Antonio at the border. The reversal demonstrates masochism's transference of character function. Either male or female plays the role of torturer within the carefully predetermined parameters of masochistic desire. Antonio, who has played The Greek to Don Pasquale's Severin, watches Concha leave without explanation. He assumes the psychic identity of the masochistic subject. This moment resembles the end of *Morocco* when La Bessiere is positioned as the helpless and abandoned child: he is left to watch Amy disappear over a hill with the camp followers. However, in *The Devil Is a Woman*, Antonio exhibits a wild, hallucinatory look of total disbelief that suggests an end to the masochistic fantasy.

In *The Scarlet Empress*, Count Alexei, Master of the Hunt, first appears as the equivalent to Sacher-Masoch's The Greek but is quickly transformed into a figure of masochistic suffering. Alexei is entrusted with bringing Sophia Frederica, a minor Prussian princess, to her fiancé, the Grand Duke Peter of Russia. Sophia has never seen her betrothed, and Alexei ridicules her expectations: "So you want him to be handsome . . . and tall, and strong. . . . well, he is all that, and more." In describing the Grand Duke, Alexei takes himself as the referent: "His eyes are like the blue sky, his hair the color of ebony . . . and he is sleepless because of his desire to receive you in his arms. . . ." The truth is that Peter is an insanely cruel and repulsive little creature who has absolutely no sexual interest in his bride. Alexei lies to protect the interests of the state, which demands a "machine of marriage" to produce a son. "Nothing less than a boy will do" declares the old Empress (Louise Dresser). The Russian royal family is desperate; unfortunately, the heirs to the throne are either female or—in the current instance—mad.

Alexei brings portraits of the Empress as gifts for Sophia's family, but Sophia's request for a picture of the Grand Duke is pointedly ignored. Sophia's determined effort to see her fiancé—to kindle desire through sight—is subverted by her attraction to Alexei, who betrays

Count Alexei brings gifts to Sophia Frederica and her family, but Sophia's request for a picture of her betrothed is pointedly ignored. Her determined effort to see her fiancé—to kindle desire through sight—is subverted by her attraction to Alexei, the Master of the Hunt. John Lodge, Marlene Dietrich, and C. Aubrey Smith in *The Scarlet Empress* (1934).

his assigned duties as royal envoy in a self-absorbed attempt to seduce her. Tossing his mane of hair away with a gloved hand, curling his lip as he spits out lies to a naive girl who waits on his every word, Alexei seems to be testing the limits of his own sex appeal. Naturally, Sophia falls in love with him.

Alexei's desire for Sophia is initially depicted as a product of male narcissism seeking validation in sexual conquest, which is also true of Tom Brown's response to Amy in *Morocco* and Lieutenant Kranau's attraction to Magda in *Dishonored*. Concha's accusation directed against Don Pasquale in *The Devil Is a Woman* also applies to Alexei: "You always mistook your vanity for love." Female desire is discounted by male narcissism. Alexei chides Sophia for inflaming his passion by looking at him. He kisses her and then hands her a whip so she may punish him for his effrontery. His response indicates that he knows the startled but obviously flattered princess will not exercise her royal prerogative.

As the film progresses, Alexei's exercise in seduction gives way to the "authentic" desire of masochism. As he bows to the rule of masochistic desire, Sophia, now Catherine II, gains control over her sexuality to achieve the political power necessary for her survival. She has discovered the truth in Foucault's statement that sexuality is "endowed with the greatest instrumentality: useful for the greatest number of maneuvers and capable of serving . . . as a linchpin for the most varied strategies."[42] She exacts revenge against Alexei's infidelities in a dialectical masochistic reversal. From behind the veiling of her bed she tantalizes him, then orders his duplication of the role she once played for the old Empress. Alexei prepares her bedchamber for the arrival of a lover,[43] and in a variation on the primal scene fantasy he is stationed as helpless spectator to a scene that produces excitement in him but that he is helpless to act upon. Forced to replay Catherine's role as servant as well as a twisted version of his own earlier role as devious matchmaker, Alexei becomes the aroused but excluded bystander to Catherine's political ascendancy through sexual mobility. The masochistic "interruption of love" has been accomplished. Alexei's psychic identity as the father/son figure is consummated through punishment.

Masquerade and Feminine Identity

The von Sternberg/Dietrich films center on performance as a way of foregrounding the meaning of the gaze. Performance also serves as the focal point for uniting the depiction of female sexuality in a patriarchal society with the formal and psychoanalytic requirements of masochistic desire. Bill Nichols unknowingly identifies the essence of masochistic performance and the formal strategies of the masochistic aesthetic when he writes: "The visual style of *Blonde Venus* deals primarily not with pleasure—self-indulgent pleasure, as many believe—but with the control of pleasure, with the mediation of desire by style and performance."[44] Masochism must control desire through the participants' theatrical ritualization of fantasy. Masquerade is imperative to the perversion's control of pleasure and delay of consummation. Providing characters with a transformational visual mode of self-definition, masquerade functions as a performance that controls the enticement of desire. Through the temporality of masquerade, gratification is delayed and masochistic suspense is formalized.

Within feminist film theory, masquerade has been defined as a process in which, as Michèle Montrelay explains, "a woman uses her own body to disguise herself." Femininity is created with "dotty objects, feathers, hats, strange baroque constructions," the purpose of which is "to say nothing."[45] According to Joan Riviere's interpretation of masquerade, feminine accoutrements are assumed in excess in order "to hide the possession of masculinity and to avert the reprisals expected if she was found to possess it."[46]

Mary Ann Doane has suggested that a potentially subversive function arises from masquerade because it answers a woman's need to manufacture a distance between the self and the constructed image of femininity demanded by the patriarchy.[47] To illustrate her point, she cites Silvia Bovenschen's description of a Dietrich stage performance in which the audience watches "a woman demonstrate the representation of a woman's body."[48] However, Doane's appropriation of Bovenschen's remarks on Dietrich to confirm her theory on excess femininity and the masquerade are somewhat misleading, for Bovenschen goes on to associate Dietrich with an "intellectual understatement." She observes the paradox in Dietrich's achievement of "mythic status," achieved despite "her subtle disdain for men."[49] Doane assigns Dietrich's masquerade to the realm of the femme fatale who is "necessarily regarded by men as evil incarnate" because she evades patriarchal law.[50] Although Dietrich has frequently been called a femme fatale, with the possible exception of *The Devil Is a Woman* she is never portrayed as "evil incarnate" in the von Sternberg/Dietrich films. Even Concha Perez, perhaps the most ruthlessly independent of all the von Sternberg/Dietrich females, is provided with ample justification for her actions.[51]

Dietrich does possess an aloofness that suggests a distanciation from her constructed image, but the complexity of that image exceeds

Is this a man, a woman, or both? In donning male attire, Dietrich transforms the spectacle of female representation into a ritualized acting out of bisexual identification. Her gestures do not soften her masculine costuming to recuperate femininity; on the contrary, she appears unequivocally butch. Marlene Dietrich and Paul Porcasi in *Morocco* (1930).

the explanation provided by masquerade defined as a mask of excess femininity, for Dietrich's aloofness is sustained in her assumption of male attire as well. In the first backstage scene in *Morocco*, Dietrich's gestures do not soften the masculine attire to recuperate "femininity"; on the contrary, she appears unequivocally butch. Later, when she dons a feather boa and tights for the song "What Am I Bid for My Apples?" she seems like an entirely different person who, for the sake of performance, has magically acquired a new gender identity.

While the predominance of feminine masquerade also may point to a certain flexibility of female identity, this is not meant to suggest that women are more bisexual than men but that they may be less committed to social stereotypes because of the solid sense of gender identity formed out of the primary identification with the mother.[52] Masquerade serves as the female's defensive strategy within the patriarchy. Protean elusiveness allows the female to survive in a society that judges and uses her according to her image. Her transformations make male pursuit more difficult. Women's changing spectacle deflects and confuses the male gaze to keep the masochistic charade alive.[53]

In the von Sternberg/Dietrich films the heroines constantly look at themselves in mirrors as they prepare for public performance. This display of female "narcissism" is undercut by Dietrich's air of detachment, by her refusal to invest in the importance of the identity forged out of public exhibitionism. In creating herself through masquerade and performance, the female in the von Sternberg/Dietrich films takes part in a dialectical process in which power is obtained through her knowledge of how others see her. In patriarchal society, female exhibitionism depends on the ability to identify with the male who views her. As John Berger explains, women survey themselves because how they appear to men will determine how they are treated. In the mirror, the female perfects the image that is the main source of sexual and economic power in patriarchal society.[54]

Aided by the mirror, Dietrich's transformations conform to the representation of woman as spectacle while they simultaneously contribute to the subversion of male control. She exhibits a cool self-awareness, confirming her knowledge that male pleasure in looking is organized around female performance. Bovenschen's remarks on a Dietrich stage performance apply to the von Sternberg/Dietrich films: "The myth is on the receiving end and consumes the audience. She gazes down from the stage not once but twice, once as an image and once as an artist, as if to say okay, if this is how you want it."[55] Dietrich displays herself in a confirmation of what Foucault refers to as "power asserting itself in the pleasure of showing off, scandalizing, or resisting."[56] In *Shanghai Express*, Lily's costumes of feathers and fur advertise her profession and her power to fascinate. The multiplicity of pleasures achieved through this exercise of power are also asserted by Amy Jolly in *Morocco* and Helen Faraday in *Blonde Venus* in their stage performances: male costuming and lesbian signifiers offer the scandal of mobile sexuality and autonomy from male domination.

In *Blonde Venus*, costume signifiers are particularly important in Helen Faraday's control of performance. In a poster advertising her Parisian nightclub appearance, she is depicted as an abstract art deco nude—an anonymous female body for the male gaze. On stage, she is discreetly covered in a gentleman's white tuxedo. Her male costuming defies the audience's expectation that her body is of central interest in her performance. Her costuming also serves to deny the sexual difference that has ensured her success in the male world. Dietrich's cross-dressing is not indicative of a flattering emulation of the "superior" male. Instead, it serves to demonstrate the fluidity of sexual identity even as it parodies male phallic narcissism. Without the phallus, Helen assumes the male prerogative of sexual freedom with only the exterior trappings of "masculinity."[57] She becomes a mirror reflection of the male's manipulative power.

In donning male attire, Dietrich transforms the spectacle of female representation into a ritualized acting out of bisexual identification. Lawrence Kubie observes that clothes provide an important way of carrying out magical body change and the wish to become both sexes without requiring the subject to completely reject the original sexual identity.[58] Helen's performance calls into question the significance of the visual perception of the presence or lack of the penis, the "visibly ascertainable difference," in differentiating the sexes.[59] Through the changing spectacle of masquerade, the limits of one gender identity and one body-ego are transcended. In her performance, clothes "make the man": Helen's tuxedo and her flirtation with the harem girls who accompany her stage entrance suggest a sliding of sexual identity. Is this a man or a woman, or both?

In guaranteeing the pleasurable pain of desire, masquerade evidences the masochistic projection of multiple mothering imagos onto the represented female. Victor Smirnoff suggests that costuming plays a vital role in separating masochism's ambivalent imagos.[60] In *Blonde Venus*, Helen Faraday is transformed from a "little water nymph" into an American housewife and mother. In rapid succession she becomes a New York club singer, a politician's mistress, a prostitute, a Paris nightclub star, a millionaire's fiancée, and a wife and mother again. In *The Devil Is a Woman*, Concha Perez metamorphoses from a nunnishly attired traveler to a cigarette factory worker to Spain's most famous singer/courtesan. As with Helen Faraday, a.k.a Helen Jones, a.k.a. Helen Blake, the name change of Princess Sophia Frederica to Catherine II in *The Scarlet Empress* marks a significant change in identity. Sophia begins life as a German princess whose every action is dictated by her mother. As Catherine, wife of the Grand Duke Peter of Russia, she becomes mother to the heir to the throne and, finally, sole ruler of all Russia. In *Morocco*, Amy Jolly is a "suicide passenger," a cabaret singer, fiancée to a wealthy painter, then camp follower. In *Dishonored*, Magda is an officer's widow turned streetwalker. She is transformed into a spy of many disguises—blackbird, leather-jacketed pianist, peasant girl—before she chooses to return to the costume of a prostitute and death as a traitor.

Dietrich's protean metamorphoses of identity may be accounted for through Deleuze's description of tripartite maternal imagos in the masochistic fantasy. The maternal imagos symbolizing the uterine (or hetaeric), Oedipal, and oral stages are supported by one figure who functions as the single object of masochistic desire. As noted in chapter 1, in fulfilling her role as masochism's good oral mother, the female assumes the bad characteristics of the Oedipal and uterine mothers in order to usurp the father's functions.[61] The Oedipal mother is usually the victim of the sadistic, superego-dominated male or the patriarchal system. In taking on the characteristics of the uterine mother (Sacher-Masoch's Grecian woman), the female displays another aspect of the masochist's projected ambivalence: she embodies the pagan life associated with the "chaotic sensuality of the hetaeric era."[62] The ideal female protagonist of masochism must maneuver between these positions, between the extremes of suffering and torturing, between subjecting herself to patriarchal denigration and defying the system's norms, between submitting to the male's domination in the name of love and dominating him. Ambivalence is resolved in the masochistic ideal that balances these extremes in the figure of the ideal cold oral mother. The female's protean transformations are carefully controlled by the perversion's psychodynamic and the formal structure of the masochistic aesthetic. Within these transformations, Dietrich's identity remains squarely fixed within the masochistic delineation of the ambivalent maternal force. She embodies "den ruhenden Pol in der Erscheinungen Flucht," the continuum within never-ceasing transformations.[63]

The oscillation between masochism's maternal imagos and the assumption of multiple masquerades is exemplified by *Blonde Venus*. The film clearly shows how post–oral phase fantasies are "brought

Clothes "make the man." Helen Faraday's performance calls into question the significance of the lack or presence of the penis as the "*visibly* ascertainable difference" between the sexes. Marlene Dietrich in *Blonde Venus* (1932).

regressively into relationship to the oral phase," so that the basic masochistic fantasy wish may be expressed.[64] Beginning as a water nymph in a Black Forest pond, Helen's splashing exit dissolves to the splashing of her five-year-old son in the bathtub of their New York flat. Now a harried, breathless housewife, she dutifully waits for her scientist husband to return home. The triangle of Helen, Ned, and little Johnny Faraday provides an open expression of Deleuze's accounting of the alliance of mother and son.

Helen and Johnny's attachment is intensely close to the point of being sexualized. The eroticized relationship of mother and child contributes to the film's subversion of its conventional "woman's film" aspects.[65] Helen's oral aggressiveness toward Johnny is contrasted with her sexual passivity toward both husband and lover. Nick Townsend's "Gimme a kiss" declaration to Helen culminates in a kiss the audience is not permitted to see. His romantic imperative echoes Helen's words to Johnny in an earlier scene, when she passionately grabs her son to plant a kiss on his mouth; she then turns to her husband, Ned, to give him a circumspect kiss on the cheek.

Helen's treatment of Johnny infantilizes him. Although he is said to be five years old, he sleeps in a crib. His mother feeds him by hand and carries him. The phallic imagery appropriate to his actual age and to the Oedipal triangle is represented in Johnny's rocking horse, toy gun, trumpet, and the numerous mechanical toys that incessantly punctuate the action with their rocking, jumping, and pecking. Their placement in the mise-en-scène often suggests a direct comment on Ned's symbolic impotence and Johnny's subversive assumption of power within the Oedipal triangle. As Ned placidly sits in his laboratory, Johnny robustly fires his play gun and rocks on his rocking horse until he mounts his mother's shoulders to be carried off to bed.

The phallic imagery in *Blonde Venus* is not incompatible with the basic masochistic infantile wish governing the drama. Deleuze says that the masochist wants to be incorporated into the mother and reborn from her alone, but without giving up his "phallic integrity."[66] Nevertheless, it is not Oedipal but masochistic desire originating from the oral stage that rules the dynamics of the characters' interaction. *Blonde Venus* demonstrates how later phases are absorbed into the rubric of the oral phase fantasies so that the basic masochistic wish might be expressed. After she loses custody of Johnny, Helen attains her greatest success. Like Catherine in *The Scarlet Empress*, she assumes male attire at the pinnacle of her success in the male world. At her lowest, in a miserable flophouse, Helen swore she would find a better bed. We are led to believe she has found several. She now resembles

Sacher-Masoch's Grecian woman, a hermaphroditic figure who confuses sexual boundaries, demands the independence of women, and dedicates herself to momentary pleasure.[67] Helen capitalizes on her ability to provoke male desire. Her performances (on stage and in bed) have led to her financial success, but her achievement is not the equivalent of liberation. A client at the nightclub tells Nick Townsend that Helen's rise to fame has been secured by her use of men as "stepping stones." "I hear she's as cold as the proverbial icicle," he mutters. On her dressing room mirror, a quotation from Kipling's "The Winners" is scrawled: "Down to Gehenna or up to the throne / He travels the fastest, who travels alone." Helen tells Nick that she has no more feelings, but her negation of feeling is a disavowal. The male costuming and the masquerade of sadistic apathy form the pattern of pretense that requires masochistic pleasure to be conditioned and hidden by pain. Her coldness "buries" her sentimentality. The chains of emotion are unbroken; Helen cannot renounce mother love.

In fulfilling her function as ideal oral mother, Helen must be reunited with her child, but this reunion is double-edged. She is saved from the sadistic negation of feeling represented by her assumption of male attire and identification with the male's manipulative power. She is reinscribed into the patriarchal construct of marriage, but the power of the father and the superego have been negated. Ned's revenge has failed; Johnny has not forgotten his mother's face, in spite of his father's efforts to erase her memory. Through the bars of his crib, Johnny turns the musical carousel that accompanied his mother's lullaby. This complex, overdetermined image ties together Johnny's control of his parents, his own fixation at an infantile state, and the motifs of imprisonment (the bars), repetition (the circular motion), and goodness (the angel figurines). All relate to Helen's sacrifice to the patriarchal institution of marriage. She has succumbed, but the guts of the institution are gone; male control has been shattered.

Blonde Venus shows how the female's transformations may lead to a subversion of the patriarchy through the transcendence of social identity that is simultaneously a masochistic sacrifice. Often, as in *Dishonored* and *Blonde Venus*, these functions merge. Magda's death before the firing squad in *Dishonored* is both a rebellious and a submissive gesture. She successfully traps double agents and, as Lieutenant Kranau says, "deals out death" with her body. She submits to patriarchal punishment for breaking the codes that define patriotism and her profession as a spy. Allowing desire to overcome professional detachment, Magda obliterates the false self of the patriarchy's imposed values and roles. Her patriotic venture as a spy is depicted as meaningless. Like

Madga awaits the firing squad in *Dishonored*. By elevating desire above the law, her voluntary submission to death suggests a hidden, masochistic pleasure that defies rather than confirms the values of the male tribunal that courtmartials her. Barry Norton, Marlene Dietrich, and Gustav von Seyffertitz in *Dishonored* (1931). Publicity still.

Helen Faraday in *Blonde Venus,* when Magda faces patriarchal law, she appears to acquiesce. When asked by the head of the secret service why she failed to redeem her miserable life in the privilege of serving her country, she says, "I guess I'm no good." Magda's voluntary submission to death suggests a rebellious, masochistic pleasure that defies rather than confirms the values of the male tribunal that courtmartials her.

Within society, the female is expected to reach self-definition through her image. In Magda's performance before the firing squad, she coolly adjusts her stocking and reapplies her lipstick as if preparing for a rendezvous with a lover. Her calculated display of female exhibitionism functions as a mode of subversion. Her insolence in controlling her appearance before her last male audience disavows her helplessness before the patriarchy. Declaring that he will not a shoot a woman (nor any more men), a young lieutenant hysterically refuses to direct Magda's execution. He is led away and quickly replaced. Magda does not react. The execution proceeds.

Idealizing Masochism's Maternal Imagos

The von Sternberg/Dietrich heroine is often a prostitute *(Blonde Venus, Dishonored, Shanghai Express)* or sexually promiscuous *(The Scarlet Empress, Morocco, The Devil Is a Woman).* Dietrich's sexually experienced woman is a paradoxical figure. Freud considered the prostitute to be the signifier of infantile, polymorphous sexual pleasure, the representative of all perverse possibilities.[68] In another sense, as Jane Gallop observes, the prostitute represents the female as "pure receptacle."[69] The male, like the narcissistic oral infant, only has to demand; his wishes are all important. Gallop continues: "The client's role is to demand his 'I want.' The whore plays out the 'he wants.' In the renunciation of mastery (of the "ich will") the woman encompasses and surpasses the man; she knows what he wants."[70] Von Sternberg's films complicate this portrait of the woman who knows and accepts male desire. The Dietrich character is more than an object renouncing her own desire. Prostitution defines her as an exploitable economic value, but her rebellious submission to the patriarchy leads her to prostitution to achieve sexual self-identity.

The masochistic fantasy of the ideal oral mother's assumption of bad mother traits shares the Romantic ideal that the uniform of the prostitute masks a woman of virtue. The Dietrich heroine acquires independence in social ruin. Beyond the boundaries of society's pretenses, she attains greater self-awareness and honesty. In *Shanghai Express,* General Chang says, "A man is a fool to trust any woman." He

Prostitution defines this Dietrich heroine as an exploitable economic value even as she acquires independence in her social ruin. Beyond the boundaries of patriarchal society's sexual pretenses, she attains greater self-awareness and honesty. Marlene Dietrich with Gustav von Seyffertitz in *Dishonored* (1931).

does believe, however, that "a word of honor would mean something" to Shanghai Lily/Madeleine, who assumes the role of the Magdalene, the holy harlot.[71]

The female's identity as prostitute also brings together masochistic fantasy with the economic realities of a system that frequently propels the female into using her body as an economic commodity, either in the street or, in the case of *The Scarlet Empress,* in the marriage bed. The latter, as well as *Dishonored* and *Blonde Venus,* depicts the female's reaction to the power structures of patriarchal society. In *Blonde Venus,* when Ned Faraday discovers Helen has been unfaithful, he threatens to take Johnny away from her. Rather than lose custody of her child, Helen flees. She discovers she cannot sing in clubs for fear of being recognized and reported to the police. Finally, she prostitutes herself to feed her child. This sequence of events conforms to Deleuze's description of how the Oedipal mother, as a transitional figure, becomes the victim of the father. The female's victimization by the father symbolically reflects the child's interpretation of parental coitus: "mother is being attacked by father." *Blonde Venus* evidences the merging of the Oedipal mother with that of the uterine mother (prostitution).[72]

When Ned accuses Helen of becoming Nick Townsend's mistress for selfish economic motives, she replies, "How else could I have made so much money so quickly?" The hard economic facts of women's value in patriarchal society exonerate her. In true oral mother fashion, Helen acts out bad mother functions (prostitution and abandoning her child), but the film idealizes those functions. She proudly maintains, "I've been a good mother to Johnny," and, as Nichols has astutely detailed, the film supports her through lighting codes that vindicate her while they reinforce Ned's condemnation.[73] Parallel to masochism's positive disavowal of the mother is a degrading disavowal of the father. As Deleuze remarks, "the father is nothing. . . . he is deprived of all symbolic function."[74] After Helen has been reduced to poverty and prostitution, her ability to role play in response to male society protects the all-important mother/child bond. Not realizing who she is, the detective tells her, "You don't look anything like these other women." "Give me time," she cynically slurs. Her masquerade is successful. Control of her performance would ensure her escape, yet Helen voluntarily decides to give up Johnny.

When Helen reveals her true identity to the detective, who does not realize that his prostitute companion is the woman he is pursuing, she smiles as she says, "I'm no good, no good at all, you get me. No good for anything except to give up the kid before it's too late." Robin

Wood describes this as "one of the most extraordinary moments" in the film and concludes that Helen's smile "can be read most easily as an expression of relief and *release*."[75] Her speech, which counters the film's endorsement of her sacrifice as one of selfless goodness, suggests that she is echoing the patriarchy's judgment that her sacrifice to keep her son is incongruous and therefore shameful because society cannot tolerate the sexual nature of her assertion of motherhood. Yet Dietrich's characters reject the male's hypocritical attitude toward sexual mobility. Like Magda in *Dishonored* and Shanghai Lily in *Shanghai Express,* Helen Faraday is visually idealized and morally exonerated even in the depths of her supposed degradation. What society would make her shame becomes her untrammeled display of sexual power.

In *Blonde Venus,* the hypocrisy of society is personified in the detective who trails Helen. Before he knows her identity he is quite ready to enjoy her sexual favors. At the very same time he denounces Helen's brand of "mother love" to his new friend: "She's not doing her kid any good," he says. Society's representatives—the detective, Helen's scientist husband, the New Orleans judge who accuses her of vagrancy —all form the critical superego that condemns her sexual mobility. The female's nonprocreative sexual capacity has been released and used for the most basic of goals—survival. To the patriarchal superego, that sexuality is incompatible with motherhood and with control of the female. Mobile desire would undermine the foundation of the family structure that guarantees paternity.

The Scarlet Empress: *Protean Metamorphosis and the "Sadistic" Female*

In *The Scarlet Empress,* Sophia Frederica's transformation into Catherine the Great exemplifies the functioning of the female in the masochistic scenario as it also demonstrates the female's protean changes of identity necessitated by patriarchal oppression. The old Empress tells Catherine that she must learn to be a "good Russian wife," which means obey her husband, serve Russia, and produce sons, but Catherine subverts patriarchal expectations long before she arranges her husband's death. By giving birth to a bastard, she undermines the marriage contract as a guarantee of paternity and destroys the "natural" link in the patriarchal chain.

This subversion of patriarchal law was partially motivated by Catherine's callous exploitation by the system. Her child was conceived as a result of misplaced, frustrated desire. When Catherine discovers that Alexei is the old Empress's lover, she impulsively throws away a locket with his picture. Running outside to retrieve it, she is stopped by a guard. He refuses to believe she is the Grand Duchess because "everybody knows she is locked up every night." Catherine petulantly insists on her royal identity. "Well, if you are the Duchess, then I am the Grand Duke," the lieutenant replies. He embraces her, and Alexei's locket falls from her hand as she returns the lieutenant's embrace. Their ironic misunderstanding of identity creates a playful masquerade with serious consequences. The lieutenant's assumption of Peter's sexual identity subverts Catherine's appointed sociopolitical function as "brood mare" for Russian royalty. The scene also signals Catherine's sexual awakening into mobile desire and her exploitation of her own body as a political tool. Through an arranged marriage, Catherine was sacrificed to the state; she now turns sacrifice into defiant personal triumph. Carried on the shoulders of the army she has seduced, dressed in the pure white uniform of a Cossack officer, she takes the throne to become the cold, ambivalent mother figure in the logical conclusion to the masochistic tale. Elevated into the position of relative good in a corrupt system, Catherine becomes a woman of stone.

Much has been made of the "sadism" of the female protagonists in the von Sternberg/Dietrich films. Raymond Durgnat reasons that Concha's "sadism" in *The Devil Is a Woman* results from "class vindictiveness." He also writes that Catherine's actions at the end of *The Scarlet Empress* transform her into "a female Sade."[76] The female's actions may appear to be sadistic, but as Deleuze insists, it is the pseudosadism required by the woman's incarnation of the "element of inflicting pain in an exclusively masochistic situation."[77] Catherine must decide whether to be destroyed by power or to wield it. Masochism's ambivalent stance toward the oral mother guarantees the female's alternation between coldness and warmth, sacrifice and torture.

If the unconscious structures of the masochistic fantasy compel the female to triumph over the male, von Sternberg's artistry gives such films as *The Scarlet Empress* the means by which the woman's ascension to power reflects the complexity of her existence in patriarchal society. In the von Sternberg/Dietrich films, the femme fatale's danger supersedes her portrayal as an amoral, sexualized female who threatens male control. She is fatal because she represents masochism's fantasy of the powerful oral mother, the site of rebirth, and the child's symbiotic merger into nonidentity.[78] She represents the dialectical unity created in masochism's fusion of pain and pleasure, liberation and death. Death and desire become mirror reflections as their mysteries dialectically unite in a disavowal of identity that is also a triumph of masochism's promise of liberation through death.

In choosing death, an ambiguous, even illusionary triumph is created, especially in masochism, where desire is secretly ruled by the infantile fixation. Death provides a victory over the limitations of repressive reality and the promise of a transcendence of socially bound identity. It offers the masochist the only possible liberation from the repetition of desire. In *Love in the Western World,* Denis De Rougemont describes Western society's traditional glorification of passion as a disguise for the "longing for death" in terms that are startlingly similar to a description of masochistic desire: "Both passion and the longing for death which passion disguises are connected with, and fostered by, a particular notion of how to reach understanding which in itself is typical of the Western psyche. . . . Because, in being the passion that wants Darkness and triumphs in a transfiguring Death, it must be repressed, for any society whatsoever, a threat overwhelmingly intolerable." [79] As a subversive desire that refuses to fear castration, pain, or death, masochism attempts to satisfy "the unconscious longing to become part of another being." [80] Masochistic desire emerges as the epitome of transcendent, transfiguring, and tragic passion.

CHAPTER FOUR

Iconicity and the Masochistic Heterocosm

This chapter explores the psychological and semiotic aspects of iconicity in film. In *Signs and Meaning in the Cinema*, Peter Wollen cites von Sternberg's films as exemplars of an iconic textuality that has largely been ignored in film studies.[1] In Wollen's view, the neglect of the iconic aspect of filmic representation can be traced to the opposition between André Bazin's and Sergei Eisenstein's theories of cinema. In these two classical paradigms, filmic representation is divided along the indexical (Bazin) and the symbolic (Eisenstein). Following these two positions, film theory has conceptually excluded a filmmaker such as von Sternberg, whose films have little aesthetic connection with those lauded by either theorist. As Wollen observes: "Von Sternberg . . . sought, as far as possible, to disown and destroy the existential bond between the natural world and the film image. But this did not mean that he turned to the symbolic. . . . It was the iconic aspect of the sign which Von Sternberg stressed, detached from the indexical in order to conjure up a world, comprehensible by virtue of resemblances to the natural world, yet other than it, a kind of dream world, a heterocosm."[2] Wollen considers von Sternberg to be an iconic filmmaker relegated to a theoretical no-man's-land, forgotten in the gap between the indexical and the symbolic, long take and montage, "realism" and ideological didacticism.

Citing the role of semiology in exacerbating the neglect of the iconic, Wollen believes film theory's reliance on Ferdinand de Saussure has created a semiological bias against the study of iconic signs. The reason for the neglect, says Wollen, is semiology's favoring "of the arbitrary and the symbolic" and "the spoken and the acoustic."[3]

Even at the most superficial level, the theoretical neglect of iconicity is a direct by-product of the fundamental premises of Saussure, who grouped signs into two general categories, unmotivated (symbolic or arbitrary) and motivated (natural signs), the latter of which merges the iconic (representation by resemblance or likeness of the signifier and the signified) and the indexical (causal relationship between signifier and signified) into one sign category. Even so, Saussure's failure to maintain a clear-cut distinction between iconic and indexical signs does not fully account for the neglect of the iconic.

Wollen suggests that the nonlinguistically biased semiotics of Charles Sanders Peirce is particularly well suited to studying the iconic sign and fills an important gap in considering how all signs are employed in the cinema. He regards Peirce's approach to signs as a more appropriate model for studying film, which is fundamentally iconic but also indexical and symbolic.[4] Peirce divided the sign into the referent (or object), the sign itself, and the interpretant (the sign created in the mind). He remarked on the relationship between these three aspects of any sign: "A sign, or *representamen*, is something which stands to somebody for something in some respect or capacity. It addresses somebody, that is, creates in the mind of that person an equivalent sign, or perhaps a more developed sign. The sign which it creates I call the *interpretant* of that first sign. The sign stands for something, its *object*. It stands for that idea, which I have sometimes called the ground of the *representamen*."[5] The sign was classified as either iconic, indexical, or symbolic, with the iconic sign representing "its object mainly by its similarity."[6] Peirce regarded the iconic sign as the most malleable of all signs; but unlike Saussure, he did not arbitrarily favor the study of any one sign. He defined the iconic sign as a broader category than that of the related icon, which he defined as "a possibility alone," determined "purely by virtue of its quality."

According to Peirce, the object of the icon could "only be a Firstness,"[7] which was one of the three *modes of being* that defined the experiential power of the sign. His triadic system extended into categorizing the "qualitative possibilities of interpretants."[8] Through these categories, Pierce attempted to account for the dynamic process of creating signs in the mind: ". . . there are three modes of being . . . positive qualitative possibility (Firstness), the being of actual fact (Secondness) and the being of the law that will govern facts in the future (Thirdness)."[9] The icon, or *qualisign*, exhibited one mode of being —Firstness, pure form. Iconic signs were impure signs that blended Firstness, Secondness, and sometimes Thirdness. Peirce recognized that sign categories tended to overlap. Hybrid or impure signs such as the iconic, also called the *hypoicon,* were much more common than pure signs such as the icon. Iconic signs were divided into three subcategories: images, diagrams, and metaphors. Peirce remarked that the photograph is a "good example of a hypoicon, i.e., of an iconic representamen" which illustrates the blending of sign categories.[10] Although iconic, the photograph also possesses an indexical element by virtue of its reproductive (photographic) basis. Peirce noted that photographs resemble the represented object because "they [are] physically forced to correspond point by point to nature."[11]

Because any iconic sign is an impure sign, iconicity, as Charles Morris has suggested, becomes "a matter of degree."[12] In film study, that "matter of degree" may be approached through the effect of style on the cinematic sign's classification as indexical, iconic, or symbolic. Sign classification becomes a matter of interpretation, just as in Christian Metz's *grande syntagmatique,* narrative syntagmas are the product of the interpreter's valuative classification of signs. It is not a foregone conclusion that a certain sign belongs in a particular category or that a filmmaker's style is dominated by a particular sign. In "Circles of Desire," Alan Williams classifies Max Ophuls's *La Ronde* as predominantly indexical, yet Wollen's brief comparison of Ophuls's films to those of von Sternberg suggests that Ophuls might more usefully be approached as an iconic filmmaker.[13]

In Peirce's notion of semiosis, all types of nonlinguistic sign systems were judged to be equally valid topics of study. Rather than consider the verbal sign system as a reflection of a superior mode of thought, Peirce actually regarded inference from similarity or resemblance as indicative of a higher type of reasoning: "Inference from continuity, or experiential connection, is the most rudimentary of all reasoning," he declared, whereas "inference from resemblance . . . involves somewhat steady attention to qualities."[14] Peirce did not ignore analogic thinking and iconic signs, but he thought the iconic dimension of signs was central to communication: "The only way of directly communicating an idea is by means of an icon; and every indirect method of communicating an idea must depend for its establishment upon the use of an icon."[15]

In focusing on iconic sign and iconicity, my first goal is to analyze the affective power of the textuality of von Sternberg's films through Peircean semiotics. My second purpose is to clarify the production of meaning through the dominant mode of sign representation in these films. Third, a discussion of iconicity, as Wollen suggests, has broader significance for modern film theory and the issue of signification. If, as Wollen argues, Saussure's semiology is linguistically preferential—biased in favor of unmotivated, arbitrary sign systems —why has film theory found its guiding mentors and models in Roland Barthes, Roman Jakobson, and Claude Lévi-Strauss, who are essentially Saussurean-based, rather than in Charles Sanders Peirce, Thomas Sebeok, Charles Morris, and George Mead? In the wake of Wollen's study, the application of Peircean semiotics to the iconic sign in film remains a neglected area of inquiry.[16]

Iconic Representation: The Context of Classical Theory

To understand what it means to be an iconic filmmaker, Bazin's and Eisenstein's theories of representation should first be examined. Bazin stressed the indexical nature of film's photographic grounding. "All the arts are based on the presence of man," he wrote; "only photography derives an advantage from his absence."[17] In Bazin's opinion, cinema is an art in which the profilmic event (the Peircean referent or Saussurean signified) can be visually represented without the filmmaker's overt intervention. The filmmaker should defer before the power of nature and strive to capture a "fragment of raw reality" on film.[18] The contiguous temporal flow of the natural world and its spatial unity deserve a respectful translation onto film. Bazin believed that German Expressionism's excessive plastic effects showed how film might be deflected from its true aim of capturing the natural world. Far more pervasive than Expressionism in its negative effects was the emphasis on image juxtaposition shared by Eisensteinian montage and Hollywood continuity editing. The shared privileging of the ordering elements over their "objective" content had "insidiously substituted mental and abstract time" for the spatial and temporal unity of the real world.[19] In addition to violating real world unities, montage violated spectatorial individualism by imposing an interpretation of the depicted event on the viewer.

In the neorealism of Roberto Rossellini and the deep focus photography of Orson Welles, Bazin found the twin poles of his aesthetic ideal. The humanism of Rossellini's films was perfectly matched by an indexical style exemplifying "self-effacement before reality."[20] Welles's deep focus camera style restored ambiguity to the image, which had been destroyed by Eisensteinian montage and Hollywood classical editing syntax. Structurally more realistic, deep focus photography radically advanced film language to bring "the spectator in a relation with the image closer to that which he enjoyed with reality."[21] Confident of film's ability to authentically represent an objective reality, Bazin placed ultimate value on the continuity of space and time as reality's primary indicators. In Bazin's theory of representation, realism is a given and the indexicality of film is the ideal means for realizing the medium's intrinsic aesthetic capacity to become a "truth of the imagination."[22]

Eisenstein did not believe in the objective realism of nature, nor did he consider the faithful imprinting of a trace of "reality" to be a filmmaker's chief responsibility. Filmic realism, or, as he called it, "representational naturalism," was a style that inevitably reflected an ideological position. Instead of investing in an idealistic notion of the real, filmmakers should place their faith in their own ideological concepts, their own theme to be embodied in the total film effort.[23] To this end, Eisenstein emphasized the importance of juxtaposing discrete units—montage cells. Cinema's potential lay in making the "qualitative leap" beyond a simple "quantitative accumulation" of shots.[24] In its ideal form, cinema worked toward an ideologically didactic function, but its effect was primarily emotional and physiological. In harnessing film's emotional power, the indexical or iconic aspect of the image sign was insignificant beside the greater symbolic meaning of the montage cell used in a language-like combination of associations. Eisenstein believed that language was "much closer to film than painting." The filmmaker was obliged to realize that the medium was "governed by the same laws as language."[25]

Von Sternberg as an Iconic Filmmaker

In contrast to Eisenstein, von Sternberg regarded himself as a painter with light and shadow who, through exacting control, turned mechanical reproduction into art. Wollen's assessment of von Sternberg as an iconic filmmaker recognizes that the director's films cannot be accounted for within Eisenstein's or Bazin's theories of representation. Von Sternberg regarded the photographic aspect of film, its inherent indexicality, not as its greatest strength but as its greatest hazard: "The artist lauds or glorifies, invents freely when he finds nothing, protests or destroys what he opposes; never does he operate without visible superiority to his subject. . . . The director is at the mercy of his camera. It writes its own language, it transliterates all that is fed into it. . . . Left to its own devices, the camera is an incisive, vivisecting, and often destructive instrument."[26] Von Sternberg's aesthetic upholds goals antithetical to Bazin's. Seeking to eradicate the trace of the profilmic event—the trace of *nature* inscribed by the indiscriminately inclusive camera—von Sternberg once rather petulantly remarked that the perfect film of the future would be totally artificial.[27]

If von Sternberg cannot be aligned with Bazin's theoretical ideal of the cinema, neither does he fit Eisenstein's aesthetic position. While Wood has done much to correct the misconception that von Sternberg's films are out of touch with ideological issues (especially with regard to women), ideological didacticism and symbolism were not part of his films.[28] Von Sternberg's model for representation was neither nature nor ideological precepts but an art model—painting: "The white canvas onto which the images are thrown is a two-dimensional flat surface. It is not startlingly new, the painter has used it for centuries."[29] Von Sternberg's use of that surface is consistent with Deleuze's delineation of the masochistic aesthetic as a supersensual fantasy world based on an art model and operating as a "protest of the Ideal against the real."[30] Deleuze explains Sacher-Masoch's doctrine of *supersensualism:* "There is a fundamental aesthetic or plastic element in the art of Masoch. It has been said that the senses become 'theoreticians'. . . . He [Sacher-Masoch] calls his doctrine 'supersensualism' to indicate this cultural state of transmuted sensuality; this explains why he finds in works of art the source and the inspiration of his loves."[31]

In *The Rise of the American Film,* Lewis Jacobs unwittingly links the von Sternbergian world to masochistic supersensuality with blind accuracy. Reacting with unmasked critical aversion to the films' stylistic excesses and insinuations of sexual abnormality, Jacobs comments: "Made up of ravishing pictorial effects, peppered with lewdness and suggestive symbols, set in a macabre, unreal world created solely for the senses, these films trace the gradual withering of a talent. . . . They abound in madonnaesque close-ups, background symbolism, striking lighting effects, exotic atmosphere, and continuous dissolves, all at the expense of other organizational devices. They are tonal tapestries, two-dimensional fabrications valuable only for their details."[32]

Von Sternberg's films do create an "unreal world . . . for the senses," as Jacobs states, but this world is neither unorganized nor worthy of appreciation only for its decorative finesse. While symbolism might be part of that aesthetic, it is a metaphorical symbolism grounded in iconic signs, not formed out of arbitrary units. The likeness between the linked terms, their formal resemblance, comes first, just as the likeness between the signifier in film and the profilmic event is subject to the artist's manipulation. Von Sternberg's film world creates a syntax that is analogical-topological and grounded in iconic representation. It stands in direct opposition to either a Bazinian nature model exalting indexical representation or an Eisensteinian montage model stressing the ideological meaning of film and the equation of cinematic language with the structuring of discrete symbolic units as found in verbal language.

The Masochistic Heterocosm and the Iconic Style

In the spirit of the masochistic aesthetic typified by Sacher-Masoch's novels, the von Sternberg/Dietrich films create a world according to the dictates of the masochistic art of fantasy and the psychodynamics of the perversion. The real world is suspended, replaced, and reflected in a unique heterocosm that creates an imaginary time and space to contain the violence and sexuality of masochism. As Deleuze remarks, the masochistic heterocosm forms a "counterpart of the world" that serves "to hold up a perverse mirror to all nature and all mankind."[33] Such a creation depends on iconic resemblance to the world to facilitate understanding, but as the von Sternberg/Dietrich films show, the masochistic heterocosm only obliquely resembles any real world referent. Von Sternberg once remarked: "Verisimilitude, whatever its virtue, is in opposition to every approach to art."[34]

These films do not pay homage to nature or political agendas but to fantasy, to desire, and to the magical thinking of primary process. Masochistic eroticism is formalized in an aesthetic that confers a "spiritual" quality on violence and the excess of perversion by putting the two "at the service of the senses."[35] As discussed in chapter 2, the masochistic and sadistic heterocosms are entirely different; the commonality of violence and excess in masochism and sadism should not collapse the distinction made between the perversions. Each defines a different, alternative world. Sadism accomplishes this with negation, masochism with disavowal. The description of heterocosmic painting by Harry Berger, Jr., provides a useful adjunct to Deleuze in explaining how the masochistic aesthetic achieves this goal: ". . . the imaginary world is both disjunctive and hypothetical. It is *not* real life, but art or artifice; *not* actuality but fiction, hypothesis, or make believe; not merely an imitation of the world . . . but a new and very different sort of world created by the mind."[36] Von Sternberg's films maintain a similar heterocosmic stance but incorporate the particular formal requirements of masochism: disavowal, fetishism, suspension. The iconic sign is the only possible means of creating the masochistic heterocosm. In iconic representation, likeness itself becomes a new object, an experiential phenomenon without parallel in the real world, though resembling that world and appealing to the spectator as a sensuous alternative world.

While Bazin presupposed film's ability to capture reality, von Sternberg's iconic relations do not value the illusion of authenticity. On the contrary, indexical transparency and the continuum of spatial and temporal reality found in the "first world" are devalued. "I do not value the fetish for authenticity. I have no regard for it . . . ," von Sternberg commented. "There is nothing authentic about my pictures. Nothing at all."[37] Iconic textuality plays with the reproductive aspect of the cinema by emphasizing the sign as a creation divorced from its referent. The reality of imagination, of sign creation, is exalted over any presupposed objective reality. There is little pretense in von Sternberg's films that the absent referent is an actuality outside the realm of the film. The referent is clearly imaginative in status.

The dominance of iconic representation in von Sternberg's films becomes the representational equivalent to the disavowal that underscores the films' psychodynamics. The iconic sign is capable of holding its absent referent in an "I-know-but-nevertheless" suspension. The sign's reference to the profilmic event, to the "I-know," is deferred in favor of the sign itself ("but-nevertheless"). Iconic textuality locks the absent referent, whose indexical trace is left on the screen, into a dialectical, disavowing relationship with the sign as an imaginative creation. It pushes the reproductive aspect of cinema into the arena of self-referentiality by emphasizing the sign as a creation divorced from its referent and exalted over any presupposed indexical trace of "nature."[38]

Von Sternberg's iconic style involves an ambiguous disavowal of cinematic representation's indexical aspect. The dominance of iconic textuality becomes the representational equivalent of the fetishistic disavowal that underscores the films' psychodynamics. An imaginary world of disavowal creates a true cinematic fetish: the substitute for the Other that "knows" but "nevertheless" sustains the illusion of its autonomy. Yet, the masochistic alternative world cannot totally dismiss its resemblance to the first world. Berger explains such heterocosmic thinking as a disjunctive withdrawal, forced to recognize the claims of actuality that "persist and must be settled, acknowledged, or evaded."[39] Von Sternberg's rejection of the "fetish for authenticity" is a rejection of a fetish that might be considered the very cornerstone of Bazin's theory. The result is a play on the paradoxical relationship between the indexical and the iconic, "authenticity" and self-conscious illusionism.

Andrew Sarris has commented on the paradoxical illusion in von Sternberg's films:

> For all its frenzied fabulousness, *Morocco* succeeded in its time as illusionism for the general public. The proof of this success is the long

remembered belief in the final image of Marlene Dietrich setting off
into the desert sands on spike heels. . . . C. A. Lejeune . . . described
this finale as one of the most absurd of all time. Yet to single out any
one detail of a film for belief is to believe in the rest, and to believe in
Morocco's California desert is to believe in Sternberg's dream decor. . . .
The complaint that a woman in high heels would not walk off into the
desert is nonetheless meaningless. A dream does not require endurance,
only the will to act.[40]

Sarris's accuracy in assessing the public's belief in the last scene is less
important than his recognition that the von Sternberg/Dietrich films
create a world much closer to dream than waking reality. The end of
Morocco is, indeed, absurd when judged by a standard of verisimilitude, but verisimilitude is not the goal of the masochistic heterocosm.
Von Sternberg's films do not provide a Bazinian window on the world;
rather, they provide a window on the dialectical play between the unconscious and the conscious, between the second-world excesses of
masochism and the so-called normative first world, between the disavowing perverse fantasy and the demands of the reality principle.

Masochistic Disavowal and Dialectical Structure

In the masochistic scenario, disavowal's dialectical union with suspended "reality" balances the interplay of infantile fantasy and adult
conflict. The fundamental masochistic disavowal of the oral mother's
separation/difference forms the substructure of masochism's rejection
of reality. Deleuze explains masochistic disavowal as a process that
leads to a liberation from superego control. Disavowal is also the decisive formal determinant in the aesthetic's use of suspense to protect
the ideal. It is, says Deleuze, "a reaction of the imagination, as negation
is an operation of the intellect. . . . [Disavowal] is nothing less than
the foundation of imagination, which suspends reality and establishes
the ideal in the suspended world."[41] Paradoxically, the structure of
disavowal guarantees a continual, suspended acknowledgment of the
very thing denied. Within masochism, fantasy's disavowing function
is constantly threatened: the father may interpose himself between
mother and child; the superego may not be fooled by the masquerade
of pain. Disavowal suspends but cannot negate reality. Similarly, the
iconic cannot negate the indexical: imagination tentatively holds the
first world in abeyance.

The centralization of disavowal within masochism explains the
importance of von Sternberg's exotic settings in creating a frame for
the masochistic heterocosm. Berger identifies the first task in creating

any heterocosm as an "original framing gesture" that shows the alternative world "is at least initially contrary to established fact." This gesture is necessary before the second world can "hold the mirror up to nature and re-admit into its cleared space the elements of actuality."[42] The masochistic heterocosm of the von Sternberg/Dietrich films accomplishes the framing gesture through several means. Title cards and blatantly artificial opening credits provide the entry into the frame of exotic settings that bear little resemblance to their real life equivalents. Von Sternberg's films frequently begin with a listing of "The Players" over an emblematic background that accentuates the aura of make-believe. While this technique was certainly not unusual for films of the 1920s or 1930s, it is essential to the heterocosmic stance of von Sternberg's films. In *Morocco,* the credits are set against a painting of a Moroccan street scene. Fading to black, the shot is replaced with a revolving globe and "Morocco" written in large letters; a dissolve then leads to the letters' superimposition over a map, the final indicator of the exotic locale. In *Shanghai Express,* the credits are superimposed over dissolving images: a huge gong, a lily pond, a scroll of Chinese calligraphy, a Buddha, and incense burners.

Silent titles introduce the action of *Dishonored, The Scarlet Empress,* and *The Devil Is a Woman.* The titles of the first two films anticipate the outcome of the drama, conforming to Smirnoff's description of the ritualistic, closed nature of the masochistic ceremony.[43] The opening title of *Dishonored* indulges masochism's romantic fatalism with a melodramatic inscription of sexual difference: "A ring of steel encases Vienna. . . . strange figures emerge from the dust of the falling Austrian Empire. One of these, listed in the secret files of the War Office as X-27, might have become the greatest spy of history . . . if X-27 had not been a woman." Similarly, the opening title of *The Scarlet Empress* is virtually a "once-upon-a-time" proclamation that marks the film as counterfactual despite its ostensibly historical subject matter: "About two centuries ago, in a corner of the Kingdom of Prussia, lived a little princess chosen by destiny to become the greatest Monarch of her scene and Tsarina of all the Russias—the ill-famed Messalina of the North."

The opening title of *The Scarlet Empress* takes its cue from the beginning of all good fairy tales to foreshadow the action as already enacted, known, closed to any phantom possibilities of pretended here-and-now existence. The ambivalence of masochism's feminine ideal is immediately conveyed through the title's paradoxical construction: the little princess will be Russia's "greatest Monarch" yet also the "ill-famed Messalina of the North."[44] The titles frame the masochistic heterocosm as autonomous, imaginary, paradoxical. In *The Scarlet Empress* the original framing mechanism is doubled. The adult life of Sophia Frederica is set apart from the introductory childhood scene by a pivotal dream (or daydream) depicting graphic scenes of violence, executions, and sexually provocative tortures that foreshadow Sophia's future as Catherine II, "the Messalina of the North." The remainder of the film, however, fails to conform to the strategy of a conventional historical epic. Rather than cause/effect motivation, incongruous dreamlike sequences link Sophia's violent dream/fantasy to her adult life. The film provides an Alice in Wonderland world complete with spatial distortion, confusing temporal gaps, an abundance of grotesques, and a wicked "Red Queen." In spite of the make-believe quality, *The Scarlet Empress* shows how the fantastical masochistic heterocosm translates the ideological realities of the material first world into its carefully defined framework.

The exoticness of the von Sternberg settings—China *(Shanghai Express)*, eighteenth-century Russia *(The Scarlet Empress)*, the North African desert *(Morocco)*, World War I Austria *(Dishonored)*, and turn-of-the-century Spain *(The Devil Is a Woman)*—indicates the framing of the masochistic second world and concurrent disavowal of the claims of the first. Von Sternberg rejected the possibility that his films could (or should) be confused with any referent beyond the frame. In response to a pasha who thought he recognized street scenes in *Morocco*, von Sternberg glibly dismissed the supposed authenticity of the scenes as "no more than an accidental resemblance, a flaw due to my lack of talent to avoid such similarity."[45] The exotic settings are not evidence, as some have suggested, of von Sternberg's attempt to avoid the censorship problems that might have resulted had his dramas been placed against familiar contemporary backdrops.[46]

The similiarities between von Sternberg's choices of setting and Sacher-Masoch's cannot be written off as a coincidence nor explained exclusively in terms of their broadly shared cultural heritage. In *The Romantic Agony*, Mario Praz finds these same settings in the work of Romantic writers, which he goes on to associate with masochism:

> It was Merimee who localized in Spain the Fatal Woman who towards the end of the century came to be placed more generally in Russia: the exotic and the erotic ideals go hand in hand. . . . a love of the exotic is usually an imaginative projection of a sexual desire. This is very clear in such cases as those of Gautier and Flaubert, whose dreams carry them to an atmosphere of barbaric and Oriental antiquity, where all the most unbridled desires can be indulged and the cruellest fantasies can take concrete form.[47]

It may be extreme to equate the "love of the exotic" with the "projection of a sexual desire," but Western eroticism has conventionally associated trangressive sexualities with the otherness of exotic locales. The framing gesture that inscribes the exotic permits the free play of masochistic fantasy within the parameters of a meticulously formalized perverse heterocosm.

The Paradox of Iconic Illusion

In discussing *Blonde Venus,* Nichols has written that von Sternberg initially promises or encourages his audience to believe "his world real, available to the mind as a plausible unity."[48] The plausibility of the created world is not an issue. Von Sternberg's framing devices say, "This is play," but the play of masochistic melodrama is no less serious than Bazin's indexical film ideal. Gregory Bateson described the message of such a framing within the realm of animals' iconic communication:

> "This is play" looks something like this: "These actions in which we now engage do not denote what those actions *for which they stand* would denote." . . .
> . . . The playful nip denotes the bite, but it does not denote what would be denoted by the bite. . . .
> Paradox is doubly present in the signals which are exchanged within the context of play, fantasy, threat, etc. . . . Not only do the playing animals not quite mean what they are saying but, also, they are usually communicating about something which does not exist.[49]

As Bateson explained, operating within a similar strategy, a mode of psychological framing tells the viewer that the framed contents demand a different kind of thinking from that employed outside the frame. The result, said Bateson, is that a "this-is-play" frame "is likely to precipitate paradox" since it attempts to discriminate between "categories of different logical types."[50]

Reik has noted that masochism "contains a playful element."[51] The masochistic alliance requires deception and the manipulation of performance to sustain masochistic desire. Like playing animals who "do not quite mean what they are saying," masochism's participant-actors play at prolonging the suspense of pleasurable suffering. The masochist acts out fantasies based on infantile desire; the perversion's most fundamental dynamics set the frame in place. Deceptive play is at the very heart of the masochist's attempt to fool the superego. The exhibition of pain becomes an iconic sign resembling real pain, but the indexical (cause/effect) outcome expected under the regime of the superego and the reality principle is subverted. Guilt is displayed as an iconic sign, but masochism turns the signifier into a parody of guilt, the masochistic play of "psychic mimicry."[52]

Masochism's paradoxical play between the first world and the world of the perversion defines von Sternberg's cinema as recreative, reflective, and triumphantly false. In Berger's view, heterocosmic framing leads to a self-reflexivity inherent in an emphasis on technique. The viewer's attention is drawn to "the exhibition of mastery of craft and technique, of medium and methodology." As a consequence, the viewer may enjoy the second world with a particular intensity since the second world is "offered simultaneously as *only* a work of art and as *triumphantly* a work of art."[53]

Radically disavowing the world beyond the filmic frame, von Sternberg engages the spectator in a dialectical and paradoxical relationship with the first world. Reflexivity is necessary to sustain the masochistic aesthetic's dialectical balancing of the second-world fantasy with the demands of the first. The excesses of von Sternberg's films, their self-conscious technical virtuosity and attitude of *sèrio ludere* contribute to the sense that the films are *art,* not life. Although all films are iconic, von Sternberg's heterocosm displays the independence of the iconic as pure recreative likeness divorced from an indexical reliance on the original photographic referent. In his self-proclaimed "relentless excursion into style," style becomes its own subject matter.[54] This strategy recalls a remark by Adrian Stokes: "Formal relationships themselves entail a representation or imagery of their own though these likenesses are not as explicit as the images we obtain from what we call the 'subject-matter.'"[55] Disavowal, suspension, fantasy, fetishism—the subject matter of masochism—become the formal elements of the aesthetic. The art model is subject as well as form.

Von Sternberg's films offer little pretense that the film image is *transparent.* Instead, the iconic sign is offered as the sign of illusion, just as the masochistic aesthetic offers illusion as its subject matter: the illusion of suffering, of freedom, of possession. Of all the signs, the iconic is most suited to the masquerade of illusion that formalizes masochistic desire. The lie and truth of illusion are balanced in a sign that represents its object by the seemingly simple, straightforward means of likeness. Iconic communication of all types is inherently paradoxical. Icons and iconic signs are deceptive because they do not depend on an indexical relationship to the referent that would imply a consistent cause/effect link. As Peirce eloquently explained: "They [the icons], one and all, partake of the most overt character of all lies and deceptions—their Overtness."[56] The iconic sign openly presents a lie: the illusion that it actually *is* the object rather than a false, recreative substitute. Simultaneously, it offers two germane truths, the truth of essential resemblance and the truth of its overt illusionism. Paradoxically, the overt illusionism of an iconic textuality allows von Sternberg's films to become anti-illusionary.

In *Ideology and the Image,* Nichols concludes that calling attention to the medium constitutes von Sternberg's modernist critique of illusionism:

> . . . the film audience watches Sternberg display his control of their desire. . . . But Sternberg controls an image that refers to objects and events no longer present. . . .
> . . . He stresses the tenuous alliance between our knowledge of the illusion and our belief in its reality. . . . he invites us to play in the gap, the wedgelike opening, his style unveils. . . .
> Sternberg can be read as a modernist, but, like Ozu, that decisive step toward Brecht and a political modernism is only threatened, never taken.[57]

Nichols is certainly correct in his claim that von Sternberg's films break with conventional Hollywood illusionism, but this is not to say that von Sternberg should automatically be classed as a modernist. To label him as such sidesteps the director's self-proclaimed adherence to painterly traditions as well as the formal and psychoanalytic basis of what Nichols identifies as the "mediation of desire by style and performance" evident in *Blonde Venus*.[58] Calling attention to the artistic medium through the manipulation of style is not exclusively a modernist preoccupation. Deconstructing illusion has a long history in painting.[59] In von Sternberg's precarious charade between illusion and anti-illusion is the trace of masochism's reliance on its formal art model and its dialectical disavowal of reality, not modernism.

By foregrounding technique in an excessively ornate visual style, and by creating a problematic dramatic tone that emphasizes the falseness of the heterocosm, the von Sternberg/Dietrich films call attention to the paradox of iconicity's play at illusionism. Jurij Lotman has characterized traditional narrative cinema as a situation in which the "different pretends to be identical."[60] Von Sternberg's films reject "realist" cinema's pretense of indexicality, which is replaced by the overtly perverse play of the iconic. Sacher-Masoch once asked, "Is a fine work of art any the less fine if it is made up of abnormality and falsehood?"[61] Undoubtedly both Bazin and Eisenstein would answer in the affirmative. To an iconic filmmaker such as von Sternberg, the answer is a resounding "no."

Iconic Textuality as Masochistic Discourse

The iconic textuality of the von Sternberg/Dietrich films reflects on questions of iconicity beyond the issue of representation. The films exhibit what might reasonably be termed a *structured iconic discourse*. In "Circles of Desire: Narration and Representation in *La Ronde*," Alan Williams employs the term *iconic discourse* but does not define it except by the implication (through use) that it consists of some type of domination by iconic signs.[62] For our purposes, iconic discourse, iconic textuality, and iconic style will be used interchangeably; however, the term *discourse* implies more than the domination by iconic representation: it is a semantic organization sharing characteristics with the iconic discourse of the unconscious, with primary process, and with the mechanisms of image formation. Dominated by imagery, such a discourse does not exclude the verbal, but the latter can be expected to assume different characteristics and functions indicative of the close relationship to primary process. The dreamlike quality of von Sternberg's films, their emphasis on feeling and fantasy, their paradoxical mise-en-scène and curiously disjointed narratives are not the result of some "mysteriousness" that is "an absolute, unsusceptible to clarification," as one recent critic of von Sternberg declares, but are the result of an iconic discourse inseparable from the masochistic-psychoanalytic structure.[63] The films' style evidences a different type of communication drawing heavily from the iconic level of thinking associated with primary process.

Freud never offered a formal definition but did note in "The Unconscious" that *primary process* was distinguished by its defining characteristic: the discharge of affect and the "mobility of cathexes" made visible through condensation, displacement, representation in concrete form, and overdetermination—the dreamwork processes.[64] Primary process was conceived as an abstract concept, never found in pure form. Although it is frequently opposed to secondary process and the thought processes of "waking life," there always is a continuum between the two. Victor Burgin notes that unconscious processes form a very important part of everyday communication even though the continuum between the conscious and unconscious is often ignored and the unconscious is regarded as some mysterious, unfathomable entity. He asserts that unconscious processes "are structurally and qualitatively different from the process of rational thought and symbolisation enshrined in linguistics and philosophical logic" and goes so far as to assert that primary process "governs the mechanisms of visual association."[65]

Many writers have suggested that the presence of dreamwork

figuration automatically indicates the attempt to overcome censorship.
How could it be regarded otherwise if the unconscious only comes into
existence simultaneous to the subject's encounter with cultural prohibi-
tion?[66] Freud considered dream's cryptic quality to be the direct result
of repression, but dream studies now point to physiological processes
rather than psychological ones as the reason for the distinctive difference from everyday thinking; these studies also directly challenge the
theory that censorship generates these mechanisms.[67] Such research
may also require the reevaluation of these mechanisms as they are
presumed to operate in film texts: Should these codes automatically
be interpreted as analogous to the operations of dream, which work
(according to Freud) to censor the latent dream wish? There is a danger in prescriptively locating and separating the latent and manifest
content of a text as if it were a dream to be decoded without regard
to stylistic nuances. The film surface thus is reduced to its function as
a repressive mechanism that hides the "true" meaning of the film.[68]

Within the von Sternberg/Dietrich films, the paradoxes of meaning and style cannot be penetrated by a methodology that reads the
film surface as a disguise for a repressed, latent text. We may talk of
fantasy versus "reality," but fantasies express psychic realities, remnants of infantile feelings that are sometimes most obvious in narrative
patterns but also affect the intensity, atmosphere, and attitude of a
film. Gaston Bachelard's remark, that fantasy "resonates" in a text in a
dynamic merger with the surface of the work, is evocative and captures
the complexity of the relationship of the unconscious to art.[69] Instead
of a literal interpretation of how dreamwork processes function in film,
an identification of the shared stylistic similarities between films and a
consideration of their governing psychodynamics may help define the
textual mechanisms that—like primary process—more freely permit
the paradox of meanings playing side by side in contradiction.[70]

The Implications of Iconic Discourse

Chapter 3 discusses how the von Sternberg/Dietrich films evidence the dialectical interaction and transformation of infantile fantasies within the framework of the masochistic aesthetic's predictable
formal strategies. Bateson has characterized art as "an exercise in communicating about the species of unconsciousness," as a message that
acts as an "interface between conscious and unconscious."[71] Perhaps
because of the openness of the perverse masochistic fantasy, the von
Sternberg/Dietrich films seem to be particularly strong examples of
such an interface.

Although Lacan remarked that "the unconscious leaves none of our actions outside its field," Metz's influential use of Lacan in forming a theory of spectatorship tends to polarize linguistic organization and primary process as the respective representatives of "thought" and "anti-thought."[72] In *The Imaginary Signifier,* Metz discounts the applicability of the term *discourse* in reference to primary process communication because he believes the image-dominated unconscious, although structured like language, is incapable of forming a true discourse: "The unconscious neither thinks nor discourses: it figures itself forth in images; conversely, every image remains vulnerable to the attraction of the primary process and its characteristic modalities of concatenation."[73] Whether images are capable of forming an organized "thought" in primary process functioning reflects on the question of whether images alone can form narrative or discourse. Metz affirms the Lacanian principle of the search for the "mark of the unconscious in all conscious discourses," but his polarization of "thought" and "anti-thought" leaves the impression that secondary and primary process are mutually exclusive in their ability to form discursive structures. Metz is fixed into a curious position: he maintains that the unconscious does not "think" but is still like a language.[74]

The relationship of iconic discourse to imagistic structures has important methodological implications for theories of narrativity and reception. Saussurean semiology adapted to film studies has tended to equate visual semantic structures with linguistic syntax. Although cine-semiological trends of the 1970s have given way to psychoanalytic semiotics, homage to linguistic structures still holds sway over theoretical discourse concerning film. We should be wary of how linguistic bias might perpetuate a distorted notion of film's inherent organizational capacities to accommodate the medium's production of meaning to a linguistically modeled methodology.

Iconicity in the von Sternberg/Dietrich Cycle

Von Sternberg's iconic style seems an appropriate place to begin a discussion of semiology, imagistic structure, and primary process. In *Structuralist Poetics,* Jonathan Culler expresses his belief that icons (and, by implication, iconic signs) are not suited to a linguistically modeled semiological explanation: "Icons differ markedly from other signs. . . . Study of the way in which a drawing of a horse represents a horse is perhaps more properly the concern of a philosophical theory of representation than a linguistically based semiology."[75] It is not surprising that, as Wollen has pointed out, film studies perpetuate

Saussurean semiology's neglect of the iconic. The Lacanian theory of subject formation has also tended to close off discussion. For Lacan, language is the key to subjectivity and to the formation of the unconscious. We are "governed" by language symbolization and only know the unconscious through the interpretation of the conscious.[76] Often, this view has tended to return us exclusively to language's repressive force. It also fosters a deterministic model of subject formation, leaving little room for the progressive potential of nonverbal artistic communication.

Numerous studies in imagery formation and perception have thrown reasonable doubt on the premise that mind and linguistic organization structures are so perfectly analogous, as often assumed. That analogy, derived in part from the work of Edward Sapir and Benjamin Lee Whorf, has been vigorously defended in Lacanian-derived theories of film's link to subjectivity. Language acquisition is explained as a recognition and representation of difference, but one might ask whether language acquisition, as a complex, multifactorial process, is interpreted as oppressively narrow. In contradistinction to Metz, investigations into imagery by Heinz Werner, M. Vernon, Ralph Berger, N. Lukianowicz, and Mardi Jon Horowitz suggest that unconscious processes do form a discourse.[77] Decio Pignatari comments: "Unconscious language is basically paralanguage, pre-verbal, iconic, paratactic, and paronomastic. . . . What is common to the languages of the arts, of children and primitive peoples, of schizophrenics and of the Unconscious, is the paratactic, iconic organization of signs. Even Lacan is too 'word'-minded. . . . A psychoanalysis of Iconic Man (not only in works of art) should be possible. Perhaps it would also be a psychosynthesis of psychoanalysis."[78]

As Pignatari suggests, iconic organization of signs may dominate certain developmental periods. Freud noted that "thinking in pictures" predated thinking through words.[74] From her empirical studies on the relationship between verbal language and thought processes, Vernon reaches a radically anti-Lacanian conclusion: "there is no functional relationship between verbal languages and cognition or thought process; verbal language is not the mediating symbol system of thought; and there is no relationship between concept formation and level of verbal language development."[80] Pignatari, in turn, attributes the neglect of the analogic or iconic to the semiological refusal to acknowledge discoveries in divided brain structure (i.e., contiguity and similarity lobes).[81]

Bateson referred to the role of the iconic in primary process discourse and the communication of *feeling* in *Steps to an Ecology of the*

Mind. He believed that art mixes secondary process messages with those of primary process, with algorithms of the iconic which dominate the communication of feeling.

> These algorithms . . . of the unconscious, are, however, coded and organized in a manner totally different from the algorithms of language. And since a great deal of conscious thought is structured in terms of the logic of language, the algorithms of the conscious are doubly inaccessible. . . . when such access is achieved, e.g., in dreams, art, poetry . . . there is still a formidable problem of translation.
>
> . . . The subject matter of dream and other primary process material is, in fact, relationship . . . between self and other persons or between self and the environment. . . .
>
> . . . the characteristics of primary process are the inevitable characteristics of any communicational system between organisms who must use only iconic communication. This same limitation is characteristic of the artist and of the dream and of the prehuman mammal or bird.[82]

Although failing to conform to linguistic logic privileged in film studies' adaptation of Saussurean semiology and Lacanian notions of subjectivity, iconic discourse demonstrates the power of the discourse of the unconscious, of iconic algorithms and analogic thinking on filmic signification.

Dream, Primary Process, and Iconicity

The iconic structures of the von Sternberg/Dietrich films raise the question of what methodologies are best for studying the connection between production of meaning through the masochistic aesthetic, iconicity, and the open fantasy of perversion. The figurative expression of dreamwork is usually thought to be the purest example of primary process functioning, though Freud was careful to point out there was always a mix of primary and secondary modes of mentation. While dream was a "cryptically coded version" of psychic reality that attained its form due to the mechanisms of censorship, Freud dubbed fantasy a "hybrid," that is, a form that was a step closer to reality and a more direct "picture of psychic reality."[83]

Both dreams and fantasies depend upon the iconic communication and iconic or analogic association between imagistic forms to produce what Pignatari calls "diagrams of meaning."[84] The symbolism of dreams results from the association of forms that often fail to conform to the contiguous, logical structures of verbal language. Instead, parataxis (coordination) and paronomasia (likeness between sign and referent) dominate. Consequently, iconic discourse in film could be expected to exhibit many of the formal characteristics of dreamwork and fantasy. These structures suggest a different message to be communicated and the special function of such iconic strategies of communication. Iconicity also raises the question of whether different physiological brain structures govern analogic or figurative thinking.

Dream clearly demonstrates the formal characteristics of iconic discourse: paratactic structures emphasizing juxtaposition, form analogy, paromorphic metaphors, and a disregard for normal spatiotemporal continuity. Even when verbal signs dominate, they can be organized into iconic syntax emphasizing sound correspondences and verbal topology. The emphasis on the concrete signifier effects a "dewording" of words, which turns symbols (word signs) into iconic signs through paranomasia or onomatopoeia. The disruption and spatialization call attention to nonlinearity and the analogical-topological—the imagistic —syntax evidenced in literary texts such as Laurence Sterne's *Tristram Shandy* and James Joyce's *Finnegans Wake* and *Ulysses*.[85] Verbal iconization is a stylistic trait observed in von Sternberg's films but never explored beyond the notation of the films' vague status as "poetry."[86] Neither has the phenomenon been considered in the context of a guiding psychoanalytic and semantic organization to narrative and visual style.

Peircean Semiotics and Signification

If Saussurean-based theory has neglected the study of iconic signs in film, is the alternative of Peircean semiotics suggested by Wollen a better approach to filmic sign systems? Can it be reconciled with a psychoanalytic methodology as offered by this study?

The gap between psychoanalysis and a study of signs may be addressed through the model of Metz's *Imaginary Signifier*. He notes that linguistics and psychoanalysis may well be considered "the only two sciences whose immediate and sole object is the fact of signification. . . . between them they cover the whole field of *signification-fact*."[87] Deleuze's approach to Sacher-Masoch is a psychoanalysis in which the form of the text—its Firstness, in Peircean terms—is interpreted in a kind of intersemiotic process of making up the representamen (or signifiers) of other signs—the signs that signify masochism as a clinical entity and a phenomenology of experience. Although Metz tends to polarize linguistic organization and primary process as the representatives of "thought" and "anti-thought" respectively, Deleuze and Peirce do not encourage us to hold to that distinction. While Peirce explored the conscious rather than the unconscious in sign perception, his philosophically and phenomenologically grounded study of sign systems is not antithetical to a psychoanalytic consideration of film. Peirce's interest in how the "sign in the mind" is created through the intersemiotic process of sign perception does not exclude a consideration of the "mark of the unconscious" on the sign perceived.[88] His focus on interpretation (as opposed to Saussure's neglect) encourages a strategy that accounts for the unconscious as well as the conscious factors involved in sign creation/perception. No doubt, the influence of the unconscious might readily be extracted from Peirce's own *modes of being,* the categorization of the affective quality of signs. These two methodologies can complement each other in delineating and describing a full range of filmic signification. In combining Peircean semiotics with psychoanalysis, the polysemy of the sign, its position as a nodal point in the dialectic between the conscious and the unconscious, can be examined with attention to both description and interpretation.

Although he accorded all the signs their own unique value, Peirce regarded the iconic sign as the "most perfect," "bringing its interpreter face to face with the very character signified."[89] The problem of interpretation and classification of signs was one of which Peirce was keenly aware. He believed the interpretant in the mind created a dynamic process of meaning. The mind created another sign (the interpretant) that, in turn, became another sign/interpretant, ad infinitum. The critic (or any sign user) was faced with the dilemma of never being able to deal directly with the original sign but only with the interpretant. John K. Sheriff explains: ". . . the literary work, like any other sign, conceals itself. . . . It is always already something else, an interpretant. . . . On this point, Roman Jakobson, Roland Barthes, Tzvetan Todorov and Girard Genette . . . make the mistake Derrida describes in *Of Grammatology.* They seem to think they are objectively treating the text itself when they are in fact interpreting their own interpretants with codes and language-games which are transformations of the text."[90] Peirce recognized that all critical enterprises cannot escape a fundamental subjectivity at work in the very act of sign processing. However, this does not mean that language must always be a deterministic patriarchal trap that "surrounds" every sign and subjects it to the contamination of the Symbolic.

While Peirce's consideration of the sign in the mind restored the role of consciousness to the relations of the sign, equally important was his belief that the signs in the mind were not necessarily verbal or logical. This is a fundamental difference separating Peirce from Saussure. The concept of a transverbal interpretant permits the consideration of how imagery perception (and creation) may function in subverting more deterministic-linguistic operations.[91] At the same time, it permits the consideration of how iconic signs are related to the unconscious and to the psychodynamics underpinning specific texts.

Recent dream theory research and studies in cognition and imagery by Eugene Ferguson, Robert Ornstein, and Mardi Jon Horowitz tend to support Peirce's transverbal intersemiotic translation of signs.[92] Horowitz's description of the perception and retention of images in *Image Formation and Cognition* is startlingly similar to Peirce's own explanation of sign processing: "Perceptions are retained for a short time, in the form of images, which allows continued emotional response and conceptual appraisal. In time, retained images undergo two kinds of transformation: reduction of sensory vividness and translation of the images into other forms of representations (such as words)."[93] By recognizing the role of signs in the mind and the transverbal interpretant, Peirce maintained the value of ambiguity and feeling. He did not attempt to explain away the elusive effect of signs but organized his system so that the affective power of signs might be classified and considered.

Although a general theory of signs, Peircean semiotics, unlike Saussurean theory, is philosophically grounded, oriented toward epistemology, and interested in the phenomenological aspects of sign relations. Peirce suggested that the individual sign categories (index, icon, symbol) were, because of their form, likely to be interpreted through a particular category from the modes of being.[94] He acknowledged the role of culture, memory, and experience in conditioning human perception to impart meaning to signs. Because iconic signs were of a mixed nature, they could be expected to evoke an interpretation that blended all three modes of being in varying degrees, in spite of the primacy of Firstness (i.e., the quality of feeling), which Peirce defined as "the immediate element of experience generalized to its utmost."[95] Firstness was dependent on the surface qualities of the sign, on its sensual affectivity. Peirce considered Firstness to be the foundation of artistic creation and experience. Other modes were evoked as well: Secondness (disturbance of feeling, the "consciousness of polarity," or consciousness of interactions), and Thirdness (the formation of a general conception, of a general law through "synthetic consciousness").[96]

Pignatari shows how Peirce's own concept of the interpretant functions as a blending of Firstness, Secondness, and Thirdness is "like a moveable verbal and iconic supersign . . . a dynamic model of signic relationships—an icon."[97] He writes: "As the meaning of a sign is another sign (cf. the dictionary), as one sign saturates into another of the same nature, so one code continually saturates into another. . . . Ultimately, thirdness saturates into firstness. . . . For Peirce, artists and scientists alike are creators of icons."[98] Interpreting iconic signs involves the translation of a sign system that tends to be analogical, nonlinguistic, paratactic, and nonlinear into another sign system that is linguistic (i.e., digital, arbitrary, and symbolic). In confronting iconic signs, we challenge the limitations of our own intersemiotic translations.

With their emphasis on surface texture, their reliance on the malleability (and deceptiveness) of the iconic sign, von Sternberg's films seem ideally suited, as Wollen suggests, to a study using Peircean semiotics. By approaching these films through such a model, a new understanding may be acquired of how iconic signs and sign relationships function as the meeting points between consciously motivated artistic communication and a unifying psychodynamic infrastructure. Consistently concerned with human relationships and feeling, compulsion and desire, von Sternberg's iconic discourse serves to illustrate a remark made in Alain Resnais's *Providence:* "Style *is* feeling in its most elegant and economic expression."

CHAPTER FIVE

Stories of Suffering,
Paradoxes of Fixation

There is only one economy of desire, and repetition is the great
law of this economy.

—Paul Ricoeur

The masochistic narrative has a very specific story to tell. At the
primary level it is the story of how "the superego was destroyed and
by whom, and what was the sequel to this destruction."[1] In Sacher-
Masoch's novels and von Sternberg's films, masochism's narrative structure and *supersensualism* are formally united. This unity is crucial to
establishing the qualitative differences between masochism and sadism
and in determining the relationship between narrativity, visual pleasure, and the enunciation of desire through the "supersensual" style
of the masochistic aesthetic. While chapter 6 will explore very specific structuring mechanisms of masochistic narrativity, this chapter
concentrates on the general structures of von Sternberg's masochistic heterocosm and the implications they hold for current narrative
theory.

The narratives of the von Sternberg/Dietrich Paramount films
are consistent with their model of experience—the guiding iconic
sign of masochistic desire that inscribes the paradoxical pain/pleasure
structure of the psychodynamic into every aspect of its aesthetic expression. In their configurations of situation and character and unfolding of time and experience, von Sternberg's films undercut the
expectations created by classical narrative cinema. These films offer
the perceptual play of a self-consciously performed spectacle that disrupts classical narrative flow and substitutes an excessive, regressive
pre-Oedipal multiplicity of textual pleasures. Through the play of
suspense and anticipation, compulsion and coincidence, von Sternberg's narratives subvert the Barthesian notion of narrative as an Oedi-

pal, phallic trajectory of seeking out, uncovering, and denuding a quest formed in the shadow of the father.[2]

The von Sternberg/Dietrich films embody a perverse narrativity that inscribes a predictable containment for masochistic desire. Masochistic narrativity demands a reassessment of Laura Mulvey's oft-quoted statement that the "sadistic side [of pleasure] fits in well with narrative. Sadism demands a story, depends on making something happen. . . ."[3] Mulvey's broad statement on the connection between narrative and sadism is taken up by Teresa DeLauretis in *Alice Doesn't*. DeLauretis eloquently avoids a crude equation of sadism and narrativity but appears to legitimate Mulvey's phrase "sadism demands a story" with her own inversion: "a story demands sadism." DeLauretis "suspects" that the connection between sadism and narrative "is constitutive of narrative and of the very work of narrative."[4] However appealing such a generalization might be, by failing to define sadism except as force or aggression, she defers crucial questions regarding the erotic nature of sadistic violence, the role of sexual difference in its enunciation, and the formal expression of a desire that is always implicitly sadistic. More important, in linking sadism and narrativity, De-Lauretis certainly encourages a theoretical determinism in approaching classical film as an inscription of Oedipal desire. For her, desire and sadism are virtually synonymous and inextricably unite to entrap women into "consenting to femininity." Although she calls for the avoidance of "the usual and universalizing generalizations" through an examination of "specific practices," DeLauretis does so after she has proceeded to reduce all cinematic narrative (and, by implication, all male desire) to the Oedipal and the sadistic.[5]

In finding pleasure in the return to loss, the masochistic economy of desire privileges the fetishistic excess of the compulsive repetition of separation/reunion, absence/presence. This strategy diverts narrative progress from a phallic trajectory of Oedipal singularity to a governing modality dominated by the oral stage dialectic of separation/reunion, taking in and rejecting.[6] The films' narratives confront us with the implications of a masochistic repetition and ritualization that refuses the self-effacing illusionism of spatiotemporal unity. Like masochistic coldness that freezes passion, the lurching, suspended narratives of the von Sternberg/Dietrich films are paradoxical constructs that express the compulsiveness and control of masochistic desire. Uniting Thanatos and Eros, the masochistic story cannot be expressed within conventional narrative structures that associate repetition with pleasure, desire with ultimate satisfaction and resolution. In fueling desire and suspending suffering, von Sternberg's narratives tell the story of the destruction of the superego and the triumph of the cold oral mother through the *bis repetita* tha is a fundamental governing form of the masochistic psychodynamic. Fixating on the plurality of the paronomastic, the decadence of detail, and the fetishistic lingering on the fragment, masochistic narrativity demands a reconsideration of what constitutes the very basis of *narrative*.[7]

Masochistic Narrative Strategy and Classical Conventions

For years, the curious narratives and extreme visual ornateness of the von Sternberg/Dietrich films were taken as prima facie evidence that they lacked a cohesion between style and narrative. In 1948, Richard Griffith bemoaned the disunity: ". . . action and continuity were progressively drained away in favor of an ordered flow of a pattern of images, often lovely in themselves, sometimes floridly vulgar, but always empty of real dramatic meaning."[8] More recently, Kevin Brownlow has echoed Griffith's assessment: "Von Sternberg's grasp of narrative was seldom more than tenuous. The majority of his sound films were carried by the visual alone."[9] The narratives of the von Sternberg/Dietrich films are decidedly implausible by conventional standards of verisimilitude and cause/effect logic: they are melodramatic and episodic, with characters' contradictory actions juxtaposed without the intervention of explanatory motivation. They abound in time gaps, or lacunae, as well as spatial dislocations, superimpositions, and extended dissolves that abstract time and space. Obscurely banal dialogue is delivered in a perplexingly emotionless style; potentially climactic events are elided. The lack of cause/effect structuring is accentuated by reduplication of scenes and unexpected reversals.

Many current writers have attempted to justify von Sternberg's narratives and their relationship to the films' visual style. For example, in *Ideology and the Image*, Bill Nichols observes: ". . . von Sternberg's visual style is not a gratuitous finish to inconsequential stories as some have claimed, but is in fact an integral quality of the textual system. . . . this visual style directly colludes in the marking of a narrative course."[10] Yet, in the course of persuasively arguing *for* von Sternberg's conscious integration of visual style and narrative strategy, Nichols affirms the director's "disinterest in narrative per se."[11] Often quoted is von Sternberg's pronouncement that "the narrative means nothing," as well as his notorious declaration that his films should be run upside down so that the narrative would not distract the viewer from the play of light and shade.[12] It should be remembered that in interviews von

Sternberg (like John Ford) was often a resistant subject; thus, these statements should not automatically be used to fuel the argument that his narratives need not be taken very seriously.

In his autobiography, *Fun in a Chinese Laundry,* von Sternberg took the position that "all the actions and the emotions that crop up again and again, always to be proclaimed as original," were to be found in the ancient myths.[13] Technique, not subject matter, had changed, he said. Therefore, the artist's contribution to these constantly retold tales must be one of style: "The skill with which a man writes makes him a master, rarely that which he writes about."[14] Von Sternberg's views on narrative are uncannily repeated in Wood's comments on the relationship of visual style and narrative in the director's films. Wood argues that the subject of the von Sternberg/Dietrich films is formed by the style: "The plot-lines might not look very inviting on paper but a story only exists when it is told and becomes a 'subject' from the manner of the telling."[15] Von Sternberg's emphasis on style is no more a dismissal of narrative than Alexandre Astruc's *camera stylo,* which sought to redress the literary tendencies of other filmmakers. In fact, Astruc parallels von Sternberg's own pronouncement that "the camera is the pen of our craft."[16]

The supposed narrative inconsistencies of the von Sternberg/Dietrich films are not mistakes of construction but the formal results of giving voice to what Deleuze calls "the history of cruelty in love."[17] The paradoxes of von Sternberg's narratives are precisely those of the masochistic economy of desire that reverses expected instinctual progress toward post-Oedipal genitality, masquerades its own polymorphous identity, and refuses the unification of sites of textual pleasure under the phallic "efficiency" of Oedipal narratives. Von Sternberg's films evidence the implausible coincidence, episodic, repetitive scenes, and abrupt elision of decisive events that are as typical of masochistic narrativity as the fetishistic suspension of action in exquisitely painful waiting.

In referring to the poorly motivated narrative of *Blonde Venus,* Nichols has proposed that the "flawed or lacunae-ridden quality" of the film's narrative evidences "Sternberg's play in/against the assumptions, and codes, of the classical narrative."[18] As discussed in earlier chapters, von Sternberg's disruption of these conventional codes is not a purely modernist stance, as Nichols asserts, but is the predictable result of an iconic discourse and masochism's formal principles. The masochistic heterocosm plays dialectically on its inability to free itself from its referential basis. The film's illusion of diegetic reality announces itself as a performance that heightens the self-consciousness of illusionism. In fusing the past, present, and future through disavowing acts of memory and imagination, these narratives reflect the masochistic "art of fantasy."[19] They create a heterocosm of desire marked by the formal requirements that distinguish masochism as an aesthetic as well as a symptomatology.

Narrative Subversion of the Patriarchal Family Romance

Patricia Mellencamp has suggested that the narrative strategy of much of classical cinema works toward one goal: "the containment of potentially disruptive sexuality."[20] The masochistic narrative acts out pre-Oedipal wishes associated with the socially disruptive, polymorphous sexuality of masochistic desire. Potentially, the masochistic desire for symbiotic reunion undermines the Oedipal trajectory of unveiling the father's truth and the son's identity in phallic signification; instead, masochism repudiates the father, patriarchal law, and superego maturation. Freud once remarked that infantile sexual life was "doomed to extinction because its wishes are incompatible with reality."[21] Masochism rebels against the reality of the Oedipal regime through fantasy.

Classical film narrative has also been associated with the Oedipal "family romance," which works to restore patriarchal order after a brief disturbance. Undermining the typical family romance, the masochistic scenario can never unconditionally meet the conventional narrative goal of "happily ever after," the promise of social and sexual order that defines classical narrative closure.[22] Von Sternberg's films present the Oedipal triangle in a qualified, perverse form that re-enacts masochism's orally based fantasies. The films do not celebrate the "containment of potentially disruptive sexuality" but the release of it.[23] The powerful oral mother is exalted; the patriarchy is undermined by the masochistic wish to eliminate the father.

Blonde Venus demonstrates the masochistic subversion of conventional narrative goals. At first glance, the film might easily be read as perfectly adhering to the description of the family romance and the containment of sexuality. Upon closer inspection, *Blonde Venus* reveals the masochistic fantasy asserting its presence within a deceptive Oedipal construct. Desublimated masochistic desire shatters the expected progress toward the idealized, stable patriarchal family structure.

In this film, the courtship of Helen Faraday and her husband Ned is interpreted by their child, Johnny, as a fairy tale with the young traveler (Ned) discovering a princess (Helen) guarded by a Black Forest Dragon (a gruff German taxi driver). This affirmation of the family romance is undercut by the sexualization of the mother/child relationship. *Blonde Venus* is ostensibly a story of mother love, but mother love is made strange by the masochistic fantasy that overlays and subverts the Oedipal triangle and its expected resolution into patriarchal normality. As noted in chapter 3, Helen's lack of responsiveness to the males in the film contrasts sharply with the erotic autonomy of the mother/child unit. The eroticization of motherhood is not the film's unconscious demonstration of the "incompatibility . . . of female sexuality and mothering," as E. Ann Kaplan writes in *Women and Film,* but a logical result of the dynamics of the masochistic alliance and its aesthetic expression.[24] Kaplan cites Helen's effort to maintain Ned's place in the family by spelling out "father" as she tries to teach Johnny to read, but she does not mention the grotesque male mechanical puppet Johnny and Helen let fly across the table during this unsuccessful lesson. Kaplan misses the insistently repeated subversive aspects of the film which are articulated visually. The film cannot be dismissed as "an unconscious exposure of the inner workings of the nuclear family," but as Wood has convincingly shown, the oppression of women by the patriarchy is exactly what the film takes as its subject.[25]

Caught between his own masochism and society's repression, Helen's husband, like many of von Sternberg's characters, blames woman's sexuality and her threat of mobile desire for the family's disintegration—just as Don Pasquale blames Concha for his ruin in *The Devil Is a Woman,* Doc blames Madeleine for their breakup in *Shanghai Express,* and Kranau accuses Magda of luring men to their death with her body in *Dishonored.* None of these films support the male's accusation. Under the guise of morality, the male projects his failure and guilt onto the female in a reaction that, in *Blonde Venus,* is clearly portrayed as repressive. Ned's vengeful reaction to Helen's infidelity reflects his own failure. He is characterized by Helen as weak, and the film confirms his weakness. Like the father in the mythical Amazon culture, Ned is required only for the act of conception; otherwise, he is economically and sexually superfluous. Helen finds more interesting work and a more interesting lover when Ned is off for his cure. When he sells the rights to his experiments to repay Helen for the cost of his treatments, he blames her for his future failure; he will be unable to "exploit" his "life's work." Helen boldly (if drunkenly) gives the money away and then builds a successful career for herself. When she returns to New York to see Johnny, Ned is making a dismal attempt at parenting in the same dingy apartment.

Mellencamp asserts that the end of *Blonde Venus* signals that Helen "has been investigated by the narrative, proven guilty in the spectacles of female performance, and found sexual."[26] Her view adheres almost word-for-word with Mulvey's definition of a sadistic voyeurism in which "woman is the leitmotif of erotic spectacle. . . . pleasure lies in ascertaining [her] guilt."[27] Helen is found to be sexual, but *Blonde Venus* assigns guilt to the father, the representatives of the superego, and repressive patriarchal power. In playing out the infantile fantasy of abandonment/separation, the mother is blameless. The father, the external force, causes the separation of mother and child and must be neutralized or expelled to permit the restoration of the mother-child bond and the transformation of the Oedipal mothering imago (victim) into the ideal oral mother of pre-Oedipal oneness.

In *Blonde Venus* the family unit with the father as nominal head is restored, albeit within the framework of Johnny's ritual retelling of his parents' courtship. Helen is reinserted into the imprisonment of marriage, but this does not necessarily mean that Ned and the superego are victorious. For all intents and purposes, the superego is functionally dead. Ned's revenge fails; mother and child are reunited. The "happy ending" of the film nonetheless undermines the triumph of the normal patriarchal family: Johnny, who is the real impetus for the restoration of the marriage, retains his infantile, narcissistic control from behind the bars of his crib. He turns the music box just as he directs his parents' reunion.

If the ending of the film does not satisfy the masochistic goal of exorcising the father's genital likeness in the son, it does satisfy masochistic fantasies on another level—the omnipotence of the infant is reaffirmed. The male child/subject marks off the limits to his reality and his parents' sexuality and joins the present to a past of his own creation (and, ironically, in which he was created). Johnny's control ensures the continued presence of the mother and forestalls his own passage out of dependent attachment to her. Mellencamp asserts that the film's ending signals that "Johnny . . . has now successfully passed through the Oedipal drama and is constructed in the identity of the symbolic father."[28] But Johnny is exactly where he was at the beginning of the film. The regressive union of mother and child triumphs. Johnny remains bound to Helen in affirmation of the compelling power of the idealized pre-Oedipal mother as a stronger attraction than the "normalizing" force of the father, who threatens the perverse alliance of mother and child.

As the ending of *Blonde Venus* suggests, the restitution of patriarchal law is either absent or clearly qualified in von Sternberg's masochistic narratives. If the given social order appears to be triumphant, as

Mother love is made strange. Helen Faraday's lack of responsiveness to men contrasts sharply with the erotic autonomy of a mother/child unit fiercely defended by her protean transformations. Although patriarchal authority intervenes, son Johnny remains bound to Helen in affirmation of the compelling power of the idealized pre-Oedipal mother as a stronger attraction than the "normalizing" force of the father. Marlene Dietrich and Dickie Moore in *Blonde Venus* (1932).

with the end of *The Scarlet Empress,* the reestablishment is infused with ambivalence.[29] Only in *Shanghai Express,* perhaps the most conventional of the von Sternberg/Dietrich films, does the ending superficially conform to the restitution of male control, but here too the masochistic sexual agenda reappropriates happily-ever-after into its perverse order: Lily may have prayed for Doc's release, but she has not abandoned her prostitute's costume of black feathers or given assurance of her future monogamy. She takes Doc's riding crop from his hand to reconfirm the power relations that have already been established between them.

Masquerades of Meaningful Coincidence

Von Sternberg's films do not adhere to classical narrative's unseamed smoothness in "realistic," contiguous storytelling. If film's illusion of "reality" is crucially dependent on the cause/effect chain of experience, as has been suggested, then the masochistic narrative strategy rejects the illusion offered through an unbroken, linear cause/effect chain.[30] Von Sternberg's interest in the film's surface texture and in the independence of the iconic signifier weakens the chain of spatiotemporal contiguity and effects a disruption of classical narrative's inscription of a unified diegetic space and temporal connections. Events are related paratactically rather than causally, as antecedent/precedent rather than as reason/result. Techniques such as dissolves, usually associated with temporal transitions, break loose of their conventional codings to articulate the timelessness of masochistic desire. Through the paradoxical masochistic repetition of shots, of scenes and sequences, the unfolding of difference becomes an unfolding of difference into sameness.

At the most general level of narrative organization, the von Sternberg/Dietrich films dispense with the apparatus of subordination and sequencing to suggest a kind of mythic inevitability. As Mircea Eliade says of myth, "the things which happen are stated with paratactic bluntness: everything must happen as it does happen, it could not be otherwise."[31] This phenomenon might be attributed to melodramatic convention, but in the masochistic aesthetic, inevitability is also related to the fixed nature of the underlying perverse psychodynamics. Helen must run into Nick in Paris, Magda must meet Kranau at headquarters, Amy must encounter and reencounter La Bessiere. Meetings, departures, actions that seem unmotivated by circumstance prolong the masochistic game of disappearance and return, separation and reunion. Synchronicity—the meaningful coincidence of accident or cosmic fate—disavows psychic compulsion. Masochistic desire acts as the *còsa mentále* that governs characters' actions and permits masochistic suffering to masquerade as the "normal temporary toleration of unpleasure."[32] Deleuze comments on this process in Sacher-Masoch's novels: "Masoch succeeds in presenting a great part of his work on a 'reassuring' note and finds justification for masochistic behavior in the most varied motivations or in the demands of fateful and agonizing situations. (Sade, on the other hand, could fool nobody when he tried this method.)"[33]

As with Sacher-Masoch's characters, von Sternberg's find justification for their masochistic behavior through plot predicaments that cannot mask the absurdity of their pursuit. In *The Devil Is a Woman*, mythic inevitability and the masquerade of synchronicity attain their apotheosis in the triangle of Don Pasquale, Antonio, and Concha Perez. When Don Pasquale first encounters Concha, she refuses his advances and exclaims, "What do you take me for?" Concha hurries off into the departing crowd, and when Don Pasquale next sees her, she is working in a cigarette factory. He has risen in station; she has fallen. "How did you get here?" he asks. Concha replies with quintessential Sternbergian detachment: "Lord knows, I don't." In this scene, Concha seems like an entirely different person, a change that Luis Bunuel treats literally in *That Obscure Object of Desire*, his version of Pierre Louys's *Woman and Puppet*.[34] Her "chilly reaction" to Don Pasquale on the snowbound train has changed to "warmth." A scantily clad Concha is now very willing to accept his attentions and his gold pieces. She pulls him close to whisper instructions for their rendezvous outside the factory gates.

Don Pasquale later tells Antonio that he believes his chance encounters with Concha "couldn't have been a succession of mere accidents." He blames fate. Masochistic characters often profess that they are at the mercy of unknown forces pushing them into a downward spiral of humiliation, pain, or sacrifice. However, the masochist's fate is not determined by a cruel lover or an indifferent divine but by the subterranean network of masochism's demands. Throughout *The Devil Is a Woman*, Don Pasquale projects his masochistic fantasy onto the world: the purely coincidental is shown to be self-willed misery.[35] He admits to Antonio that he toured the cigarette factory with government inspectors because he had heard that a pretty girl was working there. Was he looking for Concha? Later, after Concha has left him yet another time, he hardly seems surprised to see her singing in a cabaret. Surrounded by three grotesque lovers, Concha's performance onstage parallels her offstage sexual mobility. She looks at her multiple lovers and smilingly tells her audience: "I can be as true to you." Don Pasquale sits amid a decor overwhelmed by sea nets, seafaring paraphernalia, and effigies of fish and storks. When he attempts to buy Concha's contract from the club's cackling old proprietress, she tells him that Concha "packs them in like sardines."[36] Don Pasquale the phallus-fish wants to be trapped. When Concha first brings him home to introduce him to her mother, she dangles a pet fish in a suspended bowl: "Look mama, I've a fish," she breathlessly exclaims as she enters with the fish thrust out in front of her and Don Pasquale in tow behind. In Sacher-Masoch's *Venus in Furs*, Wanda threatens to use her furs to catch Severin "like a fish in a net."[37] Don Pasquale remains the fish on Concha's hook, wiggling in the nets of her charms.

Authorial Distanciation and Masochistic Desire

Von Sternberg's irony deconstructs the masochistic masquerade of normalcy, victimization, and passivity that Don Pasquale and other characters interpose as a front for their masochism. Durgnat has referred to von Sternberg's "caustic detachment" that results in the films' "cold, aloof, cryptic quality."[38] A quality of coldness is imperative to the masochistic control of desire through suspended passion. The cold irony of the films also relates to the distance that von Sternberg maintains between his authorial presence and characters who, as he remarked on more than one occasion, represent aspects of himself.[39] His provocative admission of personal involvement is more directly evidenced in his predilection for using actors who resemble himself to play the humiliated masochistic male: Don Pasquale (Lionel Atwill), General von Hindau (Warner Oland), La Bessiere (Adolphe Menjou). Von Sternberg's inscription of himself into the films is played off against an ironic humor directed against these characters' masochistic proclivities.

Rene Girard's description of Stendhalian irony applies equally well to von Sternberg: "The novelist lets his characters act and speak; then, in a twinkling of an eye, he reveals to us the mediator. He reestablishes covertly the true hierarchy of desire while pretending to believe in the weak reasoning advanced by his character in support of the contrary hierarchy."[40] The director's irony also reveals what Reik has shown, that the masochist attempts to rationalize self-humiliating behavior as a reaction to harsh reality. "Fate," says Reik, "has replaced the humiliating and beating partner."[41] Fueled by fantasy, masochistic desire is satisfied by suffering easily obtained in the world. Operating beyond the pleasure principle and beyond the reality principle,

Amy Jolly reacts to Private Brown's departure into the desert. La Bessiere, looking for all the world like a Josef von Sternberg clone, watches the spectacle of disappointment and awaits his own privileged moment in the pursuit of submission. Adolphe Menjou and Marlene Dietrich in *Morocco* (1930).

masochism uses the latter as a masquerade for secret aims that have nothing to do with the postponement of pleasure to meet the demands of self-preservation.

In *Blonde Venus,* plot predicaments cannot hide the absurdity of Ned Faraday's determined quest to suffer. His experiments to find a safe method of using radium result in his own poisoning. Ned is first seen as he attempts to sell his body to medicine for study:

> "Doctor, I have a rather peculiar request to make. You see, I want to sell you my body. . . ."
> "Tell me, are you married?"
> "I wouldn't have come here if I weren't. . . ."

The absurdity of his request is compounded by the visual treatment of the scene: the doctor sits on his desk, absentmindedly snaps the jaws of a skull, then offers Ned 50 dollars toward a cure costing 1,500. Ned later tells Helen that his scientific discoveries should be worth a fortune, but he thinks of the most absurd and humiliating solution to his financial problems. While his body is rejected as worthless to science, Helen exploits her own body as a highly valued economic commodity on the stage and in the right bed. Her immediate success at selling herself for sexual rather than scientific scrutiny increases Ned's humiliation until he lashes out against her and becomes the "sadistic" essence in the scenario.

Masochistic Suspense and Narrative Pleasure

Masochistic suspense is paradoxical. Frequently it does not depend on the question of what will happen but on when and how. Sarris has remarked that von Sternberg weaves a "fatalistic spell" and is "not concerned with how or why people get where they are as he is with how they act and feel once they get there." [42] The films destroy the indexical transparency of film as a contiguous, unfolding, present event duplicating the hermeneutic suspense of life. Conventional dramatic suspense is undermined through the insistent repetition of visual and aural motifs, predictive titles and dialogue. As a result, suspense is displaced from the dramatic to the aesthetic. [43]

The complex interplay of fate and narrative suspense is fundamental to the narrative strategy of *The Scarlet Empress.* Titles foretell the outcome of events yet to be seen. The opening titles inform the audience that Sophia Frederica was "chosen by destiny to become the greatest Monarch of her scene." The titles' emulation of historical discourse culminates in a clichéd evocation of "destiny," but the cliché acquires complexity. Throughout the film, Sophia's actions appear to be dictated by the demands of politics. She is shuttled into the "machine of marriage" to enhance the family's status in the Russian aristocracy. Political destiny appears mediated by self-determination. Sophia rebels against her powerlessness within the patriarchy's oppressive structure, but the film suggests that the decisive factor in her rise to power as czarina is independent of political causality or personal choice. Political explanation is overwhelmed by the cumulative visual details that initially seem to be of narrative insignificance but, as in dream logic, are revealed to be the displaced center of the masochistic discourse on desire.

In the opening scene of the film, seven-year-old Sophia is examined by a doctor who is revealed to be an executioner. She asks if she too can "become a hangman someday." Although the exact mode of reverie or dream is not explicit, Sophia then fantasizes/dreams of executions, sexual cruelties, and tortures. These abruptly climax in the suspension of a half-nude man who is used as the clapper of a huge bell. His image dissolves to that of the teenage Sophia on a swing in the family garden. The dream's visual motifs, such as the motion of swinging, the bell, the tortures, the galloping horses of the cossacks, occur with increasing frequency and thematic intensity in Sophia's adult life. Even the formal mechanism that connects the dream episodes—the curious optical effect of a spatial wipe that emulates the turning of a book page or the opening of a door—is reasserted in the opening and closing of the huge doors of the czarina's palace.[44] Does Sophia's dream predict the future in an uncanny way? Or does the dream merely evidence the strength of her inner compulsions that combine with external circumstances to seal her destiny as "Messalina of the North"?

The narrative suggests the interpenetration of the future into the present in Sophia's prehensive dream. Her life answers her "wish to become a hangman" and like the prophetic dream, articulates her own imaginative excess. Sacher-Masoch's *Aesthetics of Ugliness* describes a character named Lola who, "neither brutal nor eccentric, . . . [is] reasonable and kind" and shows "all the tenderness and delicacy of a sentimental nature."[45] Lola, however, dreams of executions and being an executioner. *The Scarlet Empress* depicts Sophia as a sensitive girl capable of a deep and loyal love, but her "youthful ideals" are outraged by her grotesque marriage and by Count Alexei's betrayal. She comes to resemble Wanda in *Venus in Furs*, who tells Severin: "It was you who stifled my feelings." Although Wanda is persuaded into her role, she admits that she is "aware of dangerous forces" lurking in her. Severin confidently believes that Wanda will fulfill his fantasy: "everything I have imagined is already present in your nature."[46] Educated for her role and psychologically fated, tortured and torturess, Sophia reflects the ambivalence of the masochistic fantasy ideal.

Similarly, in *Dishonored,* the opening title states that X-27 "might have become the greatest spy of history . . . if X-27 had not been a woman." The title makes sure there will be no question that Magda, war widow turned prostitute, will be X-27 and will fail in her mission. The self-willed nature of Magda's death is predicted when she is confronted with a neighbor woman's suicide in the film's very first scene. Magda announces: "I'm not afraid of life, although I'm not afraid of death either." In fantasy fulfillment of her fatalism, the head of the Austrian secret service happens to overhear her and immediately recruits her for a spy ring. In her initial assignment, Magda attends a costume ball dressed as a swaggering black bird of prey; she flirtatiously exchanges horn toots with a man costumed as a hooded executioner. Painted on his black robe is the concrete representation of his romantic vulnerability—an oversize heart. Later that night the hooded man, General von Hindau, is exposed as a traitor by Magda and commits suicide.

Like Sophia's dream in *The Scarlet Empress,* Magda's response to the suicides of her neighbor and General von Hindau anticipates her future and mirrors her own psychological compulsion toward the defiant masochistic sacrifice. She elevates desire above the law. In the transcendence of death, Magda defines herself through a masochistic triumph. She resembles the suicide victim alluded to in the film's opening sequence, but her sacrifice is portrayed as noble. Although the femme fatale of the masochistic scenario may "destroy" the male, she is often equally fatal to herself. In *Morocco,* a ship's captain tells La Bessiere that he has seen Amy Jolly's type before: "We call them suicide passengers, one-way tickets, they never return." Of course, he is right. Amy's desire for Private Brown culminates with her joining the camp followers who she had earlier condemned as mad.

The Dietrich characters in these films embark on their own "search for submission," but it is important to remember that their function in sacrifice and pain is very different from the male's in the masochistic dynamic. Magda's death in *Dishonored* and Helen's sexual "sacrifice" in *Blonde Venus* are of a very different order than Professor Rath's demise in *The Blue Angel* or the masochistic male's humiliating loss in *Morocco* or *The Devil Is a Woman.* The sacrifice of the oral mother is ennobled rather than rendered absurd. She is idealized, justified. She does not substitute for the male masochistic subject or for the expelled superego, although she superficially represents the punishing function of the latter.[47]

The fatalism of von Sternberg's films is not simply an acceptance of death as an externally imposed inevitability but the expression of the masochistic urge toward death as a self-willed liberation. In choosing death, an illusionary triumph is created: the illusion of choice.[48] Laplanche states that "every human being aspires to death by virtue of the most fundamental internal tendency."[49] Although the Death Instinct is probably the most controversial element of Freudian drive theory, masochism's obsession with death may be interpreted either as the expression of a universal instinctual urge or as the result of the masochistic wish for complete symbiosis with the mother and a return to nothingness. Within the masochistic scheme of desire, death signals the triumph of Thanatos. Eros is desexualized and resexualized; death becomes the ultimate fetish that fascinates with the promise of a mystical unity.

Barthes suggested that tragedy provides the "most perverse" of narrative readings because the end is known: the story is not dramatic. The reader participates in a fetishistic disavowal of knowledge.[50] With its fetishistic suspension of the pleasure of narrative enigma, masochistic narrative operates through a similar strategy. While the predictability of Magda's or Amy's fate might be regarded as melodramatic overstatement, masochistic fatalism ensures the narrative closure of a perverse fantasy, which, as Smirnoff writes, is best described as a closed scenario of sacrifice without a choice.[51] Whether labeled masochistic, tragic, or melodramatic, this formula affords the fetishistic, fragmented pleasure of the suspension of knowledge.

The Death Instinct and the Activity of Inertia

Leo Bersani calls repetition the "activity of inertia." The paradox of this activity is that it can be resolved only in death: the one new thing that can happen to those who are committed to repeating themselves.[52] In the masochistic narrative, repetition signals the collapse of conventional narrativity in which cause/effect action and unifying codes of spatiotemporal contiguity lead progressively to an endpoint of satisfying, nontensioned resolution. The presence of repetitive structuring on all levels of von Sternberg's films has often been observed, but its importance to narrative theory has never been pursued.

Repetition is a key formal structure of masochism. Deleuze explains: "Repetition does occur in masochism, but it is totally different from sadistic repetition: in Sade it is a function for acceleration and condensation and in Masoch it is characterized by the 'frozen' quality and the suspense."[53] Masochistic repetition charts the regressive movement toward the fantasy goal of a return to the beginning, to the womb of rebirth and nothingness. Breaking free of repetition's expected relation to the pleasure principle, the masochistic economy of desire uses compulsive repetition to privilege similarity over difference, inertia over action, stasis over change. Hence the "frozen" quality of masochistic repetition.[54] Formally, the repetitive structure creates a dialectic between stasis and motion that resembles masochism's illusionary movement between free will and psychic determinism, causality and coincidence. The power of the underlying masochistic fixation is affirmed in repetitions that weld the narrative into an iconic imitation of the perversion's formal structure. Repetition holds the fantasy structure into aesthetic coherence as it faithfully reproduces the experiential model of infantile fixation.

The repetitive narrative structuring of von Sternberg's films is inseparable from the masochistic-psychoanalytic substructure dominated by fantasy, disavowal, and fetishism. The obsessive return to the moment of separation from the oral mother is enacted again and again in the masochistic *fort/da* repetition of desire, the matrix point uniting fantasy and action. The constant activity of compulsive repetition disguises fixation, just as the masochist's passivity in the face of fate masks a self-determined return to loss.[55] The masochistic fetish repairs the disjunctive reality of the mother's separation from the child. Pleasure is achieved in the disavowing return to the point of unity, the recovering of the past through imagination, and the fetishistic acting out of ambivalent infantile desire. The "screen memory" does not shield the subject from castration anxiety but condenses the danger and pleasure of being overwhelmed by the mother.

Tableaux Vivants *and the Spectacle of Erotic Excess*

Sexuality must be diffused in masochism to delay orgasm and defer the dangers of unabated passion. Sade's language imbues the static medium of literature with the action of sex. A character in Sade's *Juliette* explains the sadistic dilemma: "It is not easy for art, which is motionless, to depict an activity the essence of which is movement."[56] Masochism reveals the stillness in movement, the edge of Thanatos in Eros, that aestheticizes the erotic into cold suspense and diverts sexuality from orgasm to an erotic contemplation at once frustrating and pleasurable. Deleuze considers Sacher-Masoch a pioneer in the use of suspense as a central aspect of romantic novels. Suspense is literal in tortures that involve "actual physical suspension" but also occurs in the "photographic scenes" that freeze the female torturer into positions "that identify her with a statue, a painting, or a photograph." These scenes are then "re-enacted at various levels in a sort of frozen progression."[57]

In the suspended world of the masochistic journey, erotic and emotional turmoil does not duplicate the frenzied movement of the Sadian heterocosm. The Sadian spectacle of excess activity is replaced by masochism's *tableaux vivants* that freeze movement entirely or isolate the rhythmic pulsation of movement: Catherine's breath against the candle during the wedding ceremony in *The Scarlet Empress,* the swing of ropes and clappers in the same film, the sway of feathers around Lily's walk in *Shanghai Express.* The masochistic formal treatment of sensual movement is totally at odds with the sadistic economy of constant sexual activity. In a further reversal of Sade, von Sternberg takes film as a temporal art to give expression to mechanisms rooted in stillness: disavowal and fetishism.

The repetition of entire scenes reenacts the past so that the masochist can replay the same scene on different levels with a reversal of roles.[58] When the old Empress discovers the relationship developing between Catherine and Alexei, she forces Catherine to prepare her bedchamber for the arrival of the Empress's lover, Alexei. When Catherine becomes empress, she leads Alexei to believe he will assume his former role as the czarina's lover, but Catherine forces him to play her old role as servant/primal scene spectator, and General Orloff enters to play Alexei's role as lover. In its perfect iconicity, the scene evokes irony and paradox. It may resemble the model, but it has an entirely different meaning for the characters. Identities are exchanged to permit the masochistic transfer of psychic function.

Similarly, in *Blonde Venus,* Helen first meets Nick backstage on her opening night. When they meet again in Paris, roles are reversed; Helen is no longer penniless and powerless. A male mannequin wedged between them serves as the rack for Helen's fur coat and top hat, recalling the statue of a nude Venus that served as a temporary hat rack for Helen's blustering manager. The reversal in the gender of the statues parallels the reversal in power between Helen and Nick. Otherwise, there is no precise, single meaning to the reversals, no exact verbal interpretant, but a cluster of correlations, a kind of Peircean Secondness in the evocation of past events and themes: the exploitation of Helen's sexuality, the association of the female with marble coldness, the reversal of power relations. Helen tells Nick she has no intention of returning to New York, yet in a typical elision of action, the next scene finds her in New York with Nick as her fiancé.[59]

Repetition occurs in the final scene of *Blonde Venus* when Helen returns to bathe Johnny and repeat their bedtime ritual, as well as in *Dishonored* when Magda returns to her prostitute's costume to repeat her provocative gesture from the film's opening. At the end of *The Devil Is a Woman*, Concha climbs back into a carriage, echoing her initial appearance in a parade carriage and the numerous other times she has blithely left one lover for another. Through these repeated departures, Concha acts out the mother's part in masochism's *fort/da* game of desire. Her disappearances set into motion another appearance, another change of identity, another repetition of loss that erases time and circles back to stasis, to the beginning, to death.

Time and movement are suspended in a fetishistic disavowal made manifest in masochism's compulsive repetition of presence/absence. Repetition freezes the syntagmatic structure of narrative into a linearization of the paradigmatic choices of the rituals of masochistic role playing and dialectical reversals. This peculiarly masochistic phenomenon results in a distinct form of narrative repetition that contributes to the films' aesthetic quality of *coldness*. Eros is desexualized as the masochistic scenario moves toward Thanatos. Ambivalence toward the oral mother precludes any unambiguous resolution of tension except in the final gratification of desire in death, a closure that places Eros in the service of Thanatos. The end of the masochistic narrative marks a fetishistic return to the point of loss. The hallucination of death becomes the locus for symbiotic reunion and an end to the ambivalence of the masochistic *fort/da* game of desire.

Masochistic Narrativity and Time

The Sadian narrative has clear-cut goals: to fuck everyone, to count the ways you can do it, to test your speed and vigor, to measure your acts and your victims in numbers. By contrast, the heightened emotion of expectation and arrested movement unify the temporality of the masochistic fantasy in which pleasure is taken in desire unfulfilled. The logic of cause/effect played out in linear time is rendered absurd by a psychodynamic in which punishment (logically, the effect) conditions pleasure (logically, the cause of the punishment).

In masochism, the future is made present in the anticipation of punishment; the past is incessantly repeated in the *fort/da* game of disappointment and desire. The dialectical interplay of masochism's anticipation of pain and suspension of orgasm creates a paradoxical ontological present that ignores the objective boundaries of linear time and resembles Maurice Merleau-Ponty's description of an ontological present in which "each present reasserts the presence of the whole past which supplants and anticipates all that is to come. . . ."[60] The von Sternberg/Dietrich films play on the dialectic between the contiguous aspect of film and the force of a desire that collapses linear progress into timeless repetition. While von Sternberg's films frequently feature the motif of clocks and timepieces, their own temporal structuring more closely resembles a cyclical, nonlinear time. Robert Ornstein has linked nonlinear time with right-hemisphere thinking (i.e., with the same brain functions that Gregory Bateson, Lawrence Marks, and others associate with metaphoric or analogic structuring, primary process, and iconic thinking).[61]

Temporality has recently gained attention in feminist film theory. Jacqueline Rose has discussed pre-Oedipal mother/child relations in the construction of female subjectivity and concludes that women have a "privileged relation to the imaginary dyad" and to the "principle of reversibility which it contains."[62] Tania Modleski argues that Max Ophuls's *Letter from an Unknown Woman* demonstrates a melodramatic ordering of time influenced by the pre-Oedipal stage.[63] It is extremely important to avoid essentialism in approaching the issue of women's subjectivity, especially within the context of a theory of masochism; nevertheless, shared formal traits and a pre-Oedipal influence on a so-called woman's time and masochistic time may, at the very least, demonstrate a subversive transgression of the trajectory of Oedipal desire. Both may be indicative of a narrative strategy that does not search for woman's phallus, play out a sadistic battle of wills, or prove feminine guilt in lack but looks backward toward the dilemma of separation/individuation and refuses displacement onto phallic signification and the syntagmatic dominance of a "progressive" linearity.

Like the Proustian hero, the masochist never loses the past, which is ever-present in memory or recaptured in the fetish that disavows objective time. Sternbergian characters' obsession with the past recalls the intensity of the infant's desire for the remembered oral plenitude and sensory oneness of symbiotic attachment. Masochistic disavowal freezes time, but, ironically, the masochistic fixation must be expressed in repeated action. Such a relationship to time is demonstrated in *Shanghai Express*. Donald ("Dọc") Harvey, physician in service to His Royal Majesty's Army, maintains a stiff facade of British propriety that represses his passion for the idée fixe of his life, Madeleine, whom he loved and lost exactly five years and four weeks before their chance reunion. Madeleine, now Shanghai Lily, tells Doc, "You haven't changed at all." Doc has suspended pleasure in pain and holds to the desire Lily once inspired in him. He claims to have avoided any involvement with a woman because he did not want to be hurt again, yet he continues to carry a picture of the woman who motivated his sexual retreat: Lily's portrait graces his watch case and provides an ironic juxtaposition of movement and stasis. The watch marks the passage of time even as the portrait freezes Lily's image (and her identity) in the past.

Doc's fetishistic prop exemplifies the masochistic rushing forward to anticipate punishment for pleasure while suspending gratification, prolonging pain, and looking to an idealized past. Time means little within the masochistic mode of experiencing events through the anticipation of future punishment and the prolongation of the pleasurable memory of the past. Although he consciously realizes he is in danger of losing her again, Doc repeats the attitudes and actions that precipitated his original loss of Madeleine. In the final scene, he spies on her as she busily buys him a new watch. The passing of time has had little effect on either of them. Madeleine remains eroticized and active. As Wood has observed, Mulvey's account of the narrative function of the fetishized female and her paralyzing effect on narrative progress does not hold true in *Blonde Venus*.[64] In *Shanghai Express*, Madeleine also usurps the male function of carrying forward the story line: she actively works to renew her relationship with Doc by asking him to accompany her to the dining car, by approaching him on the observation deck, and by negotiating with General Chang for his release. Doc is not even permitted the requisite male duty of doing in the villain.

Movement, Metamorphosis, and the Interrupted Journey

The repetitive movement of the masochistic narrative is often contained within three major narrative schemes or motifs: the interrupted or repeated journey, the rise/fall pattern, and the *fort/da* game of the female's presence/absence. As in Sacher-Masoch's novels, these three patterns frequently converge. The journey structure offers the paradox of stasis within movement and the dialectic between circular movement and linear progress. The rise/fall pattern incorporates the opportunity for character metamorphosis and the exchange of roles; it also offers a reliable guarantee of the humiliation and pain that can be expected to accompany a character's fall. The *fort/da* game is indispensable in prolonging suspended suffering.

Von Sternberg's characters are constantly engaged in the movement of journeys or in a metamorphosis of identity. In *Shanghai Express*, the train trip to Shanghai is matched by the long journey to Russia that occupies the first half of *The Scarlet Empress*. *Morocco, Blonde Venus, Dishonored,* and *The Devil Is a Woman* contain numerous shorter journeys: Amy travels to Morocco and follows Brown to Amalfi and into the desert; Helen goes from New York to the Deep South, then to South America, France, and back to New York: Magda travels from Vienna to the warfront and enemy headquarters, then returns to Vienna, metamorphosing from identity to identity, like Helen in *Blonde Venus*. *The Scarlet Empress* and *The Devil Is a Woman* give similar prominence to female mutability in response to male possession. Although constantly appearing in the midst of apparent change, characters are enmeshed in the psychic immobility and cyclic scenario of masochistic desire.

The return to previous experience through what *Cahiers du Cinéma* has called von Sternberg's "reduplicated journeys" contributes to the films' sense of mythic inevitability. These journeys depend upon temporal linearity, but objective time is obscured by the cyclic repetitive structuring that effaces the sense of the unidirectionality of narrative progress to a point of discovery. The journey structure unifies the presence/absence play of the *fort/da* game and ensures the continued masochistic pursuit. Journeys initiated by the female provide a coming and going, a hide-and-seek play of revelation and disguise that allows the masochistic male to retain an illusory cover of passivity and displace responsibility for his suffering onto the active female. Consequently, reduplicated journeys are not just "decorative," as *Cahiers du Cinéma* declares, but essential to the narrative expression of masochistic desire.[65]

Interrupted journeys function as a metaphor for the masochistic suspension of orgasmic gratification. Time and movement, like gender identity and social role, are suspended and disavowed. Von Sternberg is a master of what Jean Rousset, referring to Gustave Flaubert, called "the stagnant expanses where all movement ceases."[66] Sternbergian journeys are dominated by inaction, disappointment, boredom. In *Shanghai Express*, the characters wait for the train tracks to be cleared before they can proceed out of the city. During the journey they sit, smoke, speculate about each other. When the train is stopped by revolutionaries they wait, talk, sit, and smoke some more. In *The Devil Is a Woman*, the suspension within the journey begins when Don Pasquale and Concha first meet on a train that is literally frozen—snowbound. Stillness within movement creates a mystical suspension of time reflecting the ultimate masochistic entrapment of infantile fixation.

Sternbergian journeys provide a coming and going, hide-and-seek play of revelation and disguise that allows the masochistic male to retain an illusory cover of passivity and displace responsibility for his suffering onto the active female. Clive Brook and Marlene Dietrich on the train bound for Shanghai in *Shanghai Express* (1932).

Iconic Structure and Masochistic Narrativity

The diegetic unity of the von Sternberg/Dietrich films rests on a poetic structuring that privileges the analogic and the iconic over the logical and the contiguous, the paratactic over the syntagmatic, the metaphorical over the metonymic. These films demonstrate what Rosamund Tuve, in *Allegorical Imagery*, calls "the polyphonic nature of what is happening."[67] Von Sternberg's strategy of narrative and spectacle is illuminated through Barthes's discussion of film in "The Third Meaning." Barthes discusses a meaning that can be felt emotionally, whose site can be marked, but one that escapes articulation through language. This "third meaning" reaches beyond the levels of information and symbolism to force a reading that interrogates the signifier rather than the signified and depends "not on the intellection" but on a "poetic apprehension." It is this third, "extra" meaning, says Barthes, "both persistent and fugitive, apparent and evasive," that defines filmic signification as beginning "only where language and articulate metalanguage cease."[68]

Barthes's essay opens another avenue for approaching the relationship of spectacle and narrative in the masochistic aesthetic. Spectacle should be examined for the movement of a meaning that is not gratuitous to narrative but subverts a logical, horizontal reading to create, as Barthes suggests, "a *vertical* reading" that "flouts logical time."[69] Spectacle may shift attention to the intrashot signifier, to the individual shot, or to the repetition of shots as a paradigmatic play of alternative choices that interrupt the logical progression of their syntagmatic association.

In "Spectacle and Narrative Theory," Lea Jacobs and Richard de Cordova cite the wedding scene in *The Scarlet Empress* as an example of how von Sternberg's narrative is "dissipated into pure spectacle" as the exchange of looks between Alexei and Catherine shift the narrative "into a mode of pure repetition."[70] Although Jacobs and Cordova correctly assess the film's subversion of classical narrative's spatiotemporal relations, by continuing to divide spectacle and narrative into two "separate discursive registers" they reinforce that arbitrary division, which bears similarity to the division of description and narrative.

Relevant to a discussion of spectacle is Durgnat's contention that spatiotemporal considerations in narrative have been overvalued. He defends the link between description and narrativity denied by Metz in *Film Language*:[71] "Thus a shot which is autonomous in relation to the principal of space-time continuum of its context may be semantically nonautonomous from its overall actions or theme. It is this

semi-autonomy which permits digressions, descriptions, certain philosophical overtones. To obscure it must reduce narrative-dominated to
"telling the story," without the discursiveness which accounts for so
much of the structure and substance of the story."[72] To separate description and narrative or the articulation of spectacle and narrative
fosters the equation between the organization of written language and
film's visual language. It also confuses the differences between the discrete symbols of language and the messy narrative capability of the
image.[73] In turn, such a view fosters a belief in the interchangeability of
language processing and the perceptual/cognitive processing of film,
an issue addressed in chapter 6.

V. F. Perkins once asserted: "The only limits of the single shot
are those imposed by film theory."[74] Von Sternberg's films demonstrate a multisensory synchronic saturation of shots with an emphasis
on detail which lends credence to the accusation that the function of
individual shots has been overlooked. Like Peircean Firstness, which
tends to become evanescent when verbalized, the possibility of the single shot as a narrative unit is elusive. Kernels of action and syntagmatic
units have either explicitly (or, more recently, implicitly) dominated
the study of narrative. These units emphasize sequentiality as the privileged aspect of film and film narrative. Obviously film moves through
time—its continuous, sequential nature cannot be negated—but the
von Sternberg/Dietrich films disavow the syntagmatic through repetitive structuring. This strategy recalls Roman Jakobson's comments on
poetry: the paradigmatic is projected onto the syntagmatic; similarity
is superimposed on contiguity to give poetry its symbolic, multiplex,
polysematic essence.[75]

Fetishistic Excess and the Narrative Scene

If, as Barthes says in *A Lover's Discourse,* "The first thing we
love is a *scene,*" the masochistic narrative finds its master plot in the
primal scene.[76] It is not the control of the look that masochistic spectacle demonstrates but the narrative repetition of the infantile *lack of
control* which finds its prototype in that original scene of spectatorial
exclusion and inaction. Although the wedding sequence of *The Scarlet
Empress* might be read as confirmation of Mulvey's account of fetishistic scopophilia and the erotic look that paralyzes narrative, it is better
understood as a variation on the masochistic primal scene fantasy.
Alexei passively watches as Catherine and Peter are united in marriage. The looks exchanged between them during the ceremony reveal
the conflict between private emotion and empty public ritual. Their

exchanged looks also reveal how the "controlling male gaze," which Mulvey cites as fundamental to classical narrative cinema, is qualified in the von Sternberg/Dietrich films.[77]

The controlling gaze is qualified by its masochistic aim and by the treatment of space. Nichols has noted that in *Blonde Venus* there is a curious lack of exchanged looks between characters. He attributes this absence, also evident in *The Scarlet Empress* and other films of the cycle, to an emphasis on decor.[78] However, a careful analysis shows that this stylistic feature is the logical result of the masochistic control of desire. The lack of exchanged looks and the absence of eyeline matches contribute to a fracturing of cinematic space which compromises the controlling power of the male gaze.

Alexei helplessly oversees the union that he has been instrumental in bringing about in *The Scarlet Empress*. His impassive stare at Catherine might be interpreted as a classic example of the controlling male gaze. Her look, previously linked to her attempt to actively establish her own desire, is fragmented, confused, as is the space created between the would-be lovers. Louis Audibert describes this space as "that of a dreadful, dreamed scene . . . [where] looks can only slip away from one another . . . lost, not exchanged and . . . isolated."[79] Dietrich appears in a highly eroticized series of close-ups that fetishize her as the object for the spectator's unmediated gaze. These shots also reinforce the spectator's empathy with Catherine (and another suffering position?). Alexei is stationed as the helpless, impotent spectator. His position and gaze match the description of the primal scene provided by Laplanche: "the child impotent in his crib . . . on whom is imposed the spectacle of parental intercourse."[80] Though it might be argued that in this scene sexual difference in looking is maintained and male visual control satisfied, Alexei's gaze reaffirms his (and our) inability to prevent Catherine's possession by another. Alexei—and the film spectator—is afforded the masochistic pleasure of the suffering position.

The wedding scene in *The Scarlet Empress* exemplifies how von Sternberg's films create a perverse core of spatiotemporal relations that provides not only a surfeit of details but an alternative to conventional narrative structures. Action is displaced into the trope of visual detail; the masochistic tale is told within a spectacle that constitutes, like masochism itself, a tactic for delaying the consummation of desire. The fragment of the narrative sequence, the shot itself, attains an importance that recalls Culler's remark on Flaubert's strategy of "valuing not the completed structure but the fragment (which gains in power from its isolation). . . ."[81] The fetishistic excess and unconventional fracturing of space and temporality do not mean, as Jacobs and Cordova maintain, that the scene "loses all of its narrative implication" because "nothing comes of the glances."[82] On the contrary, quite a lot comes about because of Alexei and Catherine's inability to act on their desire. The spectacle of their separation does not displace narrative but becomes the visual context in which the smallest action gains narrative significance: the sensuous lifting of a veil, the rhythmic swing of incense pots, the binding together of Peter's and Catherine's hands. Through the hypertrophic repetition of such motifs, the masochistic narrative attains its structure: Catherine's veil is repeated in the scene in which she invites Alexei to her bedroom; the swinging motion is prefigured in Catherine's fortuitous childhood dream and in her adolescent games; the knot is repeated in Catherine's signal beginning the palace coup that ends her husband's life.

Alexei's position as the helpless child-lover does not make for a sadistic "battle of wills" but the masochistic story of the perverse pleasure to be found in the act of desiring. Fetishistic repetition within the scene becomes the paratactic, paradigmatic projection of masochistic variations on looking. The narrative shifts to representing the essence of masochistic narrativity, a repetition binding Eros and Thanatos into an excess of looking: the primal scene of desire and impotence that is at once spectacle and narrative. The film plays with the paradigmatic repetition of the signifier and its visual "interrogation," resulting in a perverse foreplay of spectacle that denies its assumed preparatory function in the phallic thrust of narrative "action." Deleuze asserts that the visual pleasure of masochism's economy of desire relies on the principle that an excess of stimulation is erotic.[83] Masochism's perverse pleasure extends into the spectacle of decorative and erotic excess that displaces conventional narrative "progress" with the lingering voluptuousness of masochistic suspense. The spectator is seduced into an excess of visual pleasure where pain and pleasure fuse in the act of a spectatorial looking that can never overcome distance. The masochistic narrative asserts itself in the spectacle of looking, of waiting, of desiring.

CHAPTER SIX

Mechanisms of Masochistic Narrativity

Metaphor serves, not to bring poetry closer to dream, but rather closer to the psychic processes underlying both art and fantasy.
—Ernst Kris

Von Sternberg's scenarios of masochistic desire relate concerns of primary process through a narrative strategy that emphasizes the perceptual possibilities of the polyvalent masochistic experience. Disrupting the conventional spatiotemporal "realities" of classical narrative cinema, the von Sternberg/Dietrich films show how carefully controlled repetition and transformation are essential to the masochistic narrative. Meaning is suspended and then carefully unveiled in a formal system that imitates the perversion's control of desire.

Within these narratives, two principal structuring mechanisms become apparent: synesthesia and metaphor. Synesthesia has rarely received attention in film studies, but metaphor has been the subject of discussion by Jean Mitry, Christian Metz, Marie-Claire Ropars, and Linda Williams, among others.[1] In *Figures of Desire*, Williams observes that modern film studies privilege the analysis of metonymy because "film has often been defined as an essentially metonymic art." She goes on to declare: "Film metaphors have been pushed aside, as if to make up for all the years metaphor reigned supreme."[2] In pursuing the connection between synesthesia, metaphor, and narrative in the von Sternberg/Dietrich Paramount cycle, this chapter explores how metaphoric structuring through iconic similarity frequently displaces cause/effect narrative organization in the films. The analysis of specific examples leads to a broader discussion of narrativity which considers the roles of imagery perception, analogic thinking, and iconographic intertextuality in the production of meaning.

Synesthesia and Metaphor: Defining Intersensory Analogy

In "Some Observations on Sternberg and Dietrich," Carole Zucker identifies the operation of synesthesia in *Shanghai Express* and defines this phenomenon as "the substitution of sensory elements for one another."[3] As her chief example, Zucker uses the juxtaposition of Shanghai Lily and Doc Harvey kissing on the observation deck with the shot of a train whistle blowing. Zucker leaves the impression that film synesthesia depends upon the contiguous relationship of discrete elements that produces synesthesia in verbal language. In the latter, metaphoric word combinations describe sensation by combining words of different modalities (i.e., bitter cold = taste and feeling; thundering dawn = sight and sound).[4] As a result, verbal synesthesia, the basis of metaphor, has been thought of as intrinsically artificial, even illogical.[5] The Firstness of the sensory modalities must go through Thirdness —through the word as abstraction—rather than being experienced in sensory directness. Additionally, words are split, separated into pho- nemes: language synesthesia cannot combine senses into one unit.

By discussing synesthesia, Zucker ventures into a valuable area of study, but her definition and examples do not establish the dif- ference between synesthesia in verbal language and synesthesia as a figurative language of the unconscious evidencing analogic thinking and a reliance on iconic signs. In film synesthesia, actual modalities of sensory experience are available through sight and sound. Film also provides the implied presence of other modalities, especially the tac- tile and the spatial. Modalities of sense are metaphorically connected by continuity (as in the juxtaposition of kiss/train whistle) or can be simultaneous (i.e., within the same shot or in the superimposition of shots). Association overcomes the illogic of difference. Trans-sensory or iconic similarities are stressed.

Zucker's example of the kiss/train whistle illustrates metaphor, not pure synesthesia. Metaphor, as an offshoot of synesthesia, relies upon recognizing some qualities of likeness between elements, upon the perception of an analogic relationship between the signs. In verbal language this likeness is usually on the level of the signified, not the signifier or representamen.

In reference to this very same example from *Shanghai Express*, Williams designates the juxtaposition of elements as an example of a classical film metaphor. In principle, such a metaphor closely resem- bles verbal metaphor which relies upon hierarchical correspondences between the *tenor* (diegetic action—the kiss) and the *vehicle* (comparison —the whistle): the kiss must come first to ground the figure's meaning; the whistle merely comments on the action. It is not the form of the elements (the signifiers) that determines the association but their imagined qualities of likeness.[6] Consequently, the continuity of tenor and vehicle becomes crucial to the recognition of the quality held in common, or, as Metz says, the metaphor depends upon the similarities "perceived or felt to exist between the *referents* of the two units. . . ."[7]

Central to Williams's thesis in *Figures of Desire* is the identification of a deconstructing alternative to classical metaphor. She finds this alternative in the famous eye-cutting sequence of Luis Bunuel's *Un Chien andalou:*

> . . . form rather than content dictates the ground of the association. Such a figure, though formally modeled on the typical metaphor, actually functions as a deconstruction of the anticipated metaphoric process in which the denotative content of the eye-cutting refuses to be absorbed immediately into the connotative expression.
>
> Unlike the classical figure, this seemingly autonomous figure refuses to be read as mere embellishment upon a discourse. It demands to be seen as the very cause of this discourse.[8]

Williams argues that the typical metaphor can be interpreted "in an instant" but that metaphors based on form, such as Bunuel's, imitate "the procedures of the unconscious" and deconstruct the normal "metaphoric process." For Williams, the similarity of form between the vehicle and tenor invites comparison, yet, as she notes, no immediate "connotative explanation" is given "on the level of signified."[9] These metaphors require the analysis of the entire text to uncover their latent meaning.

No doubt Williams might be surprised to discover that the kind of deconstructive metaphors she finds in Bunuel's films bear greater similarity to the dominant metaphoric pattern in von Sternberg films than the example she and Zucker cite from *Shanghai Express*. The von Sternberg/Dietrich films use the classical metaphor, but somewhat ironically they show an increasing reliance on metaphors of form, on *iconic metaphors* and a complex metaphoric structuring of the entire film. The metaphoric structuring of von Sternberg's films finds its culmination in *The Scarlet Empress*. The overdetermination of the film's metaphors also necessitates a reading across the entire text for their meaning, a process Paul Ricoeur argues is actually typical of poetry.[10]

Von Sternberg's metaphors also evidence the power of their synesthetic origins. In film, synesthesia does not necessarily depend upon contiguity but may occur as the simultaneous perception of differing modalities of sense. Marks defines synesthesia as "different senses

assisting each other in perception."[11] Film is always synesthetic (sight
and sound), but, as with iconicity, we also must judge the degree to
which synesthesia is implied or stressed. Marks's definition is more
appropriate to a study of film since it refers more directly to the synesthesia of imagery and sound perception. Language synesthesia offers
symbolic, abstract units that *pretend to represent* different senses. Synesthesia, as defined by Marks, suggests that the phenomenon actually
makes a unified sensory experience out of the combination of different
senses. Just as masochism is a regressive psychosexuality, synesthesia is
also a regressive functioning, a rich mode of analogic perception associated with figuration, primary process, and childhood perception.
Marks outlines the developmental process that associates synesthesia
with iconicity:

> . . . a young child tests by perceiving, by transforming perceptions into
> images, and by operating on these iconic representations. . . . because
> more children than adults exhibit sensory synesthesia it is likely that
> many synesthetic children lose their synesthesia when they grow up. This
> makes me suspect that synesthesia is a characteristic of the processes that
> dominate cognitive growth's perceptual or iconic stage. Like perception
> in general, synesthesia is a direct and economical means of cognition
> organization.[12]

Iconic thinking and childhood synesthesia have not been taken
into account in the emphasis on difference in the acquisition of verbal symbols. Piaget's studies allow us to return to the role of analogic
thinking in symbolization. In his 1945 study "Plays, Dreams, and Imitation in Childhood," Piaget observes that a child who sees a train may
subsequently make the sound "tch-tch" when other objects or people
are observed moving.[13] The child applies the sound to actions that display the dynamic of movement originally observed. In effect, the child
makes a metaphoric connection, one in which the perceived property
is recognized in a class of situations. The perception is also synesthetic
in that sound is not isolated but part of the entire event of perceiving
the train or objects/movement classified as similar. The word/sound
cannot be separated from the association of impressions.[14] Sound and
sight merge into an analogic perception that organizes the world on a
level still largely dependent on synesthesia. As a child develops, verbal signs replace synesthetic perception. Although language signs are
more flexible and precise than synesthesia, they are less salient.[15]

Synesthesia's sensory, analogic associations lead to a comparison of an event with a phenomenon occurring in another sensory
mode and eventually to metaphor. It also leads to a blurring of the

boundaries between the senses, between the animate and the inanimate, human and thing, perceived reality and imaginative projection. The mixing of sensory modes and elements (thing—thing, sign—sign) is a recognized feature of von Sternberg's films.[16]

In film, synesthesia depends upon similarity, upon an iconic relationship of Peircean Firstness that intertwines disparate phenomena into an affective experience. In adult life, metaphor is the most obvious expression of synesthesia. It permits what Marks calls the forging of "new multi-sensory meanings."[17] As with iconic sign relationships in general, synesthesia and iconic metaphors based on formal likeness privilege similarity over contiguity through intersensory analogy and, in displacing modalities of perception, may participate in a dreamlike displacement, condensation, identification, and symbolism.

In the von Sternberg/Dietrich Paramount films, synesthesia and metaphor play an important role in extending the meaning of signs and organizing the narrative discourse. Iconic sign relationships and the mixing of modalities of senses and signifiers function to express the thematic connections that give the films their "poetic" quality. Nevertheless, not all of the films' metaphors are iconic metaphors with an overt resemblance between the signifiers or representamen. In blending Peircean Firstness and Thirdness, iconic or analogic sign relationships forge a meaning that is created, shared, and transferred in a process that resembles poetry and dream. The so-called mystery of von Sternberg's films, their ambiguity and richness, can be traced to the creation of multivalent meaning through such sophisticated iconic sign relationships.[18]

Most useful to initiating a discussion of film metaphor within the von Sternberg/Dietrich films is Max Black's interaction theory. Black considers the affective power of metaphor as that of a completely new meaning created from the interaction of the metaphoric statement's individual elements (ground or vehicle and trope).[19] While his definition is compatible with the Peircean view of the blending of Firstness and Thirdness in the interpretant, it also points to the impreciseness of metaphoric thought. Peirce's own definition of metaphor is carefully phrased but difficult: "Those [icons] which represent the representative character of a representamen by representing a parallelism in something else, are metaphors."[20] Decio Pignatari offers a Peircean-derived definition of metaphor as "a hypoicon or iconic sign by contiguity, meaning a similitude or parallelism between certain supposedly observed features of the referents of the sign."[21] A verbal metaphor rests on a semantic similarity between the referents, not a formal one between the representamen (signifiers). Pignatari goes beyond the scope of this definition, expressing an interest in the unheralded role of the likeness created between signifier and signified: iconization, or paronomasia in all forms of art.[22] His and Peirce's definitions are applicable to verbal and visual signs, but the unique possibilities of visual metaphor require further explanation.

Language metaphor usually links referents (the signified); the signifier or representamen, the words as things-representations, are almost always totally dissimilar in appearance. In visual signs, similarity through form, through a parallelism of the signifiers in iconic likeness, frequently occurs to some degree. Even the kiss/train whistle "literary" metaphor contains a trace of a dynamic or kinetic likeness that underscores the resemblances perceived by the child in Piaget's example.

Peirce categorized three types of iconic signs: images, diagrams, and metaphors. He referred to verbal metaphors primarily as an expression of Thirdness, the abstracted common essence formed as an interpretant in the mind.[23] Marks regards metaphor's tie to synesthesia as indicative of its broad capacities as a "dense cognitive code," as well as of its paradoxical structure. The paradox is contained in the fact that "sensory qualities are concrete and thus specific, yet they contain a suggestion of the general."[24] Metaphoric connection, like dream figuration, reunites objects through their concrete being (the Firstness of concrete representability) to evoke a Thirdness (the abstract essence). Stylistically, visual emphasis is placed on the signifier's supersensual quality, not on its logical, contiguous aspects. Whether there are any "pure" metaphors in film untouched by metonymy is not the issue.[25] Visual metaphor can make paradigmatic relations visible by privileging not cause/effect, hierarchical continuity but the paratactic (nonhierarchical juxtaposition) and the paramorphic (similarity between forms). Even metaphor in contiguity, in syntagmatic relations, emphasizes the creation of an imaginary connection in the mind and a paratactic, analogic relationship.

Dispersed over the course of the film, either as combined vehicle and tenor (superimposition/dissolve) or with the elements separated, metaphor persists in calling attention to signifiers broken off from their momentary syntagmatic and spatiotemporal context by their relationship to past and future signifiers. In this way, the masochistic text begins to emulate the ontological time of the masochistic relationship to pain and pleasure. Through visual metaphor, contiguity's value as a marker of spatial and temporal unity is devalued, even if the tenor and vehicle belong to the same diegetic space, as they sometimes do in the von Sternberg/Dietrich films.

The organizational capacity of visual metaphor rests with the spectator's ability to read the film backward as well as forward, to reinvest earlier moments with the heightened significance of their metaphoric connection. The image is left open to function in the reverie of metaphoric thinking. Von Sternberg's technique, one critic has suggested, functions as "formal memory."[26] Genette's description of Proustian metaphor also applies to von Sternberg's use of perceived likeness between signs to create a fetishistic narrative structure obsessed with return and recovery: "Thus metaphor is not an ornament, but the necessary instrument for a recovery, through style, of the vision of essences. . . . it is the stylistic equivalence of the psychological experience of involuntary memory, which . . . by bringing together two sensations separate in time, is able to release the common essence through the miracle of analogy."[27]

The flexibility of imagistic organization and imagery processing becomes the cornerstone to a narrative employing metaphor and synesthesia. Metaphor as a structuring device to narrative circumvents and subverts the limitations of cause/effect logic and contiguity. The linear temporality of film is disavowed as the spectator is forced to utilize the synchronous processing and symmetrical associations of imagery perception/cognition. Allan Paivio's research leads him to conclude that verbal and imagistic processing are entirely different modes of brain functioning. His empirical studies lend credence to Durgnat's intuitive assessment of how film narrative is read by the spectator.[28] Paivio states:

> . . . imagery system is specialized for synchronous organization and parallel processing of nonverbal information whereas verbal processes involve sequential organization of linguistic units. . . .
> . . . information processing of the visual may be successive, but the functioning of any element in the system does not depend on the outcome of the functioning of another. . . . Synchronous organization also implies that interim associations in memory are directionally symmetrical and free from sequential constraints during retrieval. . . . Through its high memory capacity and freedom from sequential constraints, imagery contributes richness of content and flexibility in the processing of that content, so that diverse bits of information could be quickly compared.[29]

Von Sternberg's iconic discourse is very dependent on the "high memory capacity and freedom from sequential constraints" that Paivio characterizes as unique aspects of imagery processing.[30] The pervasive opinion that von Sternberg's films are flawed attempts at narrative construction may relate to the critical failure to recognize this mode of visual thinking/processing in the construction of narrative.

Von Sternberg's films depend on the symmetry of associations, the synchronous and the parallel rather than the sequential, contiguous, differentiated elements essential to linguistic organization. This process is illustrated in brief reference to *The Scarlet Empress*. The image of the iron maiden in Sophia's dream, the glimpse of the Madonna/Child figure on her bed, and the ornate relief of the Christ/Madonna on the door of the carriage that takes her to the "arms of Mother Russia" first appear to be given inordinate attention that seems explicable only as an example of von Sternberg's decadent excess or his obsession with historical detail. Later, when the connection between Madonna/Catherine/Christ has been established through the extension of the metaphor within the governing frame of Catherine's actions, these shots acquire their significance. This illustrates how metaphoric structuring undermines the unidirectionality of film narrative and transfers meaning from the syntagmatic onto the vertical axis. The search for meaning is thrown onto the reappearance of visual detail that perpetually reasserts the signifier.

In emphasizing both paramorphic (iconic) and classical metaphors, von Sternberg's thematically centered formal structures evoke the overdetermined sources and multiple meanings found in primary process thinking. As a result, the spectator is brought closer to archaic modes of iconic thought and to the algorithms of feeling expressed through fantasy and dream. Ernst Kris explains the link between metaphors and the unconscious: "Metaphor serves as a stimulus to functional regression because the primary process is itself metaphoric and imagistic. The dream life, for instance, is predominantly visual, and shows a marked tendency to note similarities (especially by way of similar emotional responses) that escape . . . waking life." [31] Although metaphor is often cited as the fundamental mechanism of primary process discourse, we need to be cautious in taking this comparison too literally. As Jean-François Lyotard reminds us, there is a danger of reductionism in equating rhetorical forms in language with dream figuration. [32]

Language's disjunction of the elements of metaphor is potentially overcome through film's ability to create the dreamlike literal fusion of iconic signs in superimpositions or dissolves. Von Sternberg's films often use both, sometimes in combination with metaphor, sometimes as traditional transitional devices, and sometimes as formal devices that dissolve time and space within a scene. For example, midway through a sequence in *Dishonored*, Lieutenant Kranau waits in a hallway. His waiting is superimposed with a meeting of army generals in the next room. These two spaces and actions would be expected to have an ultimate narrative connection, but there is never any further association made between them. The repeated superimpositions merely indicate their temporal simultaneity. In another scene, Magda's face is superimposed over the figures of a policeman and the secret service commander as they look up in response to the sound of her piano. These scenes support Metz's statement that superimposed dissolves should not be "attributed en bloc to the metaphorical principle," but Metz rather arbitrarily classifies superimpositions and lap-dissolves as metaphoric only "if one of the two images is extra-diegetic."[33] It seems undeniable that many times the impact of the dissolve's formal quality forces comparison at the slightest of pretexts.

Von Sternberg's iconic metaphors often evolve out of conventional cinematic use (i.e., form-cuts or lap-dissolves that ostensibly bridge temporal gaps à la Vorkapich with an illusion of contiguity through matching likenesses), but his metaphors frequently also emphasize the spatiotemporal illogic of such traditional devices. The essence of masochistic temporality is crystallized in the extended lap-dissolve that Metz calls the controlled visual technique par excellence and compares to the "veiling-unveiling" of the striptease.[34] The illusion of filmic representation is heightened by von Sternberg's careful control of formal technique.

Iconic Metaphors as "Germinal Image-Clusters"

The masochistic aesthetic unites style and narrativity through an iconic discourse in which metaphors give shape to the films' iconically based construction. *The Scarlet Empress* demonstrates a particularly complex use of metaphor and synesthesia. Early in the film a lap-dissolve transforms a tortured man swinging upside down as a human bell clapper into the image of the teenage Sophia on a swing. The fusion of images is transitional, but, as Durgnat and Wood have pointed out, its significance extends beyond its transitional function.[35] Durgnat remembers the dissolve as a cut and includes statues that are not seen until later in the film: "The heavy statues of agonized old men (serfs? prophets?) insistently [re-establish] the system of torture and oppression. . . . A quick cut to Marlene on her swing establishes her—ignorance of it? Indifference to it? She gives to the poor, but the contrast establishes the sublime indifference of an erotic divine."[36] His interpretation of this metaphoric transformation hinges on cause/effect contiguity, not the obvious iconic relationship between the two shots. Durgnat reads Sophia's expression as indifference or ignorance, as a reaction to the previous shot. Although stimulated by the daily residual of the servants' discussion, her vividly intense dream precludes any notion that she is either ignorant of or indifferent to suffering or sexuality. Durgnat does not recognize that these two shots are nonhierarchical, paratactically related images linked by iconic likeness. As with the moon/clouds, eye/razor shots in *Un Chien andalou*, they elude immediate interpretation.

By contrast, Wood sees the analogic relationship between the bell clapper/swing shots and acknowledges the difficulty of interpreting the two images: "The fusion, in the very complexity of its suggestions, is central to the film's meaning. Such a juxtaposition can imply either comparison or contrast, likeness or unlikeness. . . . the dissolve provides a germinal image-cluster from which various outgrowths or related imagery will develop."[37] The dreamlike compound image offers an overdetermined, concrete visualization of masochism's aesthetic and psychoanalytic principles: suspension, disavowal, fantasy, pleasure in pain and pain in pleasure. Repetition occurs in the suspended pendulum-like movement of bodies fixed in their boundaries of action. The visual metaphor of man-clapper/girl on swing encompasses contrast and likeness. There is inversion—he is upside down, she is right side up—and reversal—male to female, pain to pleasure. Both figures appear to be in a passive position, but the man has been created by Sophia as the active child dreamer. Provocatively swinging directly into the axis of the camera, she engages in a child's game, but Sophia is ready for marriage. Her pleasure is childlike, more so than her violent dream that produced the images of pain.

The ambiguity of the dissolve-fusion, clearly shown by the widely differing interpretations of Durgnat and Wood, illustrates how an iconically based metaphor blends Peircean Firstness (aesthetic/emotional) into Secondness (comparison) and Thirdness (interpretant). Wood's assessment identifies the overdetermined aspects of the metaphor as well as the manifold meaning or ambiguity, but the structuring metaphor is also an isolated, fetishistic fragment of suffering and pleasure that does not conform to conventional notions of narrative action. It does not play on hermeneutic questions but on the image as a "screen memory," a fetish that suspends immediate meaning, frustrates knowledge, and waits on the play of restatement and repetition. Achieved through metaphors or isolated metaphoric elements, suspension of meaning becomes the narrative equivalent to the masochistic suspension of pleasure.

Throughout the film, the fusion of bell clapper/Sophia is continued in Sophia/Catherine's association with bells and swings. The original elements of the metaphor are displaced into metonymy. The swinging motif comes into play when Catherine has her first romantic encounter with Alexei in a horse stable. Suspended on a rope loop, she giddily circles around until she flops into the hay. Heralded by the ringing of bells, her wedding is marked by the rhythmically insistent swinging of incense burners. The birth of her child and her ascent to the throne are proclaimed by the ringing of bells. Finally, in the last scene, Catherine assumes the role of her dream's repulsively enthusiastic bell ringer/torturer. She rings the bells of Moscow to signal an end to Peter's bloody reign; her actions also signal her husband's murder. The tolling awakens the dreamer (Peter) to send him to a sleep of death and circles inexorably back to Catherine as the bedridden child who dreams of bells and torture and state executions.

The metaphor of tortured man/swinging girl is not a direct statement but an iconic metaphor that turns Peircean Firstness into a conceptual Thirdness. In verbalizing the meaning of a visual metaphor, the metaphor's meaning is inevitably reduced, especially if it is not analyzed as an element within the film's entire network of visual associations. Nevertheless, it should not be too quickly assumed that the ambiguity of metaphor always signals uncertainty or vagueness. Kris explains: "The understanding of irony, for example, involves the recognition of distinct (indeed, opposed) meanings, which are, however, responded to conjointly. *This type of ambiguity is especially suited to the expression of ambivalent attitudes,* and this use has long attracted the attention of psychologists and linguists" (emphasis mine).[38] Whether bridging temporal gaps or isolated, without a clearly established connection to previous time and space, von Sternberg's metaphors blend Firstness and Thirdness. In doing so, they generate what Kris identifies as "a new and larger range of significance" as they also integrate and indicate "the direction along which unification of the multiple meanings is to be achieved."[39] Ambiguity or multiple meaning is a predictable result of visual metaphors. Multivalent meaning may be perceived as ambiguity, but, as Kris notes, the essence of poetry is that it "may even require ambiguities."[40]

The composite image of tortured man/playing girl expresses transverbal aspects of masochism. The film moves close to dream figuration that does not double or mirror language. Although we call upon metaphor as a descriptive term, visual imagery allows the expression of impulses that exceed explanation through rhetorical terms.[41] Metaphor can only lead us to the locus of their meaning, back to the site of signification—the paradoxical masochistic psychodynamic.

Blonde Venus: *Iconicity and Intertextuality*

In *Blonde Venus*, a similar "germinal image-cluster" reveals a wider context in the creation of the production of meaning. This crucial iconic metaphor in the film illustrates Julia Kristeva's contention that "every text is constructed as a mosaic of citations and every text is an absorption and a transformation of another text."[42] Helen swims nude in a Black Forest pond. A dissolve connects her splashing to her son's bathtub splashing five years later in a New York City tenement. Johnny promptly declares he is a fish. Here, as in the hanging/swing metaphor of *The Scarlet Empress*, a temporal and spatial shift is articulated and abstracted through the dissolve, but the main function is iconic and, consequently, thematic rather than spatiotemporal.

This dissolve image, like that in *The Scarlet Empress*, also demonstrates the limitations of a Metzian semiological analysis. The importance of these fusions lies in their evocative nature, not in their syntagmatic function. The transition linking mother to son, water to water, "fish" to "fish," ostensibly has nothing to do with narrative events on a synoptic level. It appears to be purely descriptive, but the dissolve link is actually central in establishing the film's complex web of emotional relationships and dramatic motivation. On a level of Peircean Thirdness, Helen's watery beginning evokes the iconography of Botticelli's painting of Venus rising from the sea. In turn, Botticelli's painting is iconographically dependent on the myth that Venus rose from the watery foam of Uranus's semen. Helen's later epithet as the "Blonde Venus," like Sophia's ascendancy to royal hangman, seems to be a fated occurrence with visual, intertextual signs as the motivating force.

Erwin Panofsky defined iconography as the branch of art history concerned with "the subject matter or meaning of works of art, as opposed to their form."[43] However, iconography cannot help but involve form since it must account for the meaning of visual signs in their cultural connotations. The conventionalized aspects of the iconic signs form an iconic metaphor between mother and son that requires intertextual knowledge to ascertain at least one level of its possible signification. When intertextual knowledge contributes to the understanding of the sign, then iconography, in Panofsky's terms, must be applied to determine the level of Thirdness. Just as dream imagery is rich in levels of meaning that depend upon the individual dreamer's life experience as well as the conventionalization of signs, iconic signs in film acquire conventionalized aspects that produce meaning. Iconography emerges as an aspect of Thirdness (symbolic meaning), which is in turn an aspect of the interpretant. These iconographic aspects of the image may not be absolutely necessary for a limited understanding of the film, but their presence enriches meaning. Iconographic knowledge contributes to what Culler has called the "general discursive space that makes a text intelligible."[44]

Not only is the iconographic meaning of *Blonde Venus* enriched by the association of Helen with Venus, but the dissolve is dependent on the iconographic meaning of the fish. Traditionally a symbol of renewal or rebirth, the fish's labile quality allows it to be both phallic symbol and uterine animal.[45] The duality is an iconographic slippage that expresses the masochistic male's desire for rebirth from the oral mother. Johnny is the child of the womb, the uterine animal, the fish. Jung's account of the significance of the fish in dream unexpectedly recalls the masochistic wish for symbiotic reunion and rebirth: "The fish in dream occasionally signifies the unborn child, because the child before its birth lives in the water like a fish; similarly, when the sun sinks into the sea, it becomes the child and fish at once. The fish is therefore a symbol of renewal and rebirth."[46]

The dissolve-linked images and dialogue in *Blonde Venus* contribute to the overdetermination of the mother/son relationship. Initially, Firstness dominates in the purely iconic similarity of mother and son as nude bodies in the water and in the splashing movement; mother, gliding fishlike through the water, and bathing son. Peter Lehman and William Luhr have suggested that this likeness and the dissolve fetishistically blur the distinction between the bodies to cause the male spectator's desire to momentarily shift from Helen to the legs of her son:

> The shots of Dietrich's body are also classically fetishized through fragmentation. One of these shots seems to be of her kicking her legs in the water, but the camera pulls back to reveal a boy's legs as he splashes in the bathtub. . . . The shot is shocking because for an instant the men in the audience are likely to have placed their erotic desires on the boy's legs thinking them to be Dietrich's. . . . Men in the audience, then, are potentially not only shocked by the momentary confusion of the collapse of sexual difference but also potentially disturbed by the implicit threat of homosexuality—they have been aroused by a boy's legs.[47]

Although Lehman and Luhr's reading might actually support my analysis of the masochistic text's blurring of sexual difference, the timing and visual coding of the transition makes such a transfer of desire unlikely. The transition does illustrate how, as discussed in chapter

3, the shared likeness between mother and son provides the visual
expression of an erotic relationship that gives the film its perverse
dimensions. The visual link between them is continually reinforced
through verbal references to the fetishistic objects that surround them
as metonymic extensions. For example, in preparing for her first night
on the stage, Helen takes Johnny's teddy bear as her good luck charm
for her performance as another hairy beast. When Helen and Johnny
take to the road, the bear is juxtaposed with a chicken, which, as
Wood states, offers a pun on the French slang word for prostitute,
poule (hen).[48] Helen's numerous onstage and offstage masks and masquerades are eerily repeated in the grotesque mask that Johnny wears
perched Janus-faced on the back of his head. As in a dream, such symbols in the mise-en-scène are indecipherable at their appearance but
read across the text, with reference to the possibilities of intertextual
meaning, they acquire their "poetic" significance.

Metaphoric Structuring and Primary Process

Gregory Bateson has noted that relationships form the subject
of iconic communication and the iconic figures that dominate primary
process.[49] With its emphasis on metaphoric structuring, von Sternberg's iconic discourse leads directly to and from the regressive infantile fantasy of masochism. His films offer a complex interplay of
modes of consciousness and privilege primary process thinking. As
Victor Burgin writes, "the 'closer' we approach the unconscious the
less differentiated become the modalities of thought: gesture, image
and word become compacted into dense, multi-layered and faceted
units."[50] In the von Sternberg/Dietrich cycle, the unconscious invests
the image to overdetermine its meaning and produce a synesthetic
density.

The Scarlet Empress demonstrates how the von Sternberg/Dietrich
films inscribe masochism's psychic ambivalence into the dialectical
framework of the perversion's fantasy via dialogue, the interaction of
plastic motifs in the mise-en-scène, and metaphoric linkage. The result is a system that controls desire as it expresses that desire through
the density of delayed meaning. The opening scene introduces several
major motifs, including three of the most important: the doll/human
iconic metaphor, the metonymic Sophia/horse linkage, and the metaphoric association of Sophia with doctor/hangman. The opening shot
is of a doctor probing little Sophia Frederica. The girl's mother curtly
gathers up her dolls: Sophia, almost seven years old, is too old for such
nonsense. Later, Sophia cautiously reveals a doll she has hidden be-

neath the bedcovers. She listens intently to the servants as they talk of her "hangman" doctor who has just recommended a cure for her ills: she is to be placed in a harness "for about a year." Told that the kindly "horse doctor" is really the court executioner, Sophia asks whether she can be a hangman when she grows up. A servant tells her that many monarchs become quite skillful hangmen.

There is hardly an aspect of this scene that is not developed in the course of the film, although the first impression is that little happens of narrative importance. Sophia's gesture of retrieving the doll is not given visual emphasis. In a close-up of her face, the doll is peripherally placed in the frame. Sophia's childish defiance of her mother's dictum is a prelude to her subversion of her politically determined fate as "brood mare" for the Russian royal family. The doctor's probe is repeated in her medical examination by the Russian court doctor. The female body is subjected to the gaze that observes, judges, and controls. The court doctor hastily examines Sophia and unceremoniously loses his wig under her voluminous skirts; he emerges to declare her fit to marry and confidently assures the old Empress that Sophia will give them "no trouble." Of course, Sophia will be quite troublesome; she will successfully undermine all of the empress Elizabeth's plans for the future.

Sophia's pose with her doll is iconically repeated in the scene that marks the birth of her son. Public announcements and pealing bells proclaim the long-awaited event. A crowd of courtiers surrounds what appears to be the birth bed. Slowly the camera reveals that the doting "mother" is not Catherine but the old Empress, bedridden from illness. She is, however, still domineering enough to announce her total control over her new grandson. Sophia's mother once refused her child her dolls; now the empress Elizabeth refuses Catherine access to her own son. The old Empress assumes the domineering matriarchal function of Sophia's mother yet also assumes, through iconic likeness, Sophia's earlier role as the sick child. She serves as a dreamlike condensation of these two earlier roles, but she is also a figure of startling displacement: she appears to be the child's mother but is not. The dreamlike displacement depends upon the careful manipulation of an iconic similarity that subverts audience expectation. Catherine lies in another bed, contemplating a dazzling medal, her reward for the birth of a son.

As in a child's dream, humans and toys are paratactically juxtaposed, mixed, and confused in *The Scarlet Empress*. Conversely, humans are treated like erotic toys. This synesthetic confusion forms a complex, concrete representation of the confusion of identity, a major theme in the film and throughout the von Sternberg/Dietrich cycle. Dolls have traditionally been regarded as important tools in guiding children's development of self-identity.[51] The doll/human motif also gives concrete representability to power's perversion of human sensibility. The human becomes the mechanical.[52] Catherine's doll-obsessed husband treats the mechanical and the living alike. Peter's toys bear the brunt of his madness until he can torture and kill real people. He lops off the head of a tiny effigy of his wife and drills his Hessian troops in the palace hallways as if they were the soldier figurines on his favorite toy carousel. Human relationships are represented through the plastic motifs of dolls, puppets, and statues that indicate a synesthetic confusion of representation and object, human and environmental.

Von Sternberg's fondness for using objective correlatives to carry emotion evidences synesthesia but is also typical of the masochistic aesthetic's reliance on art as a model for the frozen ideal. The statues of the martyrs, saints, and Madonna and Child in *The Scarlet Empress*, like the mannequin and statue in *Blonde Venus*, are more than carriers of atmosphere. The statues of martyrs and saints, ever present in the mise-en-scène, are often treated like furniture, and sometimes literally are furniture. While the characters dress in eighteenth-century costumes of satin, brocade, feathers, and fur, their accoutrements of a civilized court life are silently contrasted with the primitive, ghostly white statues. With candles in hand, they resemble otherwordly sentinels. Their twisted shapes and painful expressions make them the concrete representation of human suffering, the masochistic art model frozen in the ultimate suspended spectacle of pain.

Deleuze remarks that the art model suspends gesture and attitude to suggest a state of being "beyond all movement . . . closer to the sources of life and death."[53] When Alexei confronts Catherine at the palace stairs, he is juxtaposed beside a twisted statue of Saint Sebastian, the martyr pierced by arrows. Alexei's countenance is impassive, his suffering displaced onto the frozen realm of art. Sacher-Masoch's *Venus in Furs* sheds light on the connection between martyrdom and masochism which is relevant to Alexei's situation:

> Wanda: "You mean that reason has little power over you and that you
> are weak and sensuous by nature?"
> Severin: "Were the martyrs also weak and sensuous?"
> Wanda: "The martyrs?"
> Severin: "Precisely, the martyrs were supersensuous beings who found
> positive pleasure in pain and who sought horrible tortures,
> even death, as others seek enjoyment. I too am supersensual,
> madam, just as they were."

With candles in hand, the statues in *The Scarlet Empress* resemble otherworldly sentinels. Their twisted shapes and painful expressions make them the concrete representation of human suffering, the masochistic art model frozen into the ultimate suspended spectacle of pain. Marlene Dietrich in *The Scarlet Empress* (1934). Publicity still.

Wanda: "Take care that you do not also become a martyr to love, the martyr of a woman."[54]

In pursuing Catherine, Alexei is martyred to love. His desire intensifies as Catherine pursues others. The visual association of Alexei, the Master of the Hunt, with the martyred Saint Sebastian points to the similarities between masochism as a perversion and the religious martyr's consummation of sacred love in a self-annihilating esctasy of pain. Masochism's ideal subject, the willing victim in a pact of suffering, finds its prototype in Jesus Christ. Deleuze notes that Sacher-Masoch's work is permeated by "Christology."[55] This allusion's appeal to masochism is easily located in the masochistic fantasy of rebirth into the new being born of suffering and death.

Echoing Sacher-Masoch's *Venus in Furs*, the iconography of *The Scarlet Empress* appropriates Christic imagery. Catherine's identification with the ideal oral mother of masochism is reinforced by the presence of the Madonna/Child statue serving as the headboard to her bed, the figures reflecting in the mirror as Catherine prepares for her ill-fated wedding. In anticipation of the wedding night, priests bless the bed, but a tracking shot into a close-up of the Madonna/Child dissolves into a shot of a human skeleton used as the stand for wedding feast refreshments. On a level of Thirdness, the mother/child figure iconically represents the alliance of the Mother of God and the Holy Child. The dissolve also functions as a chilling prediction of a marriage that ends in murder. In the reflection of the statue, Catherine's role in the masochistic scenario is doubled in an objective correlative repeated and frozen once again in the mirror. The ironies of metaphor multiply. Catherine possesses unexpected resemblances to the Madonna: she is a mother, an innocent, a woman whose husband is not her child's father, a woman chosen to be the mother of the heir to a kingdom. Yet Catherine is also sexually promiscuous, ambitious, and involved in murder, not martyrdom. The visual analogy between Catherine and the Madonna emerges as paradoxically profane and true.

In *Venus in Furs*, Severin equates the worship of Christ with his love for Wanda: "I prostrated myself before her and kissed her feet in a way I had seen my fellow-countrymen kiss the feet of the dead savior."[56] In *The Scarlet Empress*, Catherine's likeness to the Madonna is established, but her link to the suffering Christ is also clearly made. Joanna Hubbs, who has discussed the role of the "female savior" in Russian culture, argues that rulers "were identified with the Humiliated Christ rather than the proud and distant Jehovah." Russian culture, she notes, has traditionally blended the patriarchal and the matriarchal in the myth of the Mother Goddess and her consort/son, "the dying god."[57]

The iconography of the crucifix dominates Catherine's triumph over Peter, who is killed behind a cross. Accompanied by sculptures of Christ (a blatant impossibility in the Russian Orthodox church), Catherine triumphantly enters the Moscow cathedral. At the end of the sequence, a close-up of one of these Christ figures dissolves into a close-up of Catherine's face. Deleuze explains how masochistic fantasy places the ideal maternal imago in an "elaboration of the Marian phantasy" in which Christ is put on the cross by his mother to ensure the son's parthenogenetic rebirth and resurrection. The son does not actually die, but the father in the son does, so that the cross comes to represent "the maternal image of death."[58] In Christic iconography, masochism finds its intertextual model for the alliance of the willing male victim and the ideal maternal imago.

The objective correlatives in *The Scarlet Empress* also register a dreamlike displacement of feeling or action from one character to another. Wielding a huge spiral bore, Peter accidentally drills through the eye of an icon hanging in the old Empress's bedroom, in an attempt to spy on his wife, who waits in service on the Empress. As the bore emerges through the icon's eye, Catherine stares at the blasphemously comic result of Peter's inept covert operation. Head cocked like that of a perplexed child, Catherine imitates her gesture with her doll from the opening scene. Peter's defacement of the icon destroys Catherine's symbolic likeness. Later, his murderous feelings are knowingly displaced onto a doll model of Catherine as, in a dream, he iconically acts out his violent wishes against his wife. On a level of Firstness, Peter's continual association with toys adds a bizarre quality to his mania. Ironically, his keen interest in torture was shared by the child Sophia, whose aggression remained within the confines of her dreamlife.

The objective correlatives of the masochistic aesthetic create iconically based metaphors that add to the atmosphere of suspended movement, timelessness, and coldness. The painting and statues, like masks and dolls, exemplify the iconic suspension of spatial and temporal laws, the delay of gratification, and masochistic contemplation in the art model. In *Blonde Venus* and *The Scarlet Empress* these correlatives appear in scenes that are iconically modeled on earlier ones. Dreamlike repetition of specific motifs and entire scenes demonstrates how the film disavows a sense of narrative progression and reinforces the inevitable cyclical, fetishistic remarking of the past that is a key requirement of masochism's formal expression. The "frozen progression" of repetition is paralleled in iconic likenesses that double the suspension of masochistic experience. As Deleuze says, "the plastic arts confer an eternal character on their subject" and express "a profound state of waiting."[59] In its "mystical play of flesh, fur, and mirror," the von Sternberg masochistic texts depend upon the plastic elements of mise-en-scène to transmute the sensuality of film's constant movement into the paradoxical temporality of masochistic fantasy.[60]

This transmutation is apparent in the scene in *The Scarlet Empress* in which Catherine summons Alexei to her bedroom. He approaches her bed in expectation that their mutual passion will finally be consummated. A medium close-up of Alexei dissolves into a shot of a devil statue that looms behind him. Alexei moves out from behind the statue and out of the frame (foreground exit). At this movement, a dissolve superimposes a close-up of Alexei with the head of the statue; his motion is temporarily frozen by the dissolve at midpoint in the action. Then, after Alexei has completely left the frame, another dissolve reinserts him into the same space. This visual fusion has no logical function in a coherent film space or unified time frame. The superimposition is not a transition and escapes the syntagmatic function Metz attributes to dissolves.[61] It creates a diegetic metaphor that compels the spectator to link the scene to an earlier event: Catherine's discovery of Alexei's affair with the old Empress. After preparing the Empress's bedroom, Catherine opens the door to discover Alexei in an elaborate, hooded disguise. He brushes past her, and as she stands outside the door of the secret passageway, in a moment of painful exclusion, her anguished face is superimposed over the bedroom door. The fusion does not create a metaphor but suspends forward narrative and temporal progress. The Alexei/devil metaphor becomes readable only within the context of this earlier scene and the charting of Alexei's actions over the course of the entire film. Like the masochist who freezes time through disavowal, the spectator suspends time through the memory of the film's metaphoric connective elements. As in primary process mentation, Alexei literally becomes his past self in a concrete but highly symbolic way. Connection through parataxis of visual forms (Firstness) leads to Thirdness (connection/general concept). Past and present are indistinguishably fused in a hallucinatory synesthesia, a visual condensation of the environmental and the human.

Alexei as a sign becomes another sign. These signs are connected by the interpretant which creates a diagram of present meaning out of the film's past. In fusing Alexei/devil, the film makes use of a rather clichéd symbolic analogy in a sophisticated narratological way: spatial and temporary unity are dissolved. The synesthetic blending of the environmental and the human displaces the qualities associated with the statue onto the human. A paratactic rather than a one-way hierarchical relationship is created between the human and the inanimate in a dreamlike combination.

In *The Scarlet Empress,* metaphoric repetition also serves as an ironic play on the film's iconographic intertextuality and its historical "accuracy." Wood states of the film's ending: "By associating Catherine finally not with a lover but with a magnificent white horse, Sternberg may conceivably have had in mind the legend (unsupported, apparently, by historians) of her death: that she died during attempted intercourse with a stallion which was accidentally let slip after being hauled into position."[62] Von Sternberg's possible slyness in referring to a bizarre legend is not the important factor here. What is important is that the association does not occur in one isolated scene but is woven throughout the entire film. Catherine/bed/horse are continually linked in dialogue, visual imagery, and action. Often, other events or motifs take precedence, but by the continued presence of this extreme example of Catherine's sexual desire, *The Scarlet Empress* offers a surprising substantiation of Wood's claim concerning the film's ending.

In the opening scene, Sophia Frederica shows a seductive expanse of bare shoulder in a pose rather uncharacteristic for a child. The pose is reiterated in a later bedroom scene. The harness prescribed as a cure for the sick girl and the "horse doctor" who prescribes it evoke the rigging and the animal that legend says led to Catherine's death. The concepts of control, mastery, and the restriction of physical (and sexual?) movement are also evoked. The cure will control Sophia's body; later her body will be subject to state control. Catherine breaks that domination by discovering the power in her sexuality. "I don't like to make my own bed," the teenager protests when her mother eagerly rattles off a list of her daughter's domestic attributes to Alexei. Catherine will make her bed in a different sense. Her bed becomes her political forum.

The sexualization of the horse motif is continued in the sequence in which Sophia journeys by coach to Russia. Her mother berates Alexei and compares their lodgings to a horse stable. Alexei replies that if she so wishes, he will be happy to stable the horses in her bedroom. As noted earlier, Catherine's sexual awakening occurs in a horse barn. When her lovemaking with Alexei is interrupted by the whinnying of a horse, Catherine lifts her hooped skirts and scurries off. When Alexei and Catherine confront each other on the palace stairs, Catherine is returning from horseback riding. When she and

her cossacks take the palace, they ride their horses up those same stairs
to the throne room. Breathless and smiling, Catherine is framed in
a close-up with her huge white steed. The child tended by the horse
doctor is transformed, by dream logic, into a woman whose bedroom
adventures are so polymorphous as to include bestiality.

Theoretical Implications of Metaphoric Structuring

The apparent transparency of *The Scarlet Empress* as a narrative
construct is deceptive. What seem to be casual comments, unmotivated, random actions, or frivolous choices of setting and background
detail are not careless artistic choices but are intricately interrelated in
a complex organization. Analogic relationships, not cause/effect ones,
dominate a narrative dependent on the mechanisms operative in fantasy and dream discourse.

The formal organization of iconic signs into metaphor and synesthesia makes a reading of all levels of meaning (including the iconographic and intertextual) of such a film an intricate, dynamic process.
Scenes cannot be read in isolation, nor can decoding on a cognitive
level guarantee an absolute explanatory value for the complicated
interaction of Peircean Firstness, Secondness, and Thirdness. The effect resembles the power of the metaphor as described by Black: "The
extended meanings that result, the relations between initially disparate realism created, can neither be antecedently predicted nor subsequently paraphrased in prose. . . . Metaphorical thought is a distinctive
mode of achieving insight, not to be construed as an ornamental substitute for plain thought."[63] The von Sternberg/Dietrich films are not
symbolic in the sense that Eisenstein's work is symbolic. Visual metaphor, even when it is not paronomastic, rests on iconicity at the first
level. Neither can the metaphoric structure demonstrated in *The Scarlet
Empress* and *Blonde Venus* be reduced to or equated with verbal metaphor, which rests on a primary base of symbolic association and then
iconicizes that association. Metaphor's full meaning is evasive; visual
metaphor forged from deceptive iconic signs is doubly so.

By its very nature the phenomenological effect of films is a thorny
subject. Thirdness emerges out of the Firstness of the complex surface
of von Sternberg's films. While there is obvious need to explore the
perceptual processes whereby Thirdness arises out of the perception
of filmic Firstness, Peirce's semiosis is useful in helping to define the
levels of denotation and connotation at work in a text and the affective
and cognitive response to these levels. With the application of Peircean
concepts within a governing masochistic model, I hope to show the

potential value of defining specific sign categories and applying *modes of being* in an effort to account for film's production of meaning.

Von Sternberg's iconic discourse—metaphoric, synesthetic, and imagistic in origin—reveals the power of analogic thinking and primary process mentation. The implications of this kind of thinking have been neglected for too long in film studies relying on linguistic models that privilege the contiguous over the analogic, formal description over interpretation. Out of the possibilities of analogic thinking, von Sternberg's iconic discourse gives concrete expression to the paradox and ambivalence, the extended meanings and dialectical play of masochistic narrativity.

CHAPTER SEVEN

Iconic Play and Masochistic Performance

Often described as mysterious, contradictory, complex, von Sternberg's characters, says Andrew Sarris, cannot be held to "commonsense criteria of behavior."[1] They engage in the paradoxes of masochistic behavior: transformations in fixation, theatrical exhibition in the depths of humiliation, and self-revelation through masquerade. These are the predictable patterns of masochistic communication formally realized through many levels of iconic interaction. Iconicity in the von Sternberg films is not limited to the visual organization of iconic sign relationships; it also dominates the auditory band and kinesthetic elements, the full range of verbal and nonverbal communication. In this chapter I analyze these elements of iconic discourse through a dual strategy. First I examine the role of iconic communication between characters and discuss their actions and appearance within the theoretical context of iconic communication found in human dream and zoosemiotics. Then I explore the films' iconization of speech, the dialectic between von Sternberg's naturalistic and recreative use of sound, the relationship of the films' dialogue to primary process and synesthesia, and the role of sound and silence in creating the dialectical illusion of the masochistic heterocosm.

The Paradox of Play

Characters in the masochistic narrative cannot be trusted to display a true, indexical sign of their feelings. To do so would end suspense, hasten gratification, and break the contracted alliance of suffering. The masochistic game of suffering refuses to conform to the expectations of everyday patterns of motivation and behavior set by adherence to the reality principle. Words and gestures may appear to be unified in intent or they may interplay contrapuntally in blatant contradiction, but von Sternberg's characters are not inconsistently motivated as such contradictory action might imply. Instead, they evidence the paradoxical masochistic motivation that must be played out to control desire and contain pleasure.

All types of iconic communication are inherently paradoxical. Because indexicality's consistent cause/effect link is missing, the iconic sign is deceptive; it only resembles its referent. Thomas A. Sebeok's studies in zoosemiotics note how, in nature, iconic signs of sound or appearance, such as animal mimicry, permit deceptions that can ensure a species' very survival. The animal's successful imitation of the referent, usually a more powerful or dangerous animal, depends on its enemy's "belief" that the sign presented is indexical. The animal who reads the iconic sign "misunderstands" and treats the sign as indexical, as associated with the threat of the real model.[2] Although animal play describes the framing gesture that creates iconic signs and biological isomorphism defines survival techniques that rely on iconic communication, these do not define the limits of iconicity and iconic deception. Masochistic communication sets up a framework of play in which exchanged signs are paradoxical.[3] As discussed in chapter 4, the play frame is initially set by the perversion's psychodynamics, the "psychic mimicry" of the ego that fools the superego with pain.

Gregory Bateson has pointed out that the "no," the negative, is impossible in iconic communication, at least in the pure, nonverbal type found in dream and animal play. The communicating animal or the dreamer must "say" the opposite of what is meant "in order to get across the proposition that they mean the opposite of what they say."[4] In the von Sternberg/Dietrich films, the negative is acted out rather than spoken. The "contradictory" action negates the first "yes" action. The iconic sign is the only sign capable of causing the misunderstanding that must occur for pain to precondition and mask pleasure.

In *Morocco*, Amy Jolly nods assent to La Bessiere's assumption that her affectionate gestures indicate that she wishes to thank him. La Bessiere interprets Amy's actions as a sign of love. She kisses him but then leaves; her departure does not contradict her gestures but shows that her actions were not an indexical sign of love. What La Bessiere misunderstands to be love is a deceptive iconic sign with gratitude as the probable referent. Amy's attempt to play her assigned part as loving fiancée cannot prevent her acting upon her own compulsion, which ultimately satisfies La Bessiere's masochism. Similarly, in *The Scarlet Empress*, when Catherine dismisses the royal court to invite

Alexei to her bedchamber, she, like a playing animal, does "not quite mean" what she appears to be saying. Alexei misreads her iconic communication as indexical. Catherine's actions mimic those of Alexei's former lover, the old Empress, but Catherine is playing at revenge, not reconciliation.

In *Shanghai Express*, Lily is the notorious "White Flower of China." Her actions conform to the fantasy logic of masochistic transformation and iconic communication. The events that could have turned a British officer's fiancée into an infamous courtesan may strain credulity but not the limits of the iconic. Once again, deception and iconic communication underlie the misunderstandings that ensure masochistic suspense and suffering. Madeleine (Lily) feigns attraction to another man to test Donald's love. Donald misreads her action as a sign of unfaithfulness, even though it constitutes "play." In a dreamlike transformation the scorned but innocent Madeleine changes herself into the metamorphic extreme of what Donald thought she was: she becomes the most flagrantly faithless and promiscuous of women. The transformation conforms to the masochistic ideal stated in *Venus in Furs:* "If I cannot find a noble and spirited woman . . . then give me no half-measures. . . . I prefer to be at the mercy of a woman without virtue, fidelity or pity, for she is also my ideal, in her magnificent selfishness."[5]

Lily appears to be the worst of women: she has driven men mad and to their deaths. She is the equivalent of Sacher-Masoch's Grecian woman: pagan, sensual, independent.[6] In spite of her femme fatale reputation and her cynicism, she proves herself to be loyal and loving. In the revelation of her goodness, the dialectic between revelation and concealment is maintained: Lily refuses to explain her motivation for staying with General Chang. Donald rejects her again. She waits; he watches. Reconciliation comes, but, as Sarris observes, the masquerade continues: "her face merely taunts him . . . until he surrenders to the illusion she represents, but on her terms rather than his."[7] Von Sternberg once declared: "To know what to reveal and what to conceal and in what degree and how to do this is all there is to art."[8] The players in the masochistic game of desire are artists at iconic communication and masters of the "logic of concealment" necessary to masochistic pursuit.[9]

Iconicity and the Masochistic Masquerade

Continual transcendence of personality in masquerade requires the careful control of emotion. Gestures and reactions are structured

In a dreamlike transformation, the scorned but innocent Madeleine has changed into the metamorphic extreme of what her lover thought her to be. As Shanghai Lily, her costume of feathers advertises her profession and her power to fascinate. She is now the most flagrantly faithless of women. Marlene Dietrich in *Shanghai Express* (1932).

into a complex dialectic. The look, the gesture, the word that reveals feeling still constitutes an "open mystery." The visible is paradoxically deceptive: which expression is iconic? which is indexical? Von Sternberg once called the face "an inspiring mask when not maligned." [10] In prolonging masochistic desire, the human face becomes a mask to be manipulated in a performance of disguise and deception. Masquerade incorporates the mythic connotations of the donned mask and the impassive face that reflect the stillness of fixation or death. The face becomes *le máschere dell mòrte*, which does not contradict metamorphosis but converges with it.[11]

Carole Zucker has referred to the "absence or invisibility of the process of thought" in von Sternberg's characters.[12] It is true that they rarely verbalize their feelings, and their expressions are often ambiguous. In *Blonde Venus*, Helen announces to Ned that she is returning to the stage to earn money. He protests, but she maintains that she was already planning to go back to her career before he became ill. Her delivery is passionless, her face a mask that refuses to be read. She may be lying to soften his humiliation at being unable to provide for his family, but her amazingly resourceful ability to adapt to a series of increasingly degrading roles lends credibility to her explanation. Her sacrifice is charged with the need to escape the cloistered boredom of her drab life. To interpret Helen's motivation for returning to her career, reference must be made to her physical placement in the mise-en-scène. She needlepoints within the oppressive confines of Ned's dark, dusty lab, then moves to stand next to him. She never looks at him as she speaks.

As noted in earlier chapters, the lack of direct eye contact is crucial to a reading of the characters' emotional rapport in von Sternberg's films. In *Shanghai Express*, Donald and Lily's encounter on the train's observation deck is a model of the precise gradation of looks that marks their fluctuating closeness. At first, Donald refuses to look at Lily. She stands behind him, then sits next to him. She does not look at him, but as they talk about their past, Lily begins to glance obliquely at Donald. He still refuses to look at her. Finally, as he stands to leave, he protests that he was a fool to have left her. Lily looks at him directly and pulls him down for a kiss.

The lack of direct eye contact between characters who often face the camera instead of each other has led to the criticism that von Sternberg's direction of actors was poor. In response, one critic has suggested that the acting evidences a theatricality found in stage performances.[13] The transparency of pretense in the von Sternberg/Dietrich films has little to do with a theatrical stage tradition and everything to do with the theatrical requirements of masochism. Participants in the masochistic charade continually play at the games of pretense that control desire. They act for each other, sometimes in full complicity; and sometimes the governing frame of masochism requires the act to be misunderstood.

Masochistic acting and the dialectic of concealment and revelation are particularly pronounced in the female's actions. Her capricious behavior reflects the ambivalence of masochistic fantasy. Sudden reversals—Amy Jolly's departure from her engagement party, Helen Faraday's decision to return to America with Nick Townsend, Concha Perez's return from the Spanish border, and Magda's awkwardly executed release of Lieutenant Kranau—all defy a simple explanation that would conform to normal psychological motivation. Reversals are imperative in the creation of masochism's atmosphere of expectation and suspense. The reversals in the von Sternberg/Dietrich films uncannily adhere to the model set by Sacher-Masoch's *Venus in Furs*. At one point in the novel, Wanda tells Severin: "I have played my cruel role better than you expected. Now I am sure you will be content with a nice little wife, clever and not too ugly."[14] She agrees to marry him but abruptly returns the next day to bind him and triumphantly hand him over for whipping by her new lover.[15]

In *The Devil Is a Woman*, Concha's behavior closely parallels Wanda's. Taunted to the breaking point by Concha's affairs, Don Pasquale beats her, but the power relations between them do not change. She appears the next morning to tell him, "If you loved me enough you would have killed yourself last night." Her remark confronts him with the absurd logic of his masochistic compulsion. Don Pasquale solemnly tells her he is through with her, but Concha cajoles him into again declaring his love. She agrees to leave with him and, maintaining a facade of coquettish affection, says she first must take a little carriage ride without him—he should watch from the window. With impudent cheerfulness, Concha leaves with another lover. Later, when Don Pasquale has been shot in a duel, Concha visits him at the hospital and, after pretending to leave, watches him sleep. A close-up of her face gives little clue as to her reasons for later abandoning Antonio and (presumably) returning to Don Pasquale. Linda Williams has written that in this scene von Sternberg engages in an "erotic striptease of a woman's soul" to reveal the truth of Concha's "genuine desire" for Don Pasquale.[16] On the contrary, whatever process of thought is mirrored in Concha's face is open to interpretation—so open that her motivation for returning has been variously described as the desire to murder him, the wish to keep torturing him, and even gratitude.[17]

In prolonging masochistic desire, the human face becomes a mask to be manipulated in a performance of disguise and deception. Marlene Dietrich and Cesar Romero in *The Devil Is a Woman* (1935). Publicity still.

Her return displays the ambivalent double movement of masochism in which kindness and cruelty converge in the figure of the woman. Concha deserts Antonio to rejoin Don Pasquale, but her kindness to the latter is ambiguous, as is her cruelty to the former. Her costume signifiers (black, draping, shroudlike) hint of her status as the cold oral mother of masochism who satisfies Don Pasquale's desire to finally possess her in death.

In the von Sternberg/Dietrich films feeling is transverbal. It may be mirrored in faces or gestures, but the mirroring itself is limited to a refraction, a reflection, a distortion. *The Scarlet Empress* presents a subtle, polyvalent expression of the characters' emotion, emphasizing the ambivalent, fetishistic visual pleasure to be found in what Genette refers to, in a different context, as "enigmatic transparency."[18] The scene in which Catherine receives the medal for giving birth to a son exemplifies the use of mise-en-scène in the von Sternberg/Dietrich films to reveal—but also to conceal—the motivation of characters. In this scene, lace gauze surrounds Catherine bed and separates her from the camera, which moves in for an extreme close-up. Catherine's face remains an abstraction behind the pattern of lace as the medal dangles from her hand, moves, spins, and reflects light. The camera cannot penetrate the gauze mask. Catherine's emotions also remain veiled in a literal interpretation of von Sternberg's pronouncement that "the average human being lives behind an impenetrable veil and will disclose his deepest emotions only in a crisis."[19]

Up until this scene, Catherine has been characterized as a bruised but naive pawn in the marriage game. Following the medallion scene, she is suddenly transformed into a ruthless manipulator who smilingly informs a concerned priest that she will protect herself with weapons that are "more powerful than any political machine." In Sacher-Masoch's novels, the masochistic male signs a contract with the woman and educates her into the role of torturess. In von Sternberg's films, either the individual male or patriarchal society persuades the woman to assume this same role. Catherine's assumption of power and her desire for revenge are the result of her manipulation by, then of, a system personified by Alexei. Her actions echo Wanda's words in *Venus in Furs:* "It is you who have taught me selfishness, pride and cruelty, and you who shall be my first victim."[20] Catherine has been educated by Alexei's betrayal and the cruelties of the system.

The bedroom/medallion scene is not of narrative importance if considered by syntagmatic classifications, but it is a climactic moment in Catherine's life. Does she contemplate her future and her past in the refracted light of the dazzling medallion? This can only be inferred from the reversal of behavior that follows and the medallion's iconic emulation of the portrait locket she received from Alexei: Catherine's attempt to retrieve the locket after impulsively throwing it away culminated in her encounter with the "lucky" lieutenant who fathered her child. Now she gazes at a medallion that replaces the one from Alexei. Iconic repetition is complete when Catherine again takes to a gauze-shrouded bed to arouse and then reject Alexei.

On another level, the medallion scene demonstrates the complex visual pleasure created by the masochistic aesthetic. The scene appears to perfectly match Mulvey's description of the two-dimensional, fetishistic arresting of narrative progress that permits the male spectator to exercise a controlling view over the female as fetish.[21] The scene is neither comforting nor a confirmation of viewer control. Instead, separation and distance are reaffirmed. We are allowed to look in fascination at Catherine, but we are not permitted an unobstructed view. Our gaze is increasingly frustrated rather than satisfied as the pleasure of her beauty is abstracted until she is a pattern of black and white, a vision almost unrecognizable as female or even human. Erotic contemplation is diffused into an abstraction that transforms Catherine into the ideal masochistic art model.

Moments of two-dimensional stillness are not limited to the visual treatment of female characters. In a climactic moment in *The Devil Is a Woman*, Concha takes Don Pasquale's money to pass along to her bullfighter lover. Don Pasquale stands impassive; he neither moves nor speaks. In extreme close-up, with a half shadow across his face, Don Pasquale replies to Concha's inane inquiry about the time. Her question, the extreme close-up, and his barely repressed emotional intensity combine to give the scene the bizarre quality of a dream, the sense that the question has been displaced from another scene. Yet within the logic of the masochistic scenario, Concha's question is very relevant: Don Pasquale, the supreme masochist, suspends time through desire. The spectacle of masochistic suffering is captured in a fetishizing stillness that holds the male bound to the mast of masochistic passion.

Masquerade is not an empty signifier that exists only as the male's projection of desire onto the female, whose lack must be disguised. Masquerade is also essential to the pretense that makes masochistic desire possible. As discussed in chapter 3, the tantalizing pleasures of the masquerade depend on the mobility of desire and the pleasurable exchange of identity. Males as well as females participate in masquerade that delays consummation through the changing spectacle of mobile desire.

Masks and costumes are the masochistic props par excellence. Masquerades reveals the characters' intent or emotional status while temporarily (and thinly) concealing the overdetermination of desire and the ambivalent status of the persona. Such double masquerades reveal the paradoxical nature of the iconic sign and its function in masochistic theatricality. The female's protean transformation of identity engages male desire, then defers its consummation. Iconic signs provide the means by which characters act out (iconicize) what they metaphorically resemble emotionally. Change of identity is accomplished through iconic resemblance; as in a dream, to be like the thing one must become that thing. Within the masochistic construct, masquerade frequently takes the form of animal disguises which evoke the metaphoric animality and self-abasement of masochistic desire. In *Venus in Furs*, Wanda tells Severin: "You are whatever I want you to be, a man, a thing, an animal." Severin is tied to a plough and pushed into the field.[22]

In *The Devil Is a Woman*, Don Pasquale is juxtaposed with a goose when he first meets Concha on the train. Later, the motif of storks and fish (prey/victim) dominates the cabaret scene.[23] When he finds Antonio and Concha locked in a kiss, Don Pasquale stands before an enormous painting of a wounded bull, which was identified in the ancient world with Taurus and matriarchal rule. In contrast to Don Pasquale, Antonio is first juxtaposed with a man costumed as a huge rooster during the pre-Lenten carnival celebration. The paratactic relationship of Antonio and the rooster emerges as a metaphoric projection of the character's desire onto the masqueraded figure. Desire is made concrete, displaced, and doubled. The camera slowly moves into the wild celebration. The huge rooster chases a screaming circle of women. Antonio is also engaged in an active sexual pursuit. "Where are all the pretty girls?" he asks a vendor, who points to a balcony occupied by a huge woman who flirtatiously beckons to Antonio. Concha suddenly appears as the fleeting wish fulfillment to Antonio's unsuccessful quest. She rides in a procession of carriages crisscrossing the scene through a space that is isolated and unidentifiable. Antonio uses a slingshot to break the balloons hiding her masked face. He attempts to make his way toward her but is caught in the crowd.

In the dream heterocosm of the carnival, sexual identity achieves a temporary liberation in a kind of "primordial condition" in which, as Thomas Mann once described, "glances meet and marry irresponsibility in dreamlike wantonness."[24] As in a dream, characters are themselves but are not; the false self of the mask is mixed with the repressed self. Normal social identity is meaningless. Social standing or wealth holds no value in this dream space; beauty and sexual energy do. The carnival permits the chaotic subversiveness of sexuality before religious denial. Desire is suspended within a pure fantasy creation that meets the requirements of the masochistic supersensual ideal.

Both von Sternberg's films and Sacher-Masoch's novels abound with animal imagery metaphorically associated with the protean female. Sacher-Masoch compares the female with the unpredictability of Nature: "She [woman] is like a wild animal, faithful or faithless, kindly or cruel, depending on the impulse that rules her."[25] In *Venus in Furs*, Wanda is described as a lioness, a serpent, a cat, and, as a "frightened" Severin begins to lose control of their games, a bear: "As she lay pressed against my breast in her large heavy furs, a strange and painful sensation came over me, as though I were in the clutches of a wild animal, a she-bear; I almost felt her claws gradually sinking into my flesh."[26] In the von Sternberg/Dietrich films, the female's link to Nature is given concrete representability. Helen Faraday, in *Blonde Venus*, literally becomes a wild beast in her nightclub act. She is such a perfect iconic likeness of a gorilla that nervous patrons edge their way out of the animal's path as it roams the club. Held by a slender white chain attached to an undulating line of pseudonative dancers, the creature lumbers back onto the stage, its hideousness emphasized in close-ups as it passes Nick Townsend's table. Nick has pointedly refused to look at the creature, but, ironically, the animal now looks directly at Nick. Onstage, the beast sheds its skin in a variation on the Dionysian rite of flaying. Disgusting beast is revealed as desirable beauty: Nick now gazes in fascination at Helen. The change of identity that sparks Nick's interest has the matter-of-fact tone that characterizes dream transformation. To attain her symbolic release of sexuality, Helen's masquerade as the gorilla takes the abstraction of Peircean Thirdness (animality as a concept) and makes it literal.

In *The Devil Is a Woman*, Concha's early costuming shows how iconic masquerade may initiate masochistic suspense. Her costuming also reflects the complexity of motivation and variability in tone expressed in the ambivalent masochistic fantasy as it demonstrates the perversion's structural dependence on iconic figuration and primary process mechanisms. Durgnat has remarked of the opening scene's relation to the film's structure: ". . . the plot is built on Marlene contradicting each promise with an action, each phrase with a gesture, each word with its tone of voice. Dressed like a nun, she starts a fight. . . . the film is built on a structure of dizzy contradictions."[27] Black and white flowing garments, a headpiece resembling a wimple, a cir-

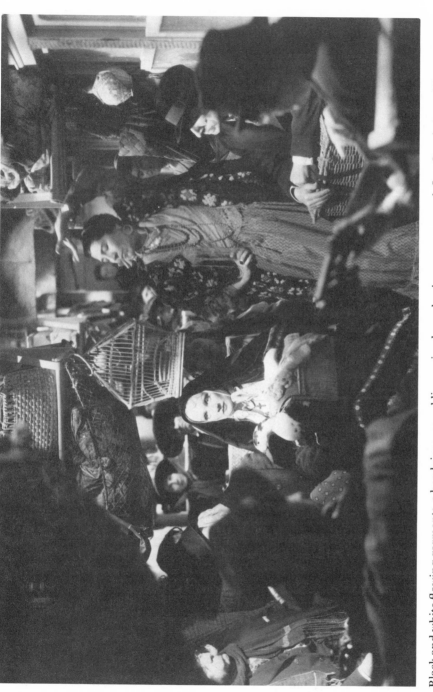

Black and white flowing garments, a headpiece resembling a wimple, and a circumspect pose define Concha's nunlike presence. Her attire should not be read as an indexical sign of what is to be expected of her—she soon starts a fight—yet it offers a humorous commentary on her sexual unavailability to the masochistic male. Marlene Dietrich in *The Devil Is a Woman* (1935).

cumspect pose, and a cross around her neck define Concha's nunlike presence as she sits amid the confusion and overcrowding of a third-class train compartment. Her exaggerated eyebrows and increasing petulance puncture the illusion of her masquerade. A woman crowds and taunts her with an improvised dance. Bird droppings fall on her from a cage suspended overhead. Patience exhausted, Concha trips the dancer, twiddles her thumbs, then trips her again. A brawl ensues.

If Concha's nunnish attire is read as an indexical sign of what should be expected of her, then her actions form an ironic contrast to her costuming signifiers. Concha's behavior and her dress have a semiotic relationship, but they do not have a causal one. Her costuming is iconic, not indexical, and provides a humorous commentary on her sexual unavailability—at least to the masochistic male. Von Sternberg plays on the conventions of costume coding and the deceptive nature of the iconic sign in structuring the spectacle of masquerade. Within these films, costuming is an independent variable that may mirror the characters' emotions or roles but can easily subvert their apparent "truth" as signifiers of personality. The audience, like the masochistic subject, is not permitted the control of knowledge; in the performance of iconic communication, the spectator is left to pursue the truth of the deceptive iconic sign.

The Voice of Masquerade

Von Sternberg's films decenter the verbal in favor of production of meaning through the kinesthetic effects of mise-en-scène. Nevertheless, verbal signs are not discounted in the texts: the construction of speech is carefully controlled to complement the films' iconic visual structure. The von Sternberg/Dietrich films iconicize words into what might be called a "nonlinear, spatial panorama—a space-sound landscape."[28] Zucker has noted that in von Sternberg's films, dialogue "exists as much for its effect as sound as for its status as meaningful utterance."[29] Sound becomes an event, a surface texture that changes but does not negate the meaning of word representation.

The style of dialogue delivery also deconstructs the relationship of speakers with their voices to create, as Maurice Blanchot says in reference to the "neutral" voice, a "nonidentification with themselves."[30] Voice becomes a masquerade, a contradiction, a way of suspending and disavowing signification. Characters play at being characters. Performance multiplies its mechanisms to inscribe itself on words and bodies as a deception, an act of exhibition and concealment. Speech contributes in confronting the spectator with a theory of character and of performance, since there is no unified pretense of a character as "I," no Shanghai Lily, but Josef von Sternberg–Shanghai Lily–Madeleine–Maria Magdalene Dietrich a.k.a. Marlene Dietrich. Identification with a unified "character" is not permitted. Instead, the irony of iconic distanciation reigns over the spectacle of characters as "iconic" representations.[31]

Although this kind of treatment of speech has been recognized as an element that links the films to poetry, the implications of the iconization of the word are much more significant in relation to iconic discourse and the masochistic heterocosm. Von Sternberg commented on speech in his films: "Dialogue cannot be permitted to carry the burden of plot movement and progression. . . . what is required is a new conception of the function of sound, to so manipulate that it does not become a barrier to the fluid language of the silent image."[32] Speech, though primarily symbolic or arbitrary, is also capable of indexicality. For example, sound may register offscreen space. It may also be iconic, as in the case of mimicry or the iconization of speech through a poetic delivery that emphasizes the spatial topography of words.

In emphasizing the word as sensory act, as a thing, von Sternberg's films return to the "concrete impact" of language.[33] The environmental and the human mix in Firstness, in form and feeling, as extensions of each other in a synesthetic cohesion that resembles dream. Synesthetic experience is recalled in mixed forms such as opera and lieder, in which rhythmic and tonal grids in music or speech iconicize words. Verbal iconicity also harkens back to a period of life in which synesthesia was the dominant mode of perception. As Hans Loewald remarks, words in primary process and in the early stages of life are "fused within the apprehended global event" as tone, as rhythm, as *things* inseparable from the total.[34] Emphasis is given to the form of the word—its rhythm, tone, placement, shape—the utterance as a sound mise-en-scène, an architecture, a body of sound in space that serves to *deword* words.[35] Words become part of a sensory environment of things. Loewald observes: "Words in their original or recovered power do not function then as signs or symbols for (as referring to) something other than themselves, but as being of the same substance, the same actual efficacy as that which they name; they embody it in a specific sensory-motor medium."[36]

In von Sternberg's fantastical heterocosm, as in the pre-Oedipal realm, words become sensory elements. They are not divorced from the environment of things that surround them, nor do their invisible referents (signified) take precedence over their immediate presence.

Speech becomes a body in the mise-en-scène of desire. Verbal signifiers serve as a masquerade for meaning. The concrete acts of speech
become yet another stage for masochistic performance.

The stylization of dialogue in the films is not indicative of a
stage-bound theatricalization but of a masochistic theatricality in the
same mode of analogic thinking that informs the films' visual iconicity.
Shanghai Express offers the most extreme example of the iconization of
speech into synesthesia: von Sternberg asked his actors to speak the
dialogue in measured phrases and a monotone delivery that would
imitate the sound of the train.[37] The dialogue becomes an iconic likeness of the mise-en-scène, just as in *The Scarlet Empress* plastic motifs
are confused with humans.

Speech and Primary Process Thinking

Dialogue also contributes directly to the film's link to the primary process. Although the language of dream is mainly visual, iconic,
and paratactic, verbal language does play a role. Burgin explains that
primary process treats words "as far as possible like images" in that
they "are just meaningful elements among others." Their relationship
to their referents is also different. He cites Freud's observation that
in dream, the meanings of words are not necessarily related to the
meaning they might have in conscious speech, "the *sense* of the things
we see is constructed across a complex of exchanges between these
various registers of representation."[38] The iconization of speech in the
von Sternberg/Dietrich films evidences synesthesia and contributes to
a treatment of the verbal which resembles that in primary process
thinking. The spatial configuration of dialogue does not counter the
meaning of words but complicates and qualifies it. Von Sternberg's dialogue is not an inane mismatch to an overwhelmingly dominant visual
style. The simplicity of the dialogue masks the emotional and formal
complexity of speech as another register of representation within the
masochistic aesthetic.

In *The Scarlet Empress*, Alexei's description of the Grand Duke
is an example of the formal, emotional, and thematic complexity of
dialogue in von Sternberg's masochistic texts; it is deceptive iconic
communication. As noted in chapter 3, Alexei takes himself as the referent of a description rooted in simile: "His eyes are like the blue sky,
his hair the color of ebony. . . . he is sleepless because of his desire to
receive you in his arms and he can also read and write." By a paratactic juxtaposition, the constructed equation of desire and literacy
destroys the conventional hierarchy and logical frame attributed to in-

dividual elements. Traits that would never be logically equated under the same category (education–emotion–desire) are associated by verbal juxtaposition. The discrepancy of category renders the statement absurdly incongruous. This rather typical example of Sternbergian humor demonstrates the formal subtlety that leaves audiences thinking, as Sarris has said, that they are "laughing at Von Sternberg" instead of "with him."[39] As is so often the case in von Sternberg's films, humor depends upon deception, iconic signs, and the juxtaposition of incongruous elements in an iconic discourse that binds the verbal and the visual in an interaction resembling their relationship in dream.

An example from *The Scarlet Empress* illustrates how an analogic, dreamlike synesthesia, displacement, condensation, and concrete representability are evoked through mise-en-scène but also through dialogue. Near the end of the film, Peter is awakened. The mise-en-scène (huge bed, the sleeper, huge room) forms an iconic recreation of the film's opening scene in which Sophia, the bedridden child, dreamed of torture. Now Catherine, living out her dream wish to be a hangman, controls another dreamer—Peter. Dressed in a long white gown, with his long blonde hair flowing like a woman's, Peter becomes the distorted mirror image of the young Sophia, just as he and Catherine were mirror images of each other at their first meeting in the throne room. In that spatially distorted tableau, they were two matched blondes in furs, the same and yet shockingly different, facing each other in horror (Catherine) or curiosity (Peter). Now Peter is the helpless child-woman. He goes to the door of his room and asks the guard, "Why are those bells ringing?" Without turning around the guard casually replies, "I don't know, Peter." The man's brusque, informal reply to the czar gives his answer the quality of inappropriateness often experienced in dreams. The tone is characteristic of the flatness of delivery that is typical of von Sternberg's films. Peter chides the guard for his lack of respect: "You're addressing the emperor. . . . Who are you?" The man responds: "My name is Orloff, and I'm on duty as guard." He is also Catherine's current lover, a former general in the army. Earlier, Peter had stripped Orloff of his rank and declared him to be "nothing." Now Orloff reverses that negation. In an unmarked monotone he says: "There is no emperor, only an empress." Without a word or any sign of anger, Orloff slowly backs Peter into the room, and, behind the silhouette of a huge cross, assassinates him.

All the elements of the mise-en-scène and the dialogue combine to provide the eerie quality of a lucid dream. Peter's costuming transforms him into the vulnerable dreamer and iconic likeness of the helpless, controlled female, the position once occupied by Catherine.

Peter is now the humiliated, the vulnerable, the negated. The huge, empty set, the cool anonymity of the guard who refuses to look at his victim, and the guard's terse, flat delivery phenomenologically recall dream experience. Like Severin's friend in *Venus in Furs*, Peter also seems to be dreaming when he is awake.[40] The dreamer asks about bells that signal his own death; his questions are unanswered. He is attacked by a man he knows but does not recognize. He who has defied the church and spit in a priest's face is killed behind a cross. Peter lives out his own nightmare. Dialogue and visual style are not at odds in *The Scarlet Empress* but evoke primary process modes of expression. This scene shows how the dialogue in von Sternberg's films may appear to be simplistic and even banal yet makes a significant stylistic contribution that requires an acknowledgment of the films' resemblance to primary process thinking and dream.

The Dialectic of Aural Illusion

The stylized delivery of von Sternberg's dialogue sounds unnatural, but it is logical that this would occur. Von Sternberg's visual fantasies must be matched by sound appropriate to their quality of otherworldliness. The complexity of the second world's relationship to the first contributes to the paradoxical, problematic tone of the films. Von Sternberg commented on the problems of achieving a match between sound and visuals:

> It [sound] had brought into what was seen another world, a world that stimulated the imagination beyond the content of what the frame of the camera had shown. . . . Sound had to counterpoint or compensate the image, add to it—not subtract from it. . . . sound was realistic, the camera was not. . . .
>
> . . . in this early stage of adding sound to the image the mobility of the camera was invalidated, it was, for the time being, a reproductive instrument, as the microphone is to this day; and to reproduce is not to create. . . .
>
> . . . The congenital tendency of the microphone to contradict the camera is not usually recognized by those who use both these instruments.[41]

Sarris has remarked that von Sternberg "refused to recognize that sound was exercising a naturalistic influence on the cinema."[42] To the contrary, von Sternberg was quite aware of the naturalistic potential of sound but consciously chose to diverge from standard sound reproduction.

While von Sternberg often chose to alter speech's naturalistic flow, he frequently employed a very realistic use of sound effects to increase the sense of space. Louis Audibert considers von Sternberg "one of the greatest deployers of sound" and attributes the director's greatness to his ability to discern sound's "suggestion of space" as its "most realistic element."[43] In *Morocco,* for example, sound is often naturalistic. In the first nightclub sequence, sound creates a sense of offscreen space that was innovative for the time, although it seems quite prosaic now: Tom Brown asks a friend to loan him money; the friend is heard answering but remains offscreen. In the same scene the reactions of the nightclub audience add to the sense of performance in the flirtation between Private Brown and Amy Jolly. At one point, when Brown refuses to accept one of Amy's apples without paying, he says, "Nothing doing. I always pay for what I get." The audience claps in approval.

The naturalistic use of sound is counterpointed by other formal, artificial uses in *Morocco.* Sound overlaps occur as the auditory parallel to the von Sternberg–signature slow dissolves used in later films. At the beginning of *Morocco,* the globe and letters that show the story's location fade to black. Before the next shot fades in, a perplexing sound is heard: the voice of a man speaking frantically in an unknown language. In the next shot a man is shown coaxing his donkey off the road as the foreign legion approaches. The soldiers march into town; the camera tracks back. The sound of the drum and bugle corps creates a sense of the patrol's placement in a "real" space, but this tendency toward an implied three-dimensionality through sound is contrasted with an abstract play of light and shadow formed by the arches and grating under which the legionnaires pass. A compelling dialectical interplay is achieved between the naturalism of sound and the creative possibilities of the camera. The irony here is that von Sternberg did use sound to give a sense of space to the film, but at the very same time the mise-en-scène fractures spatial unity or compromises three-dimensional space. Von Sternberg's films counterpoint the possibilities of space through sound with the two-dimensionality of visual space. He gave his film world a visual and auditory identity, but that world is still a second world that is not an indexical likeness of the first.

A similar dialectic between making and breaking the illusion is achieved through dialogue. The believability of the filmic world of *sèrio ludere* is often threatened by dialogue that foregrounds the falseness of the heterocosm. Wood comments: ". . . *The Scarlet Empress* belongs —somewhat uneasily—to the genre of historical romance. . . . Von Sternberg is careful to prevent our taking the film too seriously as an 'authentic' historical reconstruction: on that level, the tone—deliberately banal dialogue laced with glaring colloquialisms . . . the flat, stylized delivery . . . is that of a charade rather than of documentary."[44] Von Sternberg once remarked that sound had the tendency to impose "a world that stimulated the imagination beyond the content of what the frame of the camera had shown."[45] The masochistic heterocosm must be set apart from the real world. Dialogue becomes an iconic likeness of everyday speech made strange by the theatrical require- ments of the masochistic charade and von Sternberg's play at masking and unmasking illusion.

Because von Sternberg did not believe that dialogue should carry plot, his films also explore the expressivity of silence, an expressive capability largely ignored in the early days of sound film. Silence re- flects on the characters' *state of being* and their enigmatic nature. Char- acters may deceive by their words, through their actions, and in their masquerades, but silence directs our attention to the objects that sur- round them: Amy's collection of pictures of men from her past, Helen's pale white male mannequin, the statues that haunt the czarina's palace. The settings are more than cursory backdrops; they have a fantasy intensity that silently explains what the characters either cannot or do not wish to reveal.

In the von Sternberg/Dietrich films, silence does not arbitrarily suspend action for a moment of peripheral visual description. Like the ellipses of narrative that contain the decisive moments of the films' action, silence produces meaning that accentuates the paradoxical na- ture of masochistic experience. In the play of sound and silence, the "enigmatic transparency" of the masochistic masquerade reveals and conceals itself in all its richness and ambiguity.

CHAPTER EIGHT

Masochism and the Perverse Pleasures of the Cinematic Apparatus

> Technology cannot explain cinema. The cinema-effect can only
> be explained from the viewpoint of the apparatus, an apparatus
> which is not limited to the instrumental base but also includes
> the subject, and especially the subject of the unconscious.
> —Jean-Louis Baudry

The von Sternberg/Dietrich films raise many important issues concerning the structures of masochism and visual pleasure. The application of a Deleuzean-derived model illuminates the films' style and psychodynamics. More important, perhaps, it reveals the textual unity of the films as exemplars of iconic discourse and the masochistic aesthetic. The masochistic model transcends its value in the analysis of individual texts to provide a new way of addressing omissions and impasses in current theories of visual pleasure. Just as a theory of pre-Oedipality and masochism lifts some of the "mystery" surrounding von Sternberg's complex texts, a consideration of the relationship between masochism and the cinematic apparatus illuminates some of the central concerns in recent theoretical discourse.

Cinematic Pleasure and the Structure of Perversion

The primary appeal of the cinematic apparatus lies in its relationship to the unconscious and its ability to mobilize specific forms of pleasure. These pleasures are bound to the unique factors that make up the spectatorial experience of cinema. Jean-Louis Baudry has defined cinema's appeal as dependent on "an artificial state of regression" made possible by the darkness of the surroundings, the immense moving images projected onto the screen, and the spectator's passive, immobile positioning.[1] He locates our desire for film in the psychic link between the film apparatus and our early stages of development:

> It [the cinema] artificially leads back to an interior phase of his develop-
> ment—a phase which is barely hidden, as dream and certain pathologi-

cal forms of our mental life have shown. It is a desire, unrecognized as such by the subject, to return to this phase, an early state of development with its own forms of satisfaction which may play a determining role in his desire for cinema and the pleasure he finds in it. Return towards a relative narcissism, and even more towards a mode of relating to reality which should be defined as enveloping and which the separation between one's own body and the exterior world is not well defined.[2]

As discussed in earlier chapters, the pleasures and formal structures of masochism overlap with the psychological mechanisms that have been implicated in the functioning of the cinematic apparatus: disavowal, fetishism, fantasy, voyeurism/scopophilia. Baudry contends that the cinema-effect depends upon another psychic mechanism with pre-Oedipal origins: the *dream screen*.[3] By establishing the link between masochism and the pre-Oedipal pleasures and ambivalences described by Baudry's dream screen model, spectatorial pleasures that have been approached in earlier chapters are placed within the framework of what may constitute the governing psychological modality of cinematic experience. The presence of the dream screen as environment and the many similarities between spectatorship and masochism suggest that the oral period may be, as Baudry has argued, the privileged mode of regressive pleasures available through the cinema.[4] By pointing to an overlooked stage of psychosexual life, the masochistic model clarifies the nature of the cinematic experience in its available modes of identification and ego activity. However, as important as it is to refocus attention away from "sadistic" or Oedipal models of visual pleasure, it is equally important to state that I am not attempting to reduce cinematic pleasure to one developmental stage or to purely unconscious functioning. Nevertheless, the parallel between masochistic structures and the functioning of the cinematic apparatus requires the exploration of regressive archaic pleasures that may form the psychological substratum for our responses to the cinema.

The pleasures of cinema are, in many respects, infantile ones. They start with the pre-Oedipal pleasures of the dream screen. Both Baudry and, more recently, Robert Eberwein rely upon Bertram Lewin's definition of the dream screen in their application of this psychoanalytic concept to film.[5] In 1946, Lewin introduced the idea that all dreamers, whether aware of it or not, project their dreams upon a blank screen, a dream screen, that represents the maternal breast, the first site of falling asleep into dream. In the very act of naming his discovery, Lewin readily admitted that the similarities between film and the dream screen phenomenon were not lost on him. He theorized that in dream the sleeper's loss of ego boundaries resembles the experience of the nursing child who imagines an undifferentiated sense of "fusion with the breast." Ego boundaries are lost as the sleeper identifies with the breast/screen on which dreams are projected.[6]

In "The Apparatus," Baudry discusses how the infant's hallucination of the breast at the beginning of sleep demonstrates the "lack of distinction between representation and perception." He believes that the "lack of distinction" extends into active/passive, acting/suffering, body/breast, eating/being eaten. Baudry also contends that the specific drive phase of cinematic spectatorship is the oral phase which, from a drive theory perspective, is not sexually differentiated.[7] The spectator/cinematic environment relationship resembles the infant/mother-breast dyad of the dream screen model, which leads to an archaic kind of spectatorial identification that emulates the subject-effect of a period of development in which perception and representation were undifferentiated. By recreating the original mise-en-scène of desire and satisfaction, the cinematic dream screen simulates an oral phase drive context/environment. The cinema thus defines its desirability in pre-Oedipal terms that predate Oedipal conflict, sexual differentiation, or Lacan's mirror phase.[8]

Also working from Lewin's theory, Eberwein considers the spectatorial response to the cinema as a dream screen in "Reflections on the Breast": "Film . . . reverses the process of ego differentiation by plunging us back into memory at that moment of identification with the source of nutrition. Film's overwhelming images invite a return to the states in which the ego dissolves."[9] Expanding upon this article in *Film and the Dream Screen,* Eberwein insists that there is a crucial psychical merger, a "primal state of visual unity" created between the spectator and screen which draws upon the experience of the infant-dreamer.[10] Theoretically, he does not venture very far beyond proposing the existence of a cinematic dream screen that gives the spectator a feeling of oneness and perceptual fusion with the cinema. Instead, Eberwein concentrates on the description of films that employ images or entire dream sequences that evoke the dream screen.[11] Because the implications of the dream screen reach beyond its relevance to particular films that attempt to emulate dream experience, the structure of masochism, as an oral stage phenomenon, can be used to refine the theory of the cinematic apparatus as a dream screen.

The dream screen model helps isolate how the cinematic experience retroactively touches upon regressive perceptual modes reaching further into the archaic past of psychic life than either Oedipal conflict, the male castration complex, or the female's "negative castration complex." By evoking the pre-Oedipal realm, the cinema offers sexually undifferentiated pleasures as well as those already recognized as sexually differentiated. Its perverse pleasures are not limited to the male spectator, nor are they available to the female only if she abandons a "masochistic" identification with the passive female object to identify with the privileged "sadistic" position attributed to the male spectator. Spectatorship, like perversion, creates a limited though pleasurable object relations involvement that is akin to acting out through dream or fantasy.

As in a perversion, the cinema serves as the acting out mechanism for fantasies. Although the masochistic aesthetic is based on the pleasures and ambivalences of the oral phase and finds its central figure in the imago of the oral mother, regressive functioning is not fixed to a single object, nor is it limited to one period of development. In the masochistic aesthetic, fantasies are informed by oral stage conflict and wishes, but neither masochism nor the cinema is limited to replaying only one period of development or one unvarying source fantasy. Remnants of different periods of development are revived, but all are acted out within the specific governing modality of cinema's object relation of spectator to screen. This modality is neither psychotic nor neurotic in character but is perverse, and in its perverseness it is much closer to masochistic than to sadistic structure. If cinematic viewing is more closely allied to masochistic than sadistic pleasure, the presence of the dream screen and the many analogies between spectatorship and masochism return us to oral phase pleasures that may dominate the spectatorial experience at its most basic level of operation.

Separation is required by masochism's structure of desire, a desire that seeks to overcome individuation and restore symbiosis but cannot tolerate the danger of closing that gap. The false intimacy of perversion must suffice. Spectatorial pleasure is a limited one, like the infantile extragenital sexual pleasures that define the masochist who "gives nothing" and is defined by a body-ego "insufficiently differentiated from external reality to achieve genitality." [12] The limited or false intimacy of the perverse individual who cannot internalize the object is also that of the solitary cinema spectator who achieves one-way pleasure in the false intimacy of watching a signifier that is merely light and shadow.

M. Masud Khan explains that in a perversion the subject "remains outside the experiential climax" and "remains a deprived person whose only satisfaction has been of pleasurable discharge and intensified ego-interest" rather than true object cathexis.[13] The spectator is also the deprived observer who must be satisfied with the pleasure of expectancy and specular-distanced gratification. As in the object relations of a perversion, the spectator is incapable of true object cathexis. Overvaluation and idealization must serve as substitutes. Khan's description of the perverse mode of object relations provides a startling resemblance to the spectator's relationship to the cinematic object: "In perversions the object occupies an intermediary position: it is not-self and yet subjective; registered and accepted as separate and yet treated as subjectively created: it is needed as an actual existent not-self being and yet coerced into complying with the exigent subjective need to *invent* it. Spatially it is suspended half-way between external reality and inner psychic reality. The narcissistic magical exploitation of the object is patently visible."[14]

This description of the perverse object/subject relation is very close to the suspended reality of cinematic subjectivity: external yet also psychically grounded, disavowed but also accepted as a particular kind of magical "reality." The spectator accepts film's seductive invitation to surrender control over fantasy, over strictly defined and limited gender identification. Through disavowal, the spectator retains a measure of illusionary ego control over the autonomous fantasies presented. Only a negation can end the relationship between spectator and screen/images. The spectator could walk out; thus, if he/she chooses to continue cinema's contractual arrangement, a partial surrender of ego control is required. But the spectator's ego control cannot be threatened to the point of provoking psychosis in which the subject would begin to live out the make-believe. The cinematic apparatus is a safety net against the overwhelmingly frightening possibility of a total release of control.

Disavowal reconciles the realistic illusion of cinema with the world beyond so that the spectator's body boundaries and existence outside the theater remain separated from the screen's make-believe. Additionally, the spectator must remain outside the experiential climax of screen events. In *Sherlock Jr.*, Buster Keaton's projectionist hero literally steps into the screen to participate in the action. All spectators may wish, at some time or another, to emulate Keaton, but the separation from the screen must remain intact. This too resembles the perverse masochistic arrangement in which the individual chooses to delay and avoid the experiential climax.

On one level, the pleasures of narrative film depend upon conflict and narrative predicament. These can be compared to the masochistic masquerade that pretends to keep pleasure at bay to fool the demanding superego. The spectator suffers with the characters and braves plot predicaments because, like the masochist, he/she knows the "painful" experiences are based upon a contract promising pleasure.

A willing volunteer in cinema's perverse intimacy, the spectator, like the masochist's partner, is not coerced into the alliance. The masochist often advertises to secure the necessary partner for the contractual alliance.[15] The film spectator is also persuaded, seduced into a mutually contracted agreement. Cinema is not a sadistic institution but preeminently a contractual one based upon the promise of certain pleasures. The masochist requires an audience to make humiliation and pain meaningful. Similarly, the cinematic apparatus is meaningless without a spectator to its exhibitionistic acting out.

Enactive Remembering and the "Primordial Lure" of Repetition

Cinema provides a safe, pleasurable means of reexperiencing the archaic past, an "enactive form of remembering."[16] Loewald suggests that in such a form of remembering the person does not realize the past is being reproduced: remembering is unconscious and "shares the timelessness and lack of differentiation of the unconscious and of the primary process."[17] Archaic stages can never completely be renounced; they are retained in varying degrees by all human beings. These psychic currents, Loewald adds, are more like perversions than neuroses. Every person retains a core wish to reexperience the object relations and forms (or processes) of infantile sexuality. Therefore, every person is perverse to a degree: "Just as the Oedipus complex . . . is never actually or definitively destroyed . . . so, too, that more archaic, psychotic core tends to wane but remains with us."[18] If acted out in adult life, the pleasures and conflicts of the archaic psychic stages of life would appear decidedly psychopathological. However, the unconscious wish to act them out persists as a normal phenomenon.

The adaptation of Deleuze's theory of masochism to film has raised the question of whether the unconscious repetition of the past always is an attempt to achieve mastery. The Lacanian privileging of a mirror phase look of false mastery over the image allows only a very narrow conceptualization of cinematic pleasures. It seems noteworthy to mention that mastery was never defined by Freud as a drive, although he considered the Death Instinct and the compulsion to repeat as compelling forces that moved the subject to a return to nothingness.[19] Masochistic desire shows that pleasure of mastery or control is not the sole available pleasure in repetition. The repetition of traumatic events, either real ones or imaginary projections formed out of infantile frustration, makes available the pleasure of loss, suffering, and submission.[20] Loewald describes the primordial lure of traumatic, even self-destructive experience as the pleasure of those "ecstatic states

. . . where love and self-destruction, Eros and Thanatos are merged into one."[21] For Loewald, the essence of this lure is the resistance to giving up an intense and unique experience, "whether painful or blissful," which becomes "forever longed for."[22] If, as Laplanche claims, the wish develops out of the experience of satisfaction, then the wish to repeat painful experience speaks of the satisfaction to be found in pain.[23]

The masochist acts out what often is conscious fantasy, but these actions also have a characteristic of enactive remembering: the infantile source remains unconscious. If the cinematic fantasy offers events that coalesce with the spectator's own conscious fantasies, then the catharsis comes closer to the perverse acting out of fantasy. Cinema's fantasies either may be violently denied or accepted within the disavowing process that classifies the depicted actions as ones that do not represent the spectator's own wishes. The film's status as separate aesthetic entity ensures the enjoyment of fantasy without guilt, for the spectator is not in control of the "unbidden images."[24] Kris explains: "The maintenance of aesthetic illusion promises the safety to which we were aspiring and guarantees freedom from guilt, since it is not our own fantasy we follow. It stimulates the rise of feelings which we might otherwise be hesitant to permit ourselves, since they lead to our own reaction which, without this protection, many individuals are unwilling to admit to themselves."[25]

Immobile, surrounded by darkness, the spectator simultaneously is passive receiving object and active perceiving subject. As subject, the spectator must comprehend the images, must give them coherence, but the spectator cannot control the images, just as the nursing child cannot control the mother. On this level of pleasure the spectator receives, but no *object-related* demands are made of her/him. Sylvan Keiser explains this mode of regressive (and narcissistic) experience and its relationship to masochistic fantasies: "The wish to receive without giving is an attempt to remain in a nursing situation in which the mother is not considered as receiving any pleasure from the child. . . . in the nursing situation, to be devoured is a part of the wish to sleep."[26] To maintain, like the nursing infant, that external reality matches the subject's creation (hallucination/perception), the spectator must disavow her/his status as passive object.[27]

The spectator's misapprehension of creative control over the cinematic image is less a *méconnaissance* than a disavowal of the loss of ego autonomy over image formation. The cinema revives the memory trace of plenitude (screen/breast) and metonymic fetish of the original symbiotic attachment. The dream screen, like the fetishistic objects that follow, restores the sense of the undifferentiated ego/ego ideal of the symbiotic relationship. The imaginary visual fusion with the cinematic dream screen results in a loss of ego boundaries analogous to the child's presleep fusion with the breast. Through the dream screen, the spectator experiences a fulfillment of the wish to sleep and a sense of satisfying undifferentiation with the environment. The function of the dream screen is explained by Judith S. Kestenberg and Joan Weinstein as being like that of "a good blanket" that "shields one from distraction and maintains one's identity as a requisite for undisturbed drive satisfaction." The dream screen serves as a "framework for memory and imagery" which reunites the subject with the original object and integrates internal and external reality as it, paradoxically, "gives free rein to illusory play with space, weight, and time." [28]

The dream screen is the fundamental hallucination of gratification described by David Rapaport as "the prototype for all later thought." [29] Laplanche remarks on the relationship of wish/satisfaction to the primary process: ". . . unconscious wishes tend to be fulfilled through the restoration of signs which are bound to the earliest experience of satisfaction; this restoration operates according to the laws of primary process." [30] The dream screen as the first hallucination of gratification is essential to considering cinematic pleasure in which object/screen/images cannot be physically possessed or controlled by the spectator. In hallucination, the child creates the mother and the breast again and again. Both the hallucinated breast and the cinematic dream screen offer only a temporary and partial gratification of the symbiotic wish. Just as the hallucinated breast cannot offer real nourishment or interaction with the mother, the cinematic apparatus cannot provide intimacy or fusion with real objects. The intimacy of perversion prevails even in the pleasure of cinema: the spectator must disavow an absence.

Ego Diffusion and Visual Pleasure

For the cinematic spectator, the pleasures of film are very much like those of masochism. Resembling the infantile-fixated personality, the spectator experiences diffusion of ego identity as pleasurable. The subject participates in a regressive ego functioning similar to that of the masochist. The ego is no longer an integrated whole but resembles a "collage." In the infantile-fixated individual, a partial integration of ego function has been achieved, but the ego is not a single, coherent entity.[31] The spectator's pleasure is not analogous to Lacan's mirror phase misrecognition of bodily unity in which an overestimation of motor control is achieved through the idealized mirror-self. Mary Ann Doane has described the mirror phase as the transformation "from a fragmented body-image to an image of totality, unity, coherency."[32]

The fundamental identification generated by the cinema is not with the self as masterful likeness or, as Doane says, with "the body as a limited form," but with the fragmented self.[33] It is act of identification depending upon the loss of body-ego boundaries and abandonment of the sense of the unified/individualized self. Any diffusion of ego identity, whether experienced by the masochist, fetishist, scopophiliac, or cinematic spectator, can be accompanied by a frightening loss of control. In cinema, this potentially unpleasurable event is made pleasurable through the construction of the cinematic apparatus. The pleasure of the fragmented self as body ego is offered within an apparatus that affords the pleasure of the boundaryless self drawn into perceptual unity with the dream screen. The spectator submits to the substitute for the mothering body which lessens the anxiety of the ego loosened from body boundaries. As the cinema generates the spectator's loss of ego-body boundaries, it offers the looking/being looked at dialectic analogous to the infantile state. This is a key to overcoming the sense of differentiation between subject/object, self/environment. Yet, the dream screen also reestablishes the fluid boundaries to self and body-ego that permit the progressive polymorphous pleasures of infantile sexuality.

With the release of regressive modes of pleasure, the spectator partakes in the pleasurable possibilities of undisturbed primary identification through the dream screen and simultaneously participates in the cinema's fantasy of gender mobility through identification. If the dream screen works toward perceptual unification, mobile identification is based on the fragmentary possibilities of ego splitting. The apparatus provides the grounding that permits multiple partial, shifting, ambivalent identifications. This process defies the rigid superego control expressed in patriarchal society's standards for carefully defined sex roles and gender identification and points to the importance of bisexuality and a mobile cathexis of desire in understanding cinematic spectatorship.

Masochism, as Laplanche states, is uniquely related to the oral phase and to fantasies that center on the mothering agent. The first satisfying object is the mother who resolves the internal tension caused by the child's need to nurse. Masochism's etiology is rooted in the same phase that Margaret Mahler identifies as symbiotic. She proposes a theoretical modification of Freudian theory that integrates early object relations theory with drive theory. For Mahler, symbiosis is defined as a fantasy with libidinal as well as object relations determinants. The symbiotic relationship is a dual unity that constitutes, as Mahler explains, a "narcissistic object choice." The mother as object is not the happenstance object of "drive-derived needs."[34] Pleasure arises from a mode of object relations that is *internalized* as a libidinal drive. The mother's care libidinizes undifferentiated energy. Libido then, in Mahler's view, is a social construct rather than an innately biological one.[35]

In the symbiotic oral stage, the child is unable to fully differentiate itself from the mother as an ego formation, especially as body-ego, which Freud cited as an essential component of ego identity.[36] The pleasure of the dream screen and cinema's womblike environment contribute to the cinematic apparatus' ability to mobilize regressive ego functioning in the spectator. Both Nancy Chodorow and Edith Jacobson have written that the primary love for the mother relates to the social need for human contact as well as for food.[37] The double function of the first love object reinforces the importance of the child's visual perception of the mother in the formation of subjectivity. Chodorow writes: "The memory traces left by any kind of libidinal stimulation and gratification in the past are apt to cluster around this primitive, first, visual mother-image. . . . The images of the orally gratified or deprived self will tend to absorb the engrams of all kinds of physical and emotional stimuli, satisfactions or derivations experienced in any area of the whole self."[38]

Pleasure in looking is not only an active pleasure but encompasses the passive submission to the object that Freud discussed in relation to all children, male and female, in "Female Sexuality": "The first sexual or sexually tinged experiences of a child in relation to its mother are naturally passive in character. . . . Part of the child's libido goes on clinging to these experiences and enjoys the various gratifications associated with them."[39] This situation is duplicated in masochism and in the cinema. The pleasure of the dream screen revives the memory trace of infantile experience. Lewin's theories of the dream screen are expanded upon by René Spitz, who provides the groundwork for linking cinematic pleasure, the dream screen phenomenon, and masochism: "Therefore, the dream screen of the adult appears to be a representation of the most archaic human pleasure experience. It uses for this representation the archaic materials still available to the adult, i.e. coenesthetic sensations, and the later transition from these to the perception of the visual images in the dream screen."[40] Spitz writes that the infant perceives the "dawning awareness of 'I' and 'non-I'" when the loss of the breast is experienced and attempts to recoup the lost object through a fantasy based on sight. As Spitz asserts, ". . . from the wishful fantasy attached to what one can only see . . . the dream screen . . . is derived."[41]

The spectatorial position duplicates the infant's passive, dependent position. The viewer, like the masochist and the dreamer, adopts the "formless body image of the infant" and the feeling of animistic omnipotence that accompanies the infant's sense of oneness with the mother.[42] Omnipotence is not experienced as the power of the separate self but as the self fused with the environment in symbiotic attachment. Speaking within the framework of her study on symbiosis, Mahler theorizes that "the essential feature of symbiosis is hallucinatory or delusional somatopsychic *omnipotent* fusion with the representation of the mother and, in particular, the delusion of a common boundary between the two physically separate individuals."[43]

The spectator's position resembles that of the masochist whose fantasy of complete "passivity" and dependence is marked by a framing, imaginary control of the symbiotic alliance/fantasy. The masochist ultimately cannot guarantee control over the active partner, nor over his/her own infantile compulsion. The masochist's lack of real control over the object duplicates the situation of the infant and guarantees the necessary distance of desire. The fantasy unification of symbiosis is held within the parameters of a distanciation that prevents the subject from being overwhelmed into nonidentity. This paradoxical experience is characteristic of the masochist, the cinematic spectator, and the infant at the dream screen. The dream screen offers bliss but threatens obliteration of self as separate entity. It can endanger the infant/spectator who fails to separate from the body of the mother by clouding waking vision or coming between the child and the new reality/environment that replaces the mother as environment/part-self.[44] Normally, the dream screen maintains its separation from the subject, just as the cinematic apparatus provides the distance that holds in check the fears of incorporation accompanying this oral stage phenomenon. Soothing anxiety, the dream screen registers the universal ambivalence to the dilemma of symbiosis versus separation.

The Dream Screen and Identification

The cinematic dream screen functions as a very particular type of mirror for the spectator. It is neither the Lacanian mirror of misrecognition nor a literal mirror; rather, it is the cinema's unique mirror of bodies and faces that substitutes for the original mirror—the mother's face. As D. W. Winnicott maintains in *Playing and Reality*, the child sees itself reflected in the mother's face and later in the faces of others as perception helps establish the sense of "me"–"not-me."[45] If the mother is absent for too long, her imago fades and the child who has not yet repudiated the mother as a "not-me" object must defend its primitive ego structure. Among the defenses employed are the earliest manifestations of fetishism and masochism.

The dream screen phenomenon conforms to Robert Dickes's description of the fetish as a "screen memory."[46] Robert Bak's remarks on fetishism clarify the connection between fetishism and the pre-Oedipal trauma of separation. He observes that the fetishist clings to the object as a "symbolic substitute" that "undoes the separation from the mother." "The normal child," he goes on, "accommodates itself to separation/difference, although the wish for reunion remains."[47] The desired world of reunion cannot replace lack and separation. The symbiotic state cannot be recaptured except beyond reality—in madness, death, or fantasy.

The cinematic dream screen defines the spectator through looking, just as the infant is defined by the mother's look. The child, demanding satisfaction, is still controlled and dependent during the oral period. The subject may be all-perceiving, but that does not imply, as Metz claims, that the infant (and, therefore, the spectator) is also all-powerful.[48] According to Chodorow, a paradoxical situation occurs in development: as the child's actual dependence lessens, "felt dependence increases." In the pre-Oedipal phase the child attains "recognition of the separateness and permanence of objects . . . [but] it does not yet have an emotional certainty of the mother's permanent being, nor the emotional certainty of being an individuated whole self."[49]

Desire is born with the absence of the mother who must disillusion the infant in the developmental process into individuation.[50] The trauma of separation/individuation is one that has been undervalued in many psychological studies. Writing in *The Reproduction of Mothering*, Chodorow states that separateness evokes the anxiety of loss but also threatens "the infant's very sense of existence."[51] Mahler believes that renouncing Oedipal objects is not the most crucial in the child's development: rather, it is coping with the dilemma of separation and individuation and the loss of the original attachment to the mothering agent. She writes: "One could regard the entire life cycle as constituting a more or less successful process of distancing from and introjection of the lost symbiotic mother, an eternal longing for the actual or fantasied 'dual state of the self,' with the latter standing for a symbiotic fusion with the 'all good' symbiotic mother, who was at one time part of the self in a blissful state of well-being."[52]

The dream screen of the cinema breaks the hold of external reality and the secondary process so that the spectator may fulfill the unconscious wish for symbiosis. As Loewald states, the pleasure of this early phase is based on an environment undifferentiated from the id. Pleasure depends on a "magical participation" and a perfection found in the "incomplete distinction between inside and outside, between ego and parental object."[53] Through the cinematic apparatus, the spectator once again finds that "magical participation."

Through the dream screen and the cinematic apparatus's imagistic access to primary process, the spectator is led to a pleasurable abandonment of ego control. Reproducing the dream screen, the cinematic apparatus permits the spectator to relinquish body-ego and superego control. In "The Unrememberable and the Unforgettable," Alvan Frank discusses the psychic benefits of hallucinatory screen experiences that loosen ego boundaries and permit earlier perceptual modes to function. His views, reminiscent of those of Loewald, stress the potential psychic reparation available through such experiences: "The re-experiencing, understanding, and translation of these primitive ego states by the more developed apparatuses of the adult ego are of particular therapeutic value."[54] The alteration of ego states and re-creation of a screen phenomenon through the cinema may give access to unremembered memories of earliest childhood experience. Screen representations of the human image in larger-than-life figures evoke the differentials between parents and child. Through a mobile identification with these figures, the spectator experiences the pleasure of body-image/body-ego deconstruction/reconstruction and the reintegration of different levels of identification (primary and secondary).

The cinematic apparatus encourages multiple possibilities of identification and projection that resemble the infantile mechanisms that operate in perversions. It is important to remember that although Freud insisted that early stages of psychic development could coexist with later ones, his own work privileged the phallic and Oedipal stages to the neglect of the prephallic and the pre-Oedipal. He recognized, however, that the primitive ego of the infant, even the ego undifferentiated from the mother-as-environment, could outlive the narcissism of the infantile state. In "Civilization and Its Discontents," Freud wrote that the "primary ego-feeling" characterized by a sense of "limitlessness and of a bond with the universe" coexisted in many individuals "side by side with the narrower and more sharply demarcated ego-feeling of maturity. . . ."[55] He also admitted his own reluctance to investigate this "memorial" phenomenon which permitted the continued presence of more archaic psychological functioning in adults.[56]

The cinematic apparatus, particularly the element of the dream screen, encourages an imitation of regression to this ego-feeling. This experience occurs through (1) the emergence of the primary narcissistic stage of object relations, and (2) the emergence and dominance of a more archaic kind of ego-reality structure that does not function solely as a defense against the opposing demands of the superego and the id. Rather, this more primitive ego structure—in which ego and object are not fully differentiated—emphasizes a function that the more advanced ego also assumes but that is often overlooked—that of integration and mediation. Loewald maintains that the ego's integrative function is an essential one that reflects the continuing effort "on more and more complex levels of differentiation and objectivation of reality" to maintain the "original unity."[57]

The artificial regression of spectatorship creates the opportunity to reintegrate ego-reality on a more primitive level characteristic of the early narcissistic stage. The loss of ego boundaries experienced through the cinema recalls the loss of ego boundaries in the dual unity of mother/child. This loss, as Loewald suggests, always equals a loss of reality, the result being that "ego-reality integration sinks back, regresses to an earlier level of organization" in which reality and ego "regress to a magical level of integration."[58]

Through the dream screen—the formation of the cinematic apparatus as environment—the spectator is encouraged to play out the ambivalent oral stage conflict of union/differentiation with the fetishistic substitute for the mother. The pleasures of perversion (including the cinema) depend directly on the requirements of a splitting type of ego defense that functions to achieve a newer, more coherent integration of the ego and thereby solidify the sense of identity. Freud observed that ambivalence dominates early stages of erotic life and is retained by many people throughout their lives as the principal mode of relating to love objects.[59] The ego defense of infantile mechanisms of ambivalence found in adult perversion is not a repressive mechanism. W. Gillespie calls it a "more primitive defense of a schizoid or splitting character."[60] Chodorow has associated the splitting technique of oral stage defense to the need to hold onto primary identification with the mother. Orality or the "oral attitude" of "taking in" functions as a way of maintaining the "sense of oneness" with the mother when she is "beginning to be experienced as a separate person."[61]

The cinema offers a psychic reparation that may pleasurably restore archaic identifications and replay significant object relations as it provides an opportunity for a creative imaginary repetition of these early stages. In satisfying the compulsion to repeat archaic stages of life, the cinematic apparatus works to satisfy the need to enlarge and reintegrate the ego through different forms of ego-reality integration. As a result, the spectator experiences different forms of cathexis and identification that are normally repressed. Unconsciously repeating the past may provide a way for the spectator to cope with two primal, interrelated issues: the ambivalent response to separation from the mother and the need to stabilize a bisexually based identity. In providing an imaginary restoration of the original union with the mother through imagery as well as the dream screen, the cinematic apparatus restores a primary pleasure of the cinema that is beyond sexual differentiation and does not require conscious identification with a character. The cinema encourages secondary identifications with characters (or traits), but the spectator may also experience primary identification, not in the Metzian sense of primary identification with the act of looking, but in the more traditional psychoanalytic definition of identification with the original primary mothering agent. By restoring the original ego/ego-ideal dual unity of infant/mother, the cinematic dream screen pleasurably fulfills what Loewald suggests is one of the primary, universal goals of psychic life, that is, the struggle for "unity, symbiosis, fusion, merging, or identification—whatever name we wish to give to this sense of longing for nonseparateness and nondifferentiation." [62]

Loewald defines identification with the mother as essential to ego formation and the structuring of the personality. Like Mahler, he considers this "primary narcissistic identity" as the source of the striving toward unification and "the deepest unconscious origin and structural layer of the ego and reality." [63] Chodorow remarks that the need for primary identification is never abandoned but "leads to a preoccupation with issues of primary intimacy and merging"; as adults, we attempt to recreate the experiences of primary identification and love. [64] She also believes that preoccupation with primary merging often reflects an ambivalence that is constructed by a culture in which women traditionally are the exclusive mothering agents: "When a person's early experience tells him or her that only one unique person can provide emotional gratifications—a realistic expectation when they have been intensely and exclusively mothered—the desire to recreate that experience has to be ambivalent." [65]

The cinema restores the earliest object of desire and satisfaction through the dream screen. A primal satisfaction may also be experienced through the representation of the female, not as a lack, but as a plenitude; however, the object of the restorative wish is also the object of the child's ambivalent feelings. In a patriarchal culture, the goal of primary identification or symbiotic remerger may seem antithetical to the privileged masculine traits of separateness, self-sufficiency, and individuality. Freud's definition of identification implies that he regarded all types of identification as regressively passive and fundamentally "feminine."[66]

Male identification with likeness, with the paternal ideal ego, has often been posited as the formative core to male subjectivity, but the male's identification with the pre-Oedipal mother and his ambivalent desire to submit to/break away from her power are important—and neglected—developmental issues. The restoration of the dream screen in the structure of the cinematic apparatus permits identificatory pleasures that are particularly important to the male spectator who is encouraged by the patriarchy to "outrun" identification with the maternal body.[67]

The Visual Pleasure of Unpleasure

The cinematic apparatus and the masochistic aesthetic offer identificatory positions for male and female spectators that reintegrate psychic bisexuality, offer the sensual pleasures of polymorphous sexuality, and make the male and female one in their identification with and desire for the pre-Oedipal mother. The cinematic spectator passively surrenders to the filmic object of desire in much the same way that the masochist surrenders to his/her object of desire; but like the masochist, the spectator's passive position masks activity. The spectator and the masochist share the need to distance themselves from the anxiety of total surrender. Within the regressive structures of the cinema's perverse pleasures, ego dependence cannot be complete or disavowal would be broken. Multiple, mobile spectatorial positions alternating identification and distanciation guarantee against complete object cathexis and ego investment in the screen.

The influence of archaic stages of infantile development on the psychic reparation offered by the cinema must be explored beyond the boundaries established by the models currently dominating psychoanalytic film theory. To understand the structure of looking, visual pleasure must be connected to its earliest manifestations in infancy. The visual pleasure of archaic stages is not automatically negated by later stages of development. Consequently, many of the assumptions adopted by film theorists from Freudian metapsychology or Lacanian theory seem inadequate in accounting for the complexity and psychological significance of cinematic pleasure.

A consideration of the relationship of masochism to visual pleasure holds great promise for opening new areas of discussion in the study of film. The von Sternberg/Dietrich films suggest that out of the reenactment of the fundamental human conflict of symbiosis/separation, the masochistic aesthetic gives voice to fantasies that form the core of later dilemmas of maturation. These fantasies, and the enunciative strategies associated with them, should be explored in other films. By integrating a study of the psychic structures underlying texts with a close textual analysis, a Deleuzean model can illuminate films that offer an unrecognized alternative to "sadistic" or Oedipal narrative, including "women's films" and melodramas with the male— as well as female—positioned as the desiring subject. But it is in the relationship of the psychodynamics of masochism to spectatorial pleasure that this model holds its greatest theoretical promise. The close resemblance between the structures of masochism and the cinematic apparatus indicate that not only has masochism been an overlooked formal and psychoanalytic factor in textual systems but the fundamental vicissitudes of spectatorship appear inseparably linked to the primal "pleasure of unpleasure."[68] Masochistic pleasure reveals that our desires are not simply Oedipal ones, nor are they governed solely in terms of lack/phallus. Even when confined to the unconscious, desire cannot be renounced, just as the steps to psychic maturation are not forgotten but are retained.

Notes

Introduction

1. Sociological approaches in the 1970s included Molly Haskell's well-known *From Reverence to Rape: The Treatment of Women in the Movies* (New York: Holt, Rinehart & Winston, 1973). In addition to a privileging of psychoanalysis, feminists have frequently relied upon Marxist approaches to address the ideological implications of sexual difference. See E. Ann Kaplan, "Integrating Marxist and Psychoanalytic Approaches in Feminist Film Criticism," *Millennium Film Journal*, no. 6 (1980): 8–17; and Jane Gaines, "Women and Representation," *Jump Cut* 29 (1984): 25–27.

2. Janet Walker, "The Problem of Sexual Difference and Identity," *Wide Angle* 16 (1984): 15–23.

3. Laura Mulvey, "Visual Pleasure and Narrative Cinema," *Screen* 16 (Autumn 1975): 6–18. Bill Nichols has remarked that Lacanianism has "come to represent an authoritative theoretical discourse with which its alternatives must come to terms," and that the line of feminist film criticism that includes Mulvey "assumes that the sort of semiotic psychoanalytic theory associated with Jacques Lacan is a necessary prerequisite for a specifically feminist film theory." Nichols, "Introduction," *Movies and Methods*, Vol. 2: *An Anthology*, ed. Bill Nichols (Berkeley: University of California Press, 1985), pp. 10, 12.

4. Judith Mayne, "Feminist Film Theory and Criticism," *Signs* 11 (Autumn 1985): 83. Dudley Andrew refers to Mulvey's article as the study that "has most explicitly and influentially joined the domains of psychoanalysis and film stylistics." Andrew, *Concepts in Film Theory* (New York: Oxford University Press, 1984), p. 147.

5. Mulvey, pp. 12–13.

6. Ibid., pp. 9–11.

7. Gilles Deleuze, *Masochism: An Interpretation of Coldness and Cruelty* (New York: George Braziller, 1971).

8. Bill Nichols, *Ideology and the Image* (Bloomington: Indiana University Press, 1981), p. 110.

9. B. G. Braver-Mann, "Josef von Sternberg," *Experimental Cinema* 1 (1934): 17–21; rpt. in *Sternberg*, ed. Peter Baxter (London: British Film Institute, 1980), p. 29.

10. Richard Griffith, "Richard Griffith's Riposte," *Films in Review* 1 (November 1950): 9.

11. Andrew Sarris, *The American Cinema: Directors and Directions, 1929–1968* (New York: E. P. Dutton, 1968), pp. 74–77.

12. Ibid., p. 77; "Morocco," *Cahiers du Cinéma* (a collective text), no. 225 (November–December 1970): 5–13; rpt. in Baxter (ed.), p. 91.

13. Rather arbitrarily, I have chosen not to discuss von Sternberg and Dietrich's *The Blue Angel*, produced in Germany by Ufa and Paramount in English- and German-language versions. Although the film clearly fits within the psychodynamics and narrative patterns established in the later films, for the sake of textual unity I chose to limit my analysis to the six films made in the United States at Paramount.

14. See Richard Dyer, *Stars* (London: British Film Institute, 1979), pp. 178–80, for a brief overview of the various, conflicting considerations of the meaning of Dietrich·as sign.

15. The quoted phrase is Sarris's, from *The American Cinema*, p. 75.

16. Gregory Bateson, *Steps to an Ecology of Mind* (New York: Ballantine Books, 1972).

Chapter One: The Masochistic Aesthetic

1. For a notorious example of the speculative excesses of the nosographic approach see Sigmund Freud, "Leonardo da Vinci and a Memory of His Childhood" (1910), in *The Standard Edition of the Complete Psychological Works of Sigmund Freud*, 3d ed., trans. and ed. James Strachey, 23 vols. (London: Hogarth Press, 1953–66), 7:57–137 (hereafter cited as *SE*). Christian Metz briefly discusses the limitations of the nosographic approach in *The Imaginary Signifier*, trans. Celia Britton, Annwyl Williams, Ben Brewster, and Alfred Guzzetti (Bloomington: Indiana University Press, 1982), pp. 25–26.

2. In his own recent work on film, Deleuze rejects psychoanalysis and turns to a phenomenological approach. See his *Cinema One: Movement/Image*, tr. Hugh Tomlinson and Barbara Habberjam (Minneapolis: University of Minnesota Press, 1986).

3. Margaret Mahler's observational-based theory of symbiosis adapts classical drive theory to a relational model. She believes the child's desire to re-fuse with the primary mothering agent is matched against the urge to individuate into independence. Mahler, *On Human Symbiosis and the*

Vicissitudes of Individuation, Vol. 1: *Infantile Psychosis* (New York: International Universities Press, 1968).

4. Freud, "The Economic Problem in Masochism" (1924), in *General Psychological Theory: Papers on Metapsychology*, ed. Philip Rieff (New York: Macmillan/Collier Books, 1963), p. 193. Bernhard Berliner has referred to masochism as "one of the most complicated subjects in psychoanalytic theory and one of the most difficult problems in our therapeutic work." Berliner, "Libido and Reality in Masochism," *Psychoanalytic Quarterly* 9 (1940): 322.

5. Richard von Krafft-Ebing, *Psychopathia Sexualis*, trans. F. J. Rebman, from the 12th German ed. (n.p., n.d. [orig. ed. 1886]; rpt., New York: Special Books, 1965), p. 132.

6. Ibid., pp. 131, 215.

7. Ibid., p. 196.

8. Freud, "Instincts and Their Vicissitudes" (1915), in Rieff (ed.), pp. 91–94.

9. Freud, "Three Essays on the Theory of Sexuality" (1905), *SE* 7:133–243; Freud, "A Child Is Being Beaten" (1919), in *Sexuality and the Psychology of Love*, ed. Philip Rieff (New York: Macmillan/Collier Books, 1963), pp. 107–32; Freud, "The Economic Problem in Masochism," pp. 190–201.

10. Freud, "The Economic Problem in Masochism," p. 190.

11. Ibid., pp. 190–91.

12. Freud, "Three Essays on the Theory of Sexuality," pp. 157, 159–60. See also Freud, "Instincts and Their Vicissitudes," pp. 94–95, 97. Freud noted in "Three Essays on the Theory of Sexuality" that sadism and masochism were derived from a single sexual drive and distinguished by their passive/active differential. He theorized that only in love/hate ambivalence was there an actual change in the qualitative content of the drive rather than just the *aim*, defined as "the act to which the drive is driven," and the *object*, "the thing in regard to which or through which the drive is able to achieve its aim." Different drives were attached to certain relational modes (i.e. orality). A confusion about Freud's stance on drive reversal arises in Kaja Silverman's Freudian-based consideration of masochism and film in "Masochism and Subjectivity," *Framework* 12 (1980): 7–8. Silverman argued for a transformational process between drives, which she justified by reference to Freud's *The Ego and the Id*, trans. Joan Riviere, ed. James Strachey (New York: W. W. Norton, 1960). To ground her theory, Silverman cited Freud's remarks on love/hate reversal, but Freud considered love/hate ambivalence as an exception to the norm of drive reversal (see Freud, *The Ego and the Id* (1923), pp. 32–34). Deleuze rejects the notion of the easy transformation of sadism into masochism as abstractionism (pp. 40–41). For a thorough discussion of Freudian drive theory and the attendant problems of definition and interpretation see Jean Laplanche, *Life and Death in Psychoanalysis*, trans. Jeffrey Mehlman (Baltimore: Johns Hopkins University Press, 1976).

13. Freud, "Instincts and Their Vicissitudes," pp. 91–92.

14. Ibid., p. 92.

15. Freud, "A Child Is Being Beaten," pp. 109–11. Freud regarded perversion as one of the normal processes of development in the child's sexual life (ibid., p. 120). Laplanche suggests that perversion should not be considered a deviation from instinct because it is an exception to an undefinable norm (p. 23).

16. Freud, "Three Essays on the Theory of Sexuality," p. 165. Freud defined repression simply as "turning something away, and keeping it at a distance, from the conscious," in "Repression" (1915), *General Psychological Theory*, ed. Rieff, p. 105. In a neurosis, the infantile wish is repressed; in a perversion, fantasies connected to the wish are consciously acted upon and enjoyed.

17. Freud, "Three Essays on the Theory of Sexuality," p. 231.

18. Freud, "A Child Is Being Beaten," p. 111. Freud considered fantasy to be a key part of perversion: "A phantasy of this kind . . . retained for the purpose of auto-erotic gratification can . . . only be regarded as a primary trait of perversion" (ibid., p. 120). Although the fantasies described by Freud in this essay may be broadly defined as perverse, Laplanche has raised the question of how these fantasies function within a total symptomatology. Freud's patients were six obsessional neurotics; they were not masochistic or sadistic. The fantasies outlined in the study have often been referred to in psychoanalytic film theory as if they were characteristic of masochism and sadism as perversions, but Laplanche maintains that the fantasies must be considered within the context of their obsessional (Oedipal) basis (Laplanche, pp. 98–102). See also Miriam Hansen, "Pleasure, Ambivalence, Identification: Valentino and Female Spectatorship," *Cinema Journal* 25 (Summer 1986): 6–32. While attempting to create a space for a nonmasochistic female spectatorship, Hansen falls into the trap of confusing the "sadomasochistic" components of the three fantasies with sadism and masochism as perversions. See my reply to her article, "Dialogue," *Cinema Journal* 26 (Winter 1987): 51–53.

19. Freud, "A Child Is Being Beaten," p. 117–18.

20. Ibid., pp. 126, 128. See also Freud, "The Economic Problem in Masochism," p. 193.

21. Freud, "The Economic Problem in Masochism," pp. 191, 195.

22. Ibid., p. 200. See also Freud, "Three Essays on the Theory of Sexuality," pp. 159–60.

23. Freud, "The Economic Problem in Masochism," p. 199.

24. Ibid., pp. 192–94. See also Freud, "A Child Is Being Beaten," pp. 125–26. Freud believed that primary erotogenic masochism could "be found at the bottom in the other forms" of masochism ("The Economic Problem in Masochism," p. 192). In describing the male's active/passive orientation and "bisexual constitution," he did not consider the possibility that the boy might wish to be like the mother for reasons that have

nothing to do with the child's attempt to gain the father's love. Freud believed the boy's actions were based on his wish to "take his *mother's* place as the love-object of his *father*. . . ." Freud, "Some Psychological Consequences of the Anatomical Distinction between the Sexes" (1925), in *Sexuality and the Psychology of Love*, ed. Rieff, p. 185.

25. Deleuze, p. 65. Although he calls his approach a deductive psychoanalysis, it is actually inductive.

26. Ibid., p. 15.

27. Ibid., p. 13.

28. Ibid., p. 65. See also pp. 40–41 on the difference between sadism and masochism.

29. Heinz Hartmann, "Ego Psychology and the Problem of Adaptation," in *Organization and Pathology of Thought,* ed. David Rapaport (New York: Columbia University Press, 1951), pp. 377–78; Ernst Kris, "On Preconscious Mental Processes," in ibid., pp. 474–93. On regression's relationship to primary process functioning see Merton M. Gill, "The Primary Process," in *Psychological Issues: Motives and Thought,* ed. Robert R. Holt (New York: International Universities Press, 1967), pp. 260–98.

30. Paul Ricoeur, "Psychoanalysis and the Movement of Contemporary Culture," in *Conflict of Interpretations: Essays in Hermeneutics,* trans. Willis Domingo, ed. Don Ihde (Evanston: Northwestern University Press, 1974), p. 141. Ricoeur asks: "Do not the most innovative forms an artist, writer, or thinker can generate not have the two-fold power of concealing and revealing, of dissimulating the old, in the same way as dream, symptoms or neuroses, and of revealing the most incomplete and unrealized possibilities as symbols of the man of the future?" Marsha Kinder discusses dream's possible evolutionary function in "Dream as Art: A Model for the Creative Interplay between Visual Image and Narrative," *Dreamworks* 2 (Spring 1982): 216–25.

31. Deleuze, pp. 50–51, 54.

32. See Roy Schafer, "Problems in Freud's Psychology of Women," *Journal of the American Psychoanalytic Association* 22 (1974): 463–77. In "The Idea of Resistance," *International Journal of Psycho-Analysis* 54 (1973): 278, Schafer writes: ". . . But he [Freud] taught us virtually nothing directly about what it is to struggle endlessly with the archaic mother. He mostly neglected the real transactional aspects of particular mother-child relationships; he treated the pre-oedipal mother—and also the oedipal mother—as some combination of a warm milieu for hatching children, so to say, an almost iconic prop for the child's fantasies, and an impersonal force or agency busy with such necessities as nursing and weaning. . . ."

33. Robert J. Stoller, *Perversion: The Erotic Form of Hatred* (New York: Dell/ Delta Books, 1975), p. 99; Janine Chasseguet-Smirgel, "Freud and Female Sexuality: The Consideration of Some Blind Spots in the Exploration of the 'Dark Continent,'" *International Journal of Psycho-Analysis* 57 (1976): 275–86; Nancy Chodorow, *The Reproduction of Mothering*

(Berkeley: University of California Press, 1978). In "The Idea of Resistance," Schafer explains the source of the mother's power: ". . . anxiety over losing the mother or her love threatens to undermine the boy's and the girl's very sense of worth or right to exist. . . . The mother in pregenital life is a powerful, controlling, threatening figure against whom the child continually struggles actually and in fantasy (p. 278). On maternal authority see Irving B. Harrison, "On the Maternal Origins of Awe," *The Psychoanalytic Study of the Child* 30 (1975): 181–95.

34. Deleuze, p. 53. On ambivalence toward the mother and its effect on masochism's formal structures see Victor Smirnoff, "The Masochistic Contract," *International Journal of Psycho-Analysis* 50 (1969): 669. Smirnoff's views obviously are much indebted to Deleuze. Otto Fenichel explains identification as a defense against the anxiety of ambivalence in "Defense against Anxiety," *The Collected Papers of Otto Fenichel: First Series* (New York: W. W. Norton, 1953) p. 307. Gustav Bychowski discusses the maternal influence on masochism in "Some Aspects of Masochistic Involvement," *Journal of the American Psychoanalytic Association* 7 (1959): 263. Theodor Reik, like Deleuze, questions Freud's belief that the father "hides" behind the punishing mother figure in masochism, but he does not completely abandon Freud's stance on the father's role. Reik, *Masochism in Modern Man*, trans. Margaret H. Beigel and Gertrud M. Kruth (New York: Farrar, Straus, 1941), p. 23.

35. Berliner, pp. 323–26, 333. Does masochism ever arise out of infantile insatiability or is it always rooted in actual trauma? See Charles Brenner, "The Masochistic Character," *Journal of the American Psychoanalytic Association* 7 (1959): 203–4. H. Hartmann, E. Kris, and R. M. Loewenstein, like many others, note the link between masochism and infantile helplessness. With few defenses against loss of the mother's love, they say, the child can be expected to turn to self-punitive, masochistic maneuvers to retain that love. Hartmann, Kris, and Loewenstein, "Comments on the Formation of Psychoanalytic Structure," *The Psychoanalytic Study of the Child* 2 (1946): 11–38; and "Notes on the Theory of Aggression," *The Psychoanalytic Study of the Child* 3–4 (1949): 9–39.

36. Deleuze, p. 59.

37. Smirnoff, p. 665.

38. Deleuze, pp. 59–60. Deleuze believes the female can assume the same role as the son in the formation of a masochistic alliance with the mother. Because of the male "authorship" of the von Sternberg films, my study, like Deleuze's, focuses on the fantasy as constructed from the male viewpoint.

39. Daniel Lagache, "Situation de l'agressivité," *Bulletin Psychologie* 14 (1961): 99–112. Marsha Kinder has suggested a logical expansion of my model in which the question is not an issue of gender but of which position the fantasizing subject takes: the controlling parent (sadistic) or the child who wishes to be controlled (masochistic). Such an expansion would be consistent with Smirnoff's view that masochism cannot be ex-

plained through a pain/pleasure dynamic but must be analyzed within the governing framework of subject positioning (p. 665).

40. Freud, "The Economic Problem in Masochism," p. 193.
41. Freud, "A Child Is Being Beaten," p. 113. Laplanche provides a cogent analysis of these fantasies (pp. 99–102).
42. Deleuze, p. 49.
43. Ibid., pp. 53–55, 58.
44. Reik, p. 428. Deleuze voices a similar opinion (p. 77).
45. Deleuze, p. 95. Robert J. Stoller provides an interesting clinically oriented perspective on perversion and guilt in *Sexual Excitement: The Dynamics of Erotic Life* (New York: Simon and Schuster/Touchstone, 1979), p. 123. He rejects Freud's "sacrificial ego model" as a viable explanation of "sadomasochistic" guilt.
46. Deleuze, p. 56. For a discussion of early forms of identification with the mother from an object relations perspective see Berliner, "Libido and Reality in Masochism," p. 326; and "On Some Psychodynamics of Masochism," *Psychoanalytic Quarterly* 16 (1946): 461–62. See also Stoller, *Perversion*, p. 146; and Michael de M'Uzan, "A Case of Masochistic Perversion and an Outline of a Theory," *International Journal of Psycho-Analysis* 54 (1973): 464.
47. Freud, "The Economic Problem in Masochism," p. 193.
48. De M'Uzan, p. 462.
49. Reik, p. 428.
50. Deleuze, pp. 111–12.
51. Ibid., p. 113.
52. Ibid., pp. 77–78. See also Reik, pp. 429–30.
53. Roland Barthes, *Sade/Fournier/Loyola*, trans. Richard Miller (New York: Hill & Wang, 1976), p. 34.
54. Deleuze, pp. 52–53. Freud's view may be found in "The Economic Problem in Masochism," p. 194.
55. Leopold von Sacher-Masoch, *Venus in Furs*, trans. Jean McNeil, in Deleuze, p. 129.
56. Marquis de Sade, *One Hundred Twenty Days of Sodom and Other Writings*, trans. and ed. Austryn Wainhouse and Richard Seaver (New York: Grove Press, 1966), p. 577.
57. Ibid., p. 619.
58. See Angela Carter, *The Sadeian Woman and the Ideology of Pornography* (New York: Harper & Row/Harper Colophon Books, 1980), pp. 76–77, 24, 86.
59. Ibid., p. 37.
60. Ibid., p. 124.
61. Marquis de Sade, *The Complete Justine, Philosophy in the Bedroom and Other Writings*, trans. Austryn Wainhouse and Richard Seaver (New York: Grove Press, 1965), p. 263.
62. Klossowski, cited in Deleuze, p. 52.
63. Carter, pp. 132, 133, 135.

64. The notion of a subversive "nonsymbolic" mothering has been advanced in film theory, primarily by E. Ann Kaplan. The limitations of this theory lie in the child's gender (exclusively female), the rather vague definition of what such a mothering practice would entail, and the theoretical determinism of Kaplan's Lacanian-derived approach. See Kaplan, *Women and Film: Both Sides of the Camera* (New York: Methuen, 1983), pp. 200–206.

65. Deleuze, p. 52.

66. Ibid., pp. 16–17. See also Barthes, pp. 133–35.

67. Deleuze, p. 31.

68. Barthes, p. 18; and *The Pleasure of the Text* (New York: Hill & Wang, 1975), p. 19. He notes in *Sade/Fourier/Loyola* that "Sadian eroticism is neither sensual nor mystical" (p. 167).

69. Sacher-Masoch, p. 201.

70. Barthes, *The Pleasure of the Text*, p. 10.

71. Deleuze, pp. 36–38.

72. Ibid., p. 80.

73. Sacher-Masoch, p. 167.

74. See Smirnoff, p. 669. For a similar view see Bychowski, p. 259.

75. Sacher-Masoch, p. 228. Severin's "dephantasization" leads to his final emphatic declaration on the moral of his story: "The moral is that woman . . . is man's enemy; she can be his slave or his mistress but never his companion. This she can only be when she has the same rights as he and is his equal in education and work. For the time being there is only one alternative: to be the hammer or the anvil. I was fool enough to let a woman make a slave of me, do you understand? Hence the moral of the tale: whoever allows himself to be whipped deserves to be whipped."

76. Barthes, *Sade/Fourier/Loyola*, p. 24.

77. Sade, *Justine, Philosophy in the Bedroom, Eugenie de Franval, and Other Writings*, p. 297.

78. Deleuze, p. 18. Smirnoff parallels Deleuze's assertion that "sadomasochism" is an impossibility: ". . . in the masochistic ceremony . . . everything is settled from the very start. . . . There can be no possible sadistic-masochistic meeting: the sadist only accepts to be the tormentor of an innocent and protesting victim; the masochist can only be the victim of a reluctant executioner *malgre lui*" (p. 668). Stoller makes a similar observation in *Perversion*, p. 58.

79. Sacher-Masoch, p. 155.

80. Marquis de Sade, *Juliette*, trans. Austryn Wainhouse and Richard Seaver (New York: Grove Press, 1964), p. 118.

81. Deleuze, p. 64. Reik also stresses the importance of fantasy in masochism. In his view, not only does the masochist live out the fantasy, but masochistic fantasy is a widespread phenomenon that is "in the development of every civilized man, an unavoidable phase of transition in the conflict between instinctual demands and social claims" (p. 390).

82. Sacher-Masoch, p. 123–24.

83. On unconscious infantile fantasies see Alvan Frank, "The Unremem-berable and the Unforgettable," *The Psychoanalytic Study of the Child* 24 (1969): 62; see also Berliner, "Libido and Reality in Masochism," p. 337. On the sadistic projection of fantasy see Deleuze, pp. 63–64.

84. See Ethel Spector Person, "Sexuality as the Mainstay of Identity: Psycho-analytic Perspectives," *Signs* 5 (Summer 1980): 605–30.

85. Jacob Arlow, "Ego Psychology and the Study of Mythology," *Journal of the American Psychoanalytic Association* 9 (1961): 377. Freud details the transformational aspect of fantasies in "From the History of an Infantile Neurosis" (1918), in *Three Case Histories,* ed. Philip Rieff (New York: Macmillan/Collier Books, 1968), pp. 34–68.

86. Deleuze, p. 57.

87. Jean Laplanche and J.-B. Pontalis, *The Language of Psychoanalysis,* trans. Donald Nicholson-Smith (New York: W. W. Norton, 1973), p. 318.

88. Bychowski, p. 260.

89. Deleuze, p. 58. Bychowski offers a similar theory but centralizes the "phallic mother" as necessary to this formula so that the child may owe "her everything" (p. 260).

90. Laplanche, p. 97.

91. Metz, p. 63.

92. Laplanche, p. 102.

93. Ibid., p. 91.

94. Deleuze, pp. 91–94.

95. David Rapaport, "Psychoanalysis as a Developmental Psychology," in *Perspectives in Psychological Theory: Essays in Honor of Heinz Werner,* ed. B. Kaplan and S. Wapner (New York: International Universities Press, 1960), pp. 225–26. See also Peter H. Wolff, "Cognitive Considerations for a Psychoanalytic Theory of Language Acquisition," in *Motives and Thought: Psychoanalytic Essays in Honor of David Rapaport,* ed. Robert R. Holt (New York: International Universities Press, 1967), pp. 330–32. Rapaport argues that a change in aim of instinctual discharge must create a qualitative change in experience. This change is insufficiently accounted for in Freudian drive/dual instinct theory. Either there must be qualitatively different aims and, therefore, instincts (which then equal the aims), or one quantitative drive exists that is governed by the function of organ systems/zones, not by specific energies unique to the zones of development (i.e., oral, anal). Erik Erikson provides a complementary discussion of modes in *Childhood and Society,* rev. ed. (New York: W. W. Norton, 1963).

96. Metz, p. 60.

97. The gaze as a sadistic, controlling tool, so emphasized in recent film theory, also was the basis of Otto Fenichel's consideration of scopophilia, in "The Scoptophilic Instinct and Identification," *The Collected Papers of Otto Fenichel: First Series,* pp. 373–97.

98. Sylvan Keiser, "Body Ego during Orgasm," *Psychoanalytic Quarterly* 21 (April 1952): 162–63. In Keiser's view, the masochist retains an infantile

body image that is insufficiently distinguished from external reality. As a consequence, genitality threatens the individual's body boundaries. See also de M'Uzan on the role of suspense and orgasm as a danger to the masochist (p. 462).

99. Stephen Heath, *Questions of Cinema* (Bloomington: Indiana University Press, 1981), pp. 188–89: "It must not be forgotten that a body in cinema, in a film, is present in its absence, in the traces of an image (very different to the body in theatre). The position of the spectator of a film is often described as 'voyeuristic' but voyeurs watch people not films, though no doubt many elements of voyeurism obtain in the pleasure-in-seeking cinema engages."

Chapter Two: Masochism and Visual Pleasure

1. Chasseguet-Smirgel, pp. 281, 286. In discussing the role of oral fanta-sies, Susan Isaacs defines the term *imago* as an "*unconscious* image" that represents the part or total of a person and "includes all the somatic and emotional elements in the subject's relation to the imaged person, the bodily links in unconscious phantasy with the id, the phantasy of incorporation which underlies the process of introjection" (p. 93). In the oral stage, identification is linked to fantasies of literal incorporation of external objects. A mental taking in or *introjection* of the imago occurs that results in a *screen memory,* a mental picture that functions as a nodal point for emotional investment but is based on dream or fantasy rather than a memory of lived experience. Isaacs, "The Nature and Function of Phantasy," *International Journal of Psycho-Analysis* 29 (1948): 73–97. See also Joyce McDougall, "Primal Scene and Sexual Perversion," *International Journal of Psycho-Analysis* 53 (1972): 371–84.

2. Gilles Deleuze and Felix Guattari, *Anti-Oedipus: Capitalism and Schizophre-nia,* trans. Robert Hurley, Mark Seem, and Helen R. Lane (New York: Viking Press, 1977), p. 295.

3. See Freud, "Some Psychological Consequences of the Anatomical Dis-tinction between the Sexes," p. 193; and "Female Sexuality" (1931), *SE* 21:225–43. For counterviews see Chasseguet-Smirgel, pp. 280–81; and Schafer, "Problems in Freud's Psychology of Women," pp. 459–85. Monique Plaza calls attention to Freud's phallocentrism and misogyny in "'Phallomorphic Power' and the Psychology of 'Women': A Patriarchal Chain," in *Human Sexual Relations: Towards a Redefinition of Sexual Politics,* ed. Mike Brake (New York: Pantheon, 1982), p. 339.

4. Viola Klein, *The Feminine Character: History of an Ideology* (New York: International Universities Press, 1949), p. 83.

5. Feminists such as Juliet Mitchell have reclaimed Freud, but whether one sees Freud as dispassionately recording or complacently reproducing patriarchal dynamics, the phallic monism of his theories must be con-fronted. See Mitchell, *Psychoanalysis and Feminism* (New York: Vintage Books/Random House, 1974).

6. Plaza, pp. 327–28, 330.

7. Jacques Lacan, "The Signification of the Phallus," *Écrits: A Selection,* trans. Alan Sheridan (New York: W. W. Norton, 1977), pp. 281–91. Janet Walker discusses the relationship of the biological and the symbolic in feminist film theory in "The Problem of Sexual Difference and Identity," pp. 16–23. Jacqueline Rose explains that in Lacan, anatomical difference "comes to *figure* sexual difference" rather than permitting the latter to be "strictly deducible from the other. . . ." Rose, "Introduction II," in Jacques Lacan, *Feminine Sexuality,* ed. Juliet Mitchell and Jacqueline Rose (New York: W. W. Norton, 1985), p. 42. Deleuze and Guattari also comment on Lacan and Oedipality (pp. 82–84).

8. See Mary Ann Doane, "Woman's Stake: Filming the Female Body," *October* 17 (1981): 28–31; and Kaja Silverman, "Dis-Embodying the Female Voice," in *Re-vision,* ed. Mary Ann Doane, Patricia Mellencamp, and Linda Williams (Frederick, Md.: University Publications of America, 1984), pp. 132–49. Lacanian theory seems unable to account for how women acquire language. Rather than examine how this crucial question might reflect on the theory's validity, a deeper mystification often occurs. Doane attempts to confront the apparent impasse but backs away from directly addressing the possible implications of this theoretical contradiction: "And from a semiotic perspective, her relation to language must be deficient since her body does not 'permit' access to . . . the motor-force of language—the representation of lack. Hence, the greatest masquerade of all is that of the woman speaking (or writing, or filming), appropriating discourse. . . . How can she speak? Yet, we know that women speak, *even though it may not be clear exactly how this takes place*" ("Woman's Stake," p. 30, emphasis mine). Plaza makes the important distinction that it is not that women do not have language at their disposal but that historically they have been excluded from discourse (p. 344).

9. Mulvey, "Visual Pleasure and Narrative Cinema," p. 7.

10. Deleuze, pp. 59–60. McDougall comments in "Primal Scene and Sexual Perversion": "Thus the pervert attempts to convince himself and others that he holds the secret to sexual desire . . . that there is no difference between the sexes. More precisely put, his secret is this: *there are perceptual differences between the sexes but these are without significance;* and *above all this difference is neither the cause nor the condition of sexual desire*" (p. 378).

11. The subversive value of perversity is not agreed upon. Michel Foucault argued that perversion is implanted within society, in *The History of Sexuality, I: An Introduction,* trans. Robert Hurley (New York: Pantheon Books, 1978) pp. 45–49. Herbert Marcuse argued that perversions challenge the very basis of capitalistic society by upholding "sexuality as an end in itself," which places polymorphous perversity "outside the domination" of society's structuring "performance principle," in *Eros and Civilization* (New York: Vintage Books, 1962), pp. 45–46. In *Anti-Oedipus,* Deleuze and Guattari call for a de-Oedipalization of desiring

to be achieved in becoming a desiring machine. Guattari also makes some provocative remarks that may be applied to the subversive value of masochism in relation to the male subject: "Masculine/active therefore remains a point of reference made obligatory by power in order to permit it to situate, localize, territorialize, to control intensities of desire. Outside of this exclusive bi-pole, no salvation . . . A man who detaches himself from the promised phallic profits inherent in all power formations undertakes such a becoming-woman according to diverse possible modalities. . . . Every 'dissident' organization of the libido must therefore be directly linked to a becoming-feminine body; As an escape route from the repressive socius, as a possible access to a 'minimum' of sexed becoming, and as the last buoy vis-à-vis the established order." Guattari, "Becoming-Woman," *Semio-texte* 4 (1981): 86–88.

12. There seems to be general clinical and theoretical agreement that psychological influences have a much greater effect on the choice of sexual object or gender identification than biological ones. Evoking the concept of bisexuality may offer a positive theoretical alternative to the biological essentialism of feminists such as Luce Irigaray, who has argued for a feminine libido defined by the biology of femaleness. See Irigaray, "Women's Exile," *Ideology and Consciousness* 1 (1977): 62–77. Freud introduced his theory of bisexuality in "Three Essays on the Theory of Sexuality," p. 220: In 1938, he still affirmed its role in "Analysis Terminable and Interminable," *SE* 23:216–53. See also Robert Stoller, "An Examination of Freud's Concept of Bisexuality," in *Women and Analysis*, ed. Jean Strouse (New York: Grossman, 1974), p. 375.

13. Lawrence S. Kubie, "The Drive to Become Both Sexes," in *Symbols and Neurosis: Selected Papers of L. S. Kubie*, ed. Herbert J. Schlesinger (New York: International Universities Press, 1978), pp. 195, 202.

14. Chasseguet-Smirgel, pp. 282–83; Ernest Becker, *The Denial of Death* (New York: Free Press, 1973), p. 225; Eva Feder Kittay, "Womb Envy: An Explanatory Concept," in *Mothering: Essays in Feminist Theory*, ed. Joyce Trebilcot (Totowa, N.J.: Rowman & Allanheld, 1984), pp. 94–127; Gregory Zilboorg, "Masculine and Feminine: Some Biological and Cultural Aspects," *Psychiatry* 7 (1944): 257–96. Kubie believes orality and the drive to become both sexes are closely related: ". . . whenever we attempt to gratify mutually irreconcilable drives the gratification of either component automatically frustrates the opposite. Inevitably such insatiability has oral components. . . . the oral ingredient may be the instrument by which the unconscious drive to become both sexes is to be achieved through incorporation of breasts or penis or both or of the body as a whole" (p. 216).

15. Laura Mulvey, "Afterthoughts on 'Visual Pleasure and Narrative Cinema,' Inspired by *Duel in the Sun*," *Framework*, nos. 15/16/17 (Summer 1981): 12–15; Mary Ann Doane, "Film and the Masquerade: Theorising the Female Spectator," *Screen* 23 (1982): 74–87; Judith Mayne, "The Woman at the Keyhole: Women's Cinema and Feminist Criticism," in

Doane et al. (ed.), p. 61.; B. Ruby Rich, cited in Michelle Citron et al., "Women and Film: A Discussion of Feminist Aesthetics," *New German Critique*, no. 13 (Winter 1978): 87.

16. Mulvey, "Afterthoughts," p. 13.
17. Doane, "Film and the Masquerade," p. 87.
18. Silverman, "Dis-Embodying the Female Voice," p. 145. Silverman writes: "The felt inadequacy of the female subject in the face of these ideal images induces in her an intense self-loathing. At the same time it is impossible for her simply to turn away from them, to retreat into herself, since she has only a relational identity, knows herself only through representation. Her inability either to approximate or transcend the mirror in which she sees herself as the dim reflection of a luminous original locks her into a deadly narcissism, one more conducive to self-hatred than self-love. It must be further noted that each of the movie citations enumerated by the dirty phone-caller constitutes a masochistic inscription. . . . Classical cinema thus overdetermines the production of a docile and suffering female subject" (p. 145).
19. Mulvey, "Afterthoughts," p. 15. Mulvey emphasizes the female's ability to identify with the male gaze/spectatorial position as a result of the impossibility of forging a progressive feminine spectatorial position that can align itself with the presented female without also inevitably aligning itself with passivity and masochism, a position Doane continues in "Film and the Masquerade" (p. 80). Mulvey's use of Freud's account of feminine development to ground her theory of "masculinisation" of female spectatorship seems counterproductive, especially by evoking the feminine "phallic phase" as an explanation for the reactivation of a "phantasy of 'action'" ("Afterthoughts," p. 15). Two very recent attempts to revise this formula of female spectatorship are Hansen, "Pleasure, Ambivalence, Identification," and Jackie Stacey, "Desperately Seeking Difference," *Screen* 28 (1987): 48–61. Stacey's consideration of how the female spectator may experience simultaneous identification with and desire for women represented in film parallels some of my criticisms of feminist-psychoanalytic theory. Interesting as her argument is, Stacey still does not account for how the films she analyzes, *All About Eve* and *Desperately Seeking Susan,* obviously work to desexualize the look of potential erotic desire between women.
20. Mulvey, "Visual Pleasure and Narrative Cinema," pp. 6–18. In "Afterthoughts," Mulvey says that her reference to all spectatorship in the masculine third person was an ironic gesture (p. 12). The view that male spectatorship is Oedipally based and always sadistically controlling in classical cinema has largely remained unexamined and unchallenged. One interesting exception is Ian Green, "Malefunction," *Screen* 25 (1984): 36–48.
21. Freud, *Beyond the Pleasure Principle,* quoted in Heinz Lichtenstein, "Identity and Sexuality," *Journal of the American Psychoanalytic Association* 9 (1961): 229.

22. Laplanche and Pontalis, p. 243.
23. Nick Browne, "The Spectator-in-the-Text: The Rhetoric of Stagecoach," *Film Quarterly* 29 (Winter 1975–76): 26–38; Raymond Bellour, "Psychosis, Neurosis, Perversion," *Camera Obscura*, nos. 3–4 (Summer 1979): 106–34; Janet Bergstrom, "Enunciation and Sexual Difference (Part I)," *Camera Obscura*, nos. 3–4 (Summer 1979): 33–69.
24. Bergstrom, p. 58.
25. Kubie, pp. 195–96, 213. On the issue of androgyny see June Singer, *Androgyny: Toward a New Theory of Sexuality* (Garden City, N.Y.: Doubleday/Anchor Press, 1976).
26. Kubie, pp. 201–2, 211.
27. Reik, p. 427.
28. Paul Schilder, *Goals and Desires in Man: A Psychological Survey of Life* (New York: Columbia University Press, 1942), p. 212. Freud's use of the terms *masculine* and *feminine* in relation to *active* and *passive* come to mind as an instance of this polarization. See Freud, "An Outline of Psychoanalysis" (1940), *SE* 23:188.
29. Mulvey, "Visual Pleasure and Narrative Cinema," p. 13.
30. Ibid., p. 13.
31. Ibid., pp. 13–14.
32. Ibid., p. 14.
33. D. N. Rodowick, "The Difficulty of Difference," *Wide Angle* 5 (1982): 7. Becker discusses perversion as a process of magical thinking and overinvestment in which, "if you fix the terror of life and death magically on one person as the source of pain, you control that terror, but you also overinflate that person" (p. 246).
34. Rodowick, p. 7.
35. Ibid., p. 7. See Freud, "Three Essays on the Theory of Sexuality," pp. 150–51.
36. The role of castration fear in masochism is extremely controversial. While some researchers believe that castration fear is symptomatic of the perversion, most still relate it to the fear of losing the symbiotic attachment to the mother. Charles Socarides approaches the problem of pre-Oedipality and castration anxiety in his discussion of fetishism: "Preoedipal fantasies served as defenses against the emergence of oedipal material and vice versa. . . . castration anxiety, the direct result of the oedipal conflict, may be utilized also as a defense against anxieties of the preoedipal phase. Likewise preoedipal drives may have a defensive importance in warding off oedipal wishes and fears. There is always an interplay between the two." Socarides, "The Development of a Fetishistic Perversion: The Contribution of Preoedipal Phase Conflict," *Journal of the American Psychoanalytic Association* 8 (April 1960): 281–311.
37. Deleuze says that fetishistic rituals in sadism are not indicative of a true fetishism because they are not based on disavowal but on a mechanism of pure negation (p. 29). Freud associated a "castrating" treatment of the fetish with a "strong father-identification," which provides interest-

ing similarities to Deleuze's theory of sadism as a father/child alliance against the mother. Freud, "Fetishism" (1927), *SE* 21:157.

38. Kaja Silverman, *The Subject of Semiotics* (New York: Oxford University Press, 1983), p. 183.

39. Freud, "Fetishism," p. 153.

40. Freud, "Some Psychological Consequences of the Anatomical Distinction between the Sexes," p. 187; see also "Three Essays on the Theory of Sexuality," p. 96.

41. Freud, "The Infantile Genital Organization of the Libido" (1923), p. 174.

42. Mulvey, "Visual Pleasure and Narrative Cinema," p. 13; Freud, "Fetishism," pp. 154–55.

43. See Socarides, pp. 281–311; W. H. Gillespie, "The General Theory of Sexual Perversion," *International Journal of Psycho-Analysis* 37 (1956): 396–403; Joseph C. Solomon, "Transitional Phenomena and Obsessive-Compulsive States," in *Between Reality and Fantasy: Transitional Objects and Phenomena,* ed. Simon A. Grolnick, Leonard Barkin, and Werner Muensterberger (New York: Jason Aronson, 1978), pp. 248–56; M. Wulff, "Fetishism and Object Choice in Early Childhood," *Psychoanalytic Quarterly* 15 (1945): 465–68.

44. There has been little serious consideration of the possibilities for a progressive male spectatorship. Peter Gidal's radical rejection of any representation of women is one answer, albeit a negative one, to the perceived psychological determinism of male spectatorship. Gidal, "Against Sexual Representation in Film," *Screen* 25 (1984): 24–29.

45. John Ellis, "Photography/Pornography/Art/Pornography," *Screen* 21 (Spring 1980): 120; Freud, "Fetishism," p. 154. In Freud's view, the fetish "saves the fetishist from becoming a homosexual by endowing women with the characteristic which makes them tolerable as sexual objects" (ibid., p. 154). Metz's explanation of fetishism duplicates Freud's interpretation of the absolute *terror* evoked by the mother's supposed castration. Metz, *The Imaginary Signifier,* pp. 69–70.

46. Ellis, p. 101–2. Of importance to a consideration of this are Freud's remarks in "Some Psychological Consequences of the Anatomical Distinction between the Sexes," p. 187.

47. Erik Erikson, "Womanhood and the Inner Space," in *Identity, Youth and Crisis* (New York: W. W. Norton, 1965), p. 296. The problem of when and how the child interprets his supposed glimpse of the mother's difference is addressed by Rose in "Introduction II" p. 42. Walker briefly reviews this issue within the context of feminist film theory (p. 19).

48. Griselda Pollock, "What's Wrong with Images of Women," *Screen Education* 24 (Autumn 1977): 30.

49. Robert Dickes, "Fetishistic Behavior: A Contribution to Its Complex Development and Significance," *Journal of the American Psychoanalytic Association* 11 (1963): 320. In "Fetishism: A Review and a Case Study," *Psychiatric Quarterly* 31 (1957): 725, S. Nagler rejects castration as formative in fetishism as well as the notion of the phallic mother.

50. Dickes, p. 327.
51. Wulff, pp. 465–68.
52. P. J. Van der Leeuw, "The Preoedipal Phase of the Male, " *The Psychoanalytic Study of the Child* 13 (1958): 369. Socarides stresses the importance of identification with the powerful mother in fetishism (p. 285). The fetish is often cited as a mechanism for undoing separation. R. M. Brunswick, J. Lampl–de Groot, E. Jacobson, J. S. Kestenberg, C. Socarides, and a number of other researchers link fetishistic perversion to the pre-Oedipal period and to symptomatology associated with masochism and primary identification. Wulff qualifies the link between commonly observed childhood fetishism and adult fetishism by noting the inconsistent relationship between the two and the need for further research (pp. 450–71). See also Jacobson, "Development of the Wish for a Child in Boys," *The Psychoanalytic Study of the Child* 5 (1950): 139–52; Kestenberg, "On the Development of Maternal Feelings in Early Childhood," *The Psychoanalytic Study of the Child* 11 (1956): 257–91.
53. Socarides, pp. 306–7.
54. Socarides, p. 309; see also Dickes, p. 320.
55. Solomon, p. 250. Solomon suggests that: "Fetishism . . . may have its pregenital origin in a threatened loss of the mother. Here both survival and erotic powers are transferred to the object" (p. 250).
56. Zilboorg, pp. 259–65; Kittay, p. 125; Socarides, p. 308; Van der Leeuw, pp. 369–72.
57. M. E. Romm, "Some Dynamics of Fetishism," *Psychoanalytic Quarterly* 19 (1949): 146–47. Romm's description of one case resembles the fantasy of bisexuality and also is reminiscent of Deleuze's description of masochism's 'new man': "At times the patient would fantasy [*sic*] during masturbation that he was able to take his penis in his mouth and in so doing he would be a *complete circle*. At this period he dreamed that he was looking at his body and discovered that he had breasts like a woman and male genitals. . . . The Greek priest, in his cassock with his hair flowing over his shoulders, represented to him a neuter person, celibate and bisexual" (pp. 146–47).
58. Dickes, "Parents, Transitional Objects, and Childhood Fetishes," in Grolnick et al. (ed.), p. 315. For an interesting discussion of fetishism that centralizes the role of death anxiety see Becker, pp. 221–48.
59. Robert Bak, "The Phallic Woman: The Ubiquitous Fantasy in Perversion," *Psychoanalytic Study of the Child* 23 (1968): 16.
60. Freud, "An Analysis of a Phobia in a Five-Year-Old Boy" (1909), *SE* 10:1–147.
61. Ibid., p. 95.
62. Kittay, p. 125.
63. Ibid., p. 99.
64. Solomon links fetishism to the child's sense of body intactness derived from the relationship to the mother and the breast: ". . . this is an inheritance from the original mothering experience. The presence of

a penis is equivalent to, *and a derivative of* the presence of the mother (p. 250, emphasis mine). August Stärcke expresses a similar view in "The Castration Complex," *International Journal of Psycho-Analysis* 2 (1921): 192.

65. Margaret Mahler, "Symbiosis and Individuation: The Psychological Birth of the Human Infant," in *The Selected Papers of Margaret S. Mahler*, Vol. 2 (New York: Jason Aronson, 1974), p. 158; Mahler, "A Study of the Separation-Individuation Process and Its Possible Application to Borderline Phenomena in the Psychoanalytic Situation," *The Psychoanalytic Study of the Child* 26 (1971): 403–24; Mahler, "On the First Three Subphases of the Separation-Individuation Process," *International Journal of Psycho-Analysis* 53 (1972): 333–38.

66. Claire Pajaczkowska, "The Heterosexual Presumption: A Contribution to the Debate on Pornography," *Screen* 22 (Spring 1981): 86.

67. Deleuze, p. 29.

68. See M. Mahler, F. Pine, and A. Bergman, *The Psychological Birth of the Human Infant: Symbiosis and Individuation* (New York: Basic Books, 1975), pp. 4–9; D. W. Winnicott, *Playing and Reality* (London: Tavistock, 1971), p. 11. In reference to film as a dream screen and the I/not-I conceptualization of the mother/child dyad see Robert T. Eberwein, "Reflections on the Breast," *Wide Angle* 4 (1981): 14. Winnicott refers to the "subjective object" (the mother's breast) as the first object that is not rejected as a "not-me phenomenon" (p. 80).

The term *ideal ego* or *ego ideal* is quite confusing because of the variability in its applied meanings and because Freud's own definition evidenced considerable slippage. At times he seemed to equate it with positive, non-superego power exercised by the parents; at other times he equated it with the superego. Mulvey defines the ideal ego as a projection that is "re-introjected as an ego ideal" and occurs in connection with the misrecognition of the mirror stage, a misrecognition (into subjectivity) that is available only to the male ("Visual Pleasure and Narrative Cinema," pp. 9–10). In Deleuze's construct, masochism accords power to the female through a disavowal that abolishes the father's primacy and positions the female as the ideal ego (p. 111). It seems safest to follow Hans Loewald's definition of the ego ideal as the more primitive ego development of the pre-Oedipal stage which involves the child's attempt to attain (or reattain) infantile narcissistic perfection and the satisfaction of well-being. See Loewald, *Papers on Psychoanalysis* (New Haven: Yale University Press, 1980), pp. 46–48; and Alex Holder, "Preoedipal Contributions to the Formation of the Superego," *The Psychoanalytic Study of the Child* 37 (1982): 250–53.

69. Dickes, "Fetishistic Behavior," p. 305.

70. Deleuze, p. 110. Although Deleuze believes disavowal depends upon castration, he does not define it as an evitable indicator of feminine lack: "The masochist practices three forms of disavowal at once: the first magnifies the mother, by attributing to her the phallus instrumental

to rebirth; the second excludes the father, since he has no part in this rebirth; and the third relates to sexual pleasure, which is interrupted, deprived of its genitality and transformed into the pleasure of being reborn" (p. 87).

71. Deleuze, p. 110.

72. Chasseguet-Smirgel writes: "Freud attributed to man a 'natural scorn' for women. This scorn originated in the fact of their lack of a penis. My experience has shown me that underlying this scorn one always finds a powerful maternal imago, envied and terrifying" (p. 283). See also Kittay, pp. 98–99; and Chasseguet-Smirgel, "The Feminine Guilt and the Oedipus Complex," in *Female Sexuality: New Psychoanalytic Views,* ed. Janine Chasseguet-Smirgel (Ann Arbor: University of Michigan Press, 1970).

73. Nancy Chodorow, *The Reproduction of Mothering* (Berkeley: University of California Press, 1978), pp. 193–96.

74. Chasseguet-Smirgel, "Freud and Female Sexuality," pp. 281–84; Ralph Greenson, "Dis-identifying from Mother: Its Special Importance for the Boy," *International Journal of Psycho-Analysis* 49 (1968): 370–74; Chodorow, pp. 193–96.

75. Silverman, "Masochism and Subjectivity," p. 2–3.

76. Ibid., pp. 5–6. See also Dickes, "Fetishistic Behavior," p. 327.

77. Socarides, p. 304. On female voyeurism see Stoller, *Sexual Excitement,* pp. 90–91. On female fetishism see Dickes, "Parents, Transitional Objects, and Childhood Fetishes," pp. 315–16; N. T. Spiegel, "An Infantile Fetish and Its Persistence into Young Womanhood," *The Psychoanalytic Study of the Child* 22 (1976): 402–25; and Phyllis Greenacre, "Further Considerations Regarding Fetishism," *The Psychoanalytic Study of the Child* 10 (1955): 188.

78. For Doane, the construction of the difference between male and female looking hinges on the female's "closeness" to her mother's body: "This body so close, so excessive, prevents the woman from assuming a position similar to the man's in relation to signifying systems. For she is haunted by the loss of a loss, the lack of that lack so essential for the realisation of the ideals of semiotic systems" ("Film and the Masquerade," p. 79).

79. Mulvey, "Visual Pleasure and Narrative Cinema," p. 12.

80. Mary Ann Doane, "Misrecognition and Identity," *Cine-Tracts* 1 (Fall 1980): 28–30. Doane states: "Contemporary film theory delineates certain structures of seeing—scopophilia or voyeurism, fetishism, primary identification—which align themselves with the psychoanalysis of the male" (p. 31). In "Film and the Masquerade," she asserts that film spectatorship for the female can only be defined as a negative field in relation to narrative cinema: "Given the structures of cinematic narrative, the woman who identifies with a female character must adopt a passive or masochistic position, while identification with the active hero necessarily entails an acceptance of . . . a certain 'masculinisation' of spectatorship" (p. 80). See René A. Spitz, *No and Yes: On the Genesis of Human Communi-*

cation (New York: International Universities Press, 1957), and Renato J. Almansi, "The Face-Breast Equation," *Journal of the American Psychoanalytic Association* 8 (1960): 43–70, on the developmental importance of oral phase looking and its lack of sexual differentiation.

81. Doane, "Film and the Masquerade," p. 80.

82. Freud, "Female Sexuality," p. 233. Doane borrows from Irigaray to establish a theory in which the female cannot separate herself from the "over-presence" of the female body and so cannot assume a reflective position toward sexual difference. She skirts biological essentialism in her discussion of the girl's relation to the maternal body and the construction of a feminine structure of the look dependent on the discovery of sexual difference and "the visibility of the penis" ("Film and the Masquerade," p. 79). Although Doane rhetorically distances herself from her citation of Freud and French feminists in explaining why women have an "inability to fetishise" (ibid., p. 80), and is careful to define femininity as a "cultural construction," she does not address exactly how cultural pressures are brought to bear on the girl's interpretation of sexual difference through looking.

83. Doane, "Film and the Masquerade," pp. 80–82.

84. Ibid., p. 87; see also Mulvey, "Afterthoughts," pp. 12–15.

85. Doane, "The 'Woman's Film': Possession and Address," in Doane et al. (ed.), pp. 78–80.

86. Ibid., p. 79. Doane continues this line of thinking in *The Desire to Desire* (Bloomington: Indiana University Press, 1987).

87. Laplanche makes this point in *Life and Death in Psychoanalysis* when he states that masochism and sadism "necessarily involve, either consciously or unconsciously, an element of *sexual* excitement or enjoyment" (p. 87). He criticizes the theoretical reduction of sadism into nothing more than a nonsexual aggression (p. 143).

88. Doane, "The 'Woman's Film'," p. 78.

89. Freud gave a qualified account of the third phase of the fantasy and noted that "only the *form* of this fantasy is sadistic; the gratification which is derived from it is masochistic" ("A Child Is Being Beaten," p. 119). Doane emphasizes that the male subject in Freud's case never assumes the spectatorial position that the woman takes up in relation to her third phase fantasy, a relation Doane says corresponds with the woman's loss of "her sexual identity in the context of the scenario" as well as "her very access to sexuality" ("The 'Woman's Film'," pp. 78–79). Yet male spectatorship would seem to entail a "feminization" of the male through the imposition of a spectatorial structure associated (in Freud's description) only with female fantasy.

90. Almansi, p. 69.

91. Ibid., p. 68. The *dream screen* is defined as the blank screen on which dreams are projected.

92. Socarides, p. 301; Almansi, p. 68.

93. Mulvey, "Visual Pleasure and Narrative Cinema," pp. 14–15.

94. I must give credit to Miriam Hansen for first suggesting that Mulvey's point might be used to consider the subversive aspect of the unmediated gaze. See Hansen, "Visual Pleasure, Fetishism and the Problem of Female Discourse: Ulrike Ottinger's *Ticket of No Return*," *New German Critique*, no. 31 (Winter 1984): 102.

95. Doane, "The 'Woman's Film'," p. 82. Mayne briefly discusses Dietrich's role in *Morocco* in "The Woman at the Keyhole," p. 60.

96. Lesage, quoted in Silvia Bovenschen, "Women and Film," *New German Critique*, no. 13 (Winter 1978): 89–90.

97. Kathryn Weibel, *Mirror Mirror: Images of Women Reflected in Popular Culture* (New York: Doubleday, 1977), p. 105; Haskell, pp. 101, 112.

98. On overidentification see Doane, "Film and the Masquerade," p. 80. For women's reaction to Dietrich see Silvia Bovenschen, "Is There a Feminine Aesthetic?," *New German Critique*, no. 10 (Winter 1977): 128–29, and the roundtable discussion in "Women and Film," pp. 87–90. In Judy Whitaker, "Hollywood Transformed," *Jump Cut*, nos. 24/25 (March 1981): 33–35, an interview with nine lesbian women focuses on their experience with the cinema and produces some interesting remarks regarding Dietrich. One women mentions being "enthralled with Dietrich" and says:

    > Dietrich had substance. . . . I'm not particularly a fan of German film, but of Marlene Dietrich. She has a sustaining quality about her that I know has turned on thousands of women in this world. I can't say I identified with her. I wasn't thinking racially in terms of black and white in those days. But there was no identification.

    What was your fascination:

    > Lust, childhood lust, I'm sure (p. 35).

    Dietrich is also a recognized gay icon for males. In Hector Babenco's *Kiss of the Spider Woman*, pictures of Dietrich grace the cell wall of the homosexual prisoner Molina.

99. Irving Buchen, *The Perverse Imagination* (New York: New York University Press, 1970), p. 85.

100. Mulvey, "Visual Pleasure and Narrative Cinema," p. 11.

Chapter Three: Masochistic Masquerade in the Performance of Identity

1. Lichtenstein, p. 202.

2. Person, p. 627. Monique Plaza also refers to the "violence of dependence" marking sexual relations with an inevitable governing frame of the dominant/submission structure (p. 331).

3. Maria Ramas, "Freud's Dora, Dora's Hysteria," *In Dora's Case: Freud-Hysteria-Feminism*, ed. Charles Bernheimer and Claire Kahane (New York: Columbia University Press, 1985), pp. 155–56. Ramas asserts that the omnipotent mother who blocks the child's individuation is an actuality within the patriarchal family structure because of Western society's "exaggerated centripetal tendencies in the mother-child relationship"

(p. 155). She criticizes object relations theory for ignoring the triadic structure of the patriarchal family and does not recognize that such theory seeks to account for the strength of the mother/child dyad as a "material" reality and as a psychic reality. This does not mean that the father is absent or that patriarchal relations have no role in the formation of gender identity; rather, it means that the influence of the mother/child relationship is formidable—and continuing.

4. Mike Brake, "Sexuality as Praxis—a Consideration of the Contribution of Sexual Theory to the Process of Sexual Being," in Brake (ed.), pp. 14–15. Brake discusses the development of theories of sexuality and the implications of genitality and alternative sexualities. Freud discussed the arbitrary norms established against perverse sexuality (and sexuality in general) in "Civilization and Its Discontents" (1930), SE 21:104–5.

5. Laplanche, p. 104.

6. Deleuze and Guattari, p. 116.

7. The superego is not synonymous with morality. Freud theorized that it took its repressive power from the id ("The Economic Problem in Masochism," p. 197). Holder discusses the development of the superego prior to the phallic phase. (pp. 252–72).

8. Some feminists regard sadism and masochism, or "sadomasochism," not as a subversive of dominant power relations but as a confirmation of patriarchal influence. However, Pat Califia argues that by breaking through conventional sexual practices, "sadomasochism" as a feminist practice is a "deliberate, premediated erotic blasphemy . . . a form of sexual extremism and sexual dissent." Califia, "Unravelling the Sexual Fringe: A Secret Side of Lesbian Sexuality," The Advocate 27 (December 1979): 19. For a detailed overview of the feminist debate concerning sadomasochistic practice see Marie France, "Sadomasochism and Feminism," Feminist Review, no. 16 (April 1984): 35–42.

9. Leo Bersani, A Future for Astyanax: Character and Desire in Literature (Boston: Little, Brown, 1976), p. 29. Bersani remarks within the context of his discussion of Charles Mauron's psychoanalytic study of Racine: "Racine's characters . . . enjoy the freedom of simultaneously being different partial impulses. . . . And the pleasure which such literary representations give to us may be the equivalent to a liberating participation in the dissolving of fixed identities. Perhaps even stronger than the anguish of returning to frightening desires and murderous conflicts is—at least in the experience of art—the delight of returning to the multiple identities among which those desires allow us to move."

10. Deleuze, pp. 21, 37–38.

11. Ibid., p. 21.

12. Laplanche and Pontalis, p. 318.

13. Daniel Weiss has observed that even if the artist does recognize the controlling obsession present in his/her work and uses art to explore the unconscious, the conscious exploration can only be incomplete and cannot account for all the effects in the work. Weiss, Oedipus in Nottingham:

D. H. Lawrence (Seattle: University of Washington Press, 1962), p. 10. Von Sternberg once stated that a film revealed the director's intellectual prowess, not his emotional makeup, but it is of some interest that one of his unfinished film projects was about "man's fixation on an infantile level." Von Sternberg, *Fun in a Chinese Laundry: An Autobiography* (New York: Macmillan/Collier Books, 1965) p. 279. The paradox, the dialectic of control evident in the films' characters, extends even to the creator. By desublimating desire in the artistic work, the artist too is both liberator and slave to the masochistic structure of desire. It is in this light that von Sternberg's work must be approached, rather than assuming, as Kaplan does, that the subversive aspects of *Blonde Venus* are the result of "the incompatibility, in dominant representation, of female sexuality and mothering, and, from the film's focus on fetishism as a strategy for lessening male fears of female sexuality." Kaplan, *Women and Film*, p. 56.

14. Laplanche, p. 102.
15. Robin Wood, "Venus de Marlene," *Film Comment* 14 (March–April 1978): 62.
16. Peter Bogdanovich, "Encounters with Josef von Sternberg," *Movie* 13 (Summer 1965): 24.
17. Sigmund Freud, *An Outline of Psychoanalysis*, trans. and ed. James Strachey (New York: W. W. Norton, 1949), p. 5.
18. "Morocco," pp. 5–13; rpt. in Baxter (ed.), pp. 83–85, 89–90. It is interesting to speculate how American audiences read this "taboo of class" vis-à-vis the star system's functional displacement of class onto the aesthetics of physicality.
19. Baxter (ed.), p. 88.
20. Ibid., pp. 81–82.
21. La Bessiere's actions are contrasted with those of Adjutant Caesar, whose wife, like Amy, is romantically involved with Brown. Caesar publicly exposes his wife's infidelity, not as a masochistic exhibition of the resilience of desire, but as a sadistic, accusatory gesture. To save face and exact revenge, Caesar attempts to kill Brown but is himself killed. *Morocco's* "double inscription" of desire through its pairings of characters (Amy/Brown, Amy/La Bessiere, Brown/Madame Caesar, Madame Caesar/Caesar) fulfills the masochistic scheme on several levels, including the iconization of desire which guarantees the impossibility of consummation.
22. Reik, p. 312.
23. Alain Robbe-Grillet, "Nature, Humanism, Tragedy," *For a New Novel: Essays on Fiction*, trans. Richard Howard (New York: Grove Press, 1962), p. 61. Alain Resnais's *Last Year at Marienbad* (scripted by Robbe-Grillet) seems to *consciously* play on many conventions and situations that might be considered characteristic of a masochistic text.
24. Reik, p. 398.

25. Ibid., p. 160.
26. Deleuze, pp. 108–9. Deleuze explains the need for pain in terms of masochism's superego/ego structuring and the punishment of the father. As a result, humor shows the ego's triumph over the superego, which remains only as a "caricature" in the beating woman. Henry Hart has suggested that the triumph of the ego is demonstrated in the masochist's ability to control pain and defeat humiliation by ritualizing the two into self-administered innoculations. Hart, "The Meaning of Passivity," *Psychiatric Quarterly* 29 (1955): 605. See also Reik, p. 119. The problem of why pain is necessary to masochism's dynamic remains one of the most controversial in psychoanalysis. For a discussion of various theories see Abram Kardiner, Aaron Karushy, and Lionel Ovesey, "A Methodological Study of Freudian Theory: III. Narcissism, Bisexuality, and the Dual Instinct Theory," *Journal of Nervous and Mental Disorders* 129 (1959): 215–20.
27. Deleuze, p. 87. Deleuze's theory, that the father is guilty, is not as unusual as it might first seem. Claude Lévi-Strauss has also noted certain circumstances under which Oedipal guilt is qualified and subverted: "The initial theme of the key myth is the incest committed by the hero with the mother. Yet the idea that he is guilty seems to exist mainly in the mind of the father, who desires his son's death and schemes to bring it about. . . . In the long run it is the father who appears guilty through having tried to avenge himself, and it is he who is killed. . . . This curious indifference toward incest appears in other myths." Lévi-Strauss, *The Raw and the Cooked*, trans. Johan and Doreen Weightman (New York: Harper & Row, 1969), p. 48.
28. Frequently *The Blue Angel* is referred to as a film in which the male is destroyed by the female. In an interview, Peter Bogdanovich asked von Sternberg: "Wouldn't you say that *The Blue Angel* was the only time Dietrich really destroyed a man?" Von Sternberg's reply is telling: "She did not destroy him—he destroyed himself. It was his mistake—he should never have taken up with her. That's what the story is" (p. 25).
29. Andrew Sarris, *The Films of Josef von Sternberg* (New York: Museum of Modern Art, 1966) p. 41. Sarris writes: "Inevitably there is the misunderstanding: the younger man thinks the older man is motivated by his own lecherous designs, and the older man sighs wearily about such unfounded suspicions. Here Sternberg pulls the switch: Atwill *is* motivated by his own lecherous designs, and the whole narration is revealed as dishonest in its didactic intention."
30. Sacher-Masoch, p. 169.
31. Sylvan Keiser, "The Fear of Sexual Passivity in the Masochist," *International Journal of Psycho-Analysis* 30 (1949): 167.
32. Silverman, "Masochism and Subjectivity," p. 6.
33. Deleuze, pp. 56–59.
34. Ibid., p. 81. Deleuze explains that "interrupted love" permits the mas-

ochist to identify sexuality with incest and with rebirth. This "not only saves him from the threat of castration but actually turns castration into the symbolic condition of success."

35. Ibid., p. 81.
36. Sacher-Masoch, p. 210. See also Norman Holland, *The Dynamics of Literary Response* (New York: Oxford University Press, 1968), on abandonment fear and family rivalry.
37. Sacher-Masoch, p. 210.
38. Sarris, *The Films of Josef von Sternberg*, pp. 29–30.
39. "To-be-looked-at-ness" is a much-used phrase borrowed from Mulvey, who asserts in "Visual Pleasure and Narrative Film" that the male star is not glamorized in the same fashion as the female. His characteristics, she says, are those of the ideal ego, "not those of the erotic object of the gaze . . ." (p. 12). This generalization certainly does not hold true for all Hollywood films, especially those produced for predominately female audiences, such as the "women's films," and increasingly for films in the 1980s. Linda Williams asserts that the female gaze in classical Hollywood film either elicits punishment (and is turned into "masochistic fantasy") or is undermined by the woman's lack of moral authority. If these were the sole criteria for judging the power of the gaze, then many male protagonists would not fare well either. (In this respect, film noir seems a ripe area for a more specific examination of the complexities of male looking and masochism.) Williams, "When the Woman Looks," in Doane et al. (ed.), p. 85.
40. Mulvey, "Visual Pleasure and Narrative Cinema," pp. 12–13. Mulvey's key argument regarding space is that the male commands a "stage of spatial illusion in which he articulates the look and creates the action" (p. 13).
41. There are several possible interpretations of Brown's change of mind. *Cahiers du Cinéma* interprets his gestures as a rejection of the "castration" which a return to Europe would inevitably mean, signified by the top hat he tries on (no. 225, p. 91). His fondling of the bracelet La Bessiere has given Amy also suggests that he realizes he cannot give her material possessions. Nevertheless, as to be expected from von Sternberg, the performance of the actor (Gary Cooper) gives little definitive weight to any of these possibilities.
42. Foucault, p. 103.
43. *Pagisme* is a common element of masochistic ritual in which one of the partners acts the role of the servant. In *Venus in Furs*, Severin is bound by contract into the role of servant to Wanda. He must occupy servants' quarters, ride third-class (much to his chagrin), and grovel at the appropriate moments. See Deleuze, p. 67.
44. Nichols, *Ideology and the Image*, p. 110–11.
45. Michèle Montrelay, "Recherches sur la féminité," *Critique*, no. 278, quoted in *Cahiers du Cinéma*, no. 225, p. 93. Montrelay writes: "Within this piling up of dotty objects, feathers, hats, strange baroque construc-

tions which rise like many silent insignia, a dimension of femininity takes shapes which Lacan, taking up Joan Riviere's term, designates as *masquerade*. But it must be seen that the end of such a masquerade is to say nothing. Absolutely *nothing*. And in order to produce this nothing a woman uses her own body to disguise herself."

46. Joan Riviere, "Womanliness as a Masquerade," *Psychoanalysis and Female Sexuality*, ed. Hendrik M. Ruitenbeek (New Haven, Conn.: College and University Press Services, 1966), p. 213.

47. Doane, "Film and the Masquerade," pp. 81–82.

48. Bovenschen, "Is There a Feminine Aesthetic?," p. 129.

49. Ibid., pp. 128–29.

50. Doane, "Film and the Masquerade," p. 82.

51. In *The Devil Is a Woman*, Concha Perez comes nearest to the stereotypical femme fatale. Even if she is not given moral justification for her actions, Don Pasquale's masochism is so outrageously provocative that one cannot blame her for exploiting him. Many writers have observed that von Sternberg's films do not present Dietrich as an unvarying femme fatale. Nevertheless, the critical "myth" of her image is often sustained in casual references. For an example, see Christine Gledhill, "Klute 1: A Contemporary Film Noir and Feminist Criticism," *Women in Film Noir*, ed. E. Ann Kaplan (London: British Film Institute, 1980), p. 18.

52. Freud maintained that women were more bisexual than men, in "Femininity" (1933), *SE* 22:113. Doane qualifies this by stating that women only seem more bisexual than men, in "Film and the Masquerade," p. 81. Female identity formation is discussed by Greenson, pp. 370–71; and Person, p. 619.

53. Doane makes a similar observation in "Film and the Masquerade," p. 83.

54. John Berger, *Ways of Seeing* (London: Penquin Books, 1972), p. 46. Berger states: ". . . a woman must continually watch herself. She has to survey everything she is and everything she does because how she appears to others and ultimately how she appears to men, is of crucial importance for what is normally thought of as the success in her life. . . . how a woman appears to a man can determine how she will be treated. Consequently, to acquire some control over this process, a woman must contain it and interiorize it."

55. Bovenschen, "Is There a Feminine Aesthetic?," pp. 129–30.

56. Foucault, p. 45.

57. Freud, quoted in Klein, *The Feminine Character*, p. 86.

58. Kubie, pp. 251–52.

59. Mulvey, "Visual Pleasure and Narrative Cinema," p. 13.

60. Smirnoff, p. 669.

61. Deleuze, pp. 58–59. Deleuze explains that the transfer of all maternal functions onto one figure throws paternal functions onto the tripartite figure as well. This is one way masochism cancels out the father (pp. 54–55).

62. Ibid., p. 47.

63. Frederich Schiller, *Schiller Works*, trans., 7 vols. (London: G. Bell, 1887–1903), 5:89.

64. Alex Blumstein, "Masochism and Fantasies of Preparing to Be Incorporated," *Journal of the American Psychoanalytic Association* 7 (1959): 296.

65. Dietrich is not punished for her sexual "misconduct" at the end of *Blonde Venus;* von Sternberg fought Paramount to prevent a punitive ending. Bill Nichols also claims that von Sternberg wanted to end the film at the conclusion of Helen's meeting with Nick in Paris. *Ideology and the Image,* p. 132.

66. Deleuze is contradictory on this point and ambiguous as to what constitutes "phallic integrity" if castration is not an obstacle but is symbolically necessary to achieving the masochistic goal of symbiotic refusion (pp. 58–59).

67. Ibid., p. 42.

68. Freud, "Three Essays on the Theory of Sexuality," p. 191.

69. Jane Gallop, *Intersections: A Reading of Sade* (Lincoln: University of Nebraska Press, 1981), p. 82.

70. Ibid.

71. Carole Zucker compares Dietrich's presentation in the von Sternberg films with paintings of the Madonna from the Middle Ages. On the basis of superficial similarities in style (i.e., backlighting) and from their respective lack of emotion, she concludes that Dietrich is linked to these earlier depictions. Her analysis is interesting, but the characteristics she considers are much too broadly drawn. Zucker, "Some Observations on Sternberg and Dietrich," *Cinema Journal* 19 (Spring 1980): 21. The paradox of von Sternberg's presentation of Dietrich is that of the "holy harlot," the Magdalen (which also plays on Dietrich's given name, Maria Magdalene). Dietrich does become an object of worship, as Zucker maintains, but it is a masochistic worship that displays all the ambivalence of the idealization of the cold oral mother. For a discussion of representations of the Magdalen, see Marjorie M. Malvern, *Venus in Sackcloth: The Magdalen's Origins and Metamorphosis* (Carbondale: Southern Illinois University Press, 1975).

72. Deleuze, p. 49.

73. Nichols, *Ideology and the Image*, pp. 116–18; Zucker, p. 20. Zucker claims that Dietrich's "physiognomy is deprived of human characteristics . . . her sexuality neutralized . . . her morality impossibly exalted" (p. 21). Dietrich is idealized in these films, but she can hardly be accused of having her sexuality neutralized. However, her sexuality does conform to the masochistic ideal of sensual coldness.

74. Deleuze, p. 56.

75. Wood, p. 62.

76. Raymond Durgnat, "Six Films of Josef von Sternberg," *Movie* 13 (Summer 1965): 29–30.

77. Deleuze, p. 38.

78. Carter, *Sadeian Woman*, p. 108. Carter says the mother is considered

fatal because she represents the powerful fantasy of the oral mother, the site of the womb, "the First and Last Place, Earth, the greatest mother of them all, from whom we come, and to whom we go." For a similar description of this archetypal figure of female representation see Freud, "The Theme of the Three Caskets" (1913), *SE* 12:299.

79. Denis De Rougemont, *Love in the Western World*, trans. Montgomery Belgion, new and augmented ed. (New York: Pantheon Books, 1956), pp. 22–23.

80. Blumstein, p. 296.

Chapter Four: Iconicity and the Masochistic Heterocosm

1. Peter Wollen, *Signs and Meaning in the Cinema* (Bloomington: Indiana University Press, 1969), pp. 136–40. In *The Subject of Semiotics*, Silverman comments that Wollen's book "makes some very suggestive remarks about particular examples of iconicity and indexicality, but the topic has not been widely pursued by other film theoreticians." Silverman finds the neglect of Peircean semiotics "surprising" because the Peircean emphasis on the icon "would seem to have special pertinence to the analysis of cinematic signification" (p. 24).

2. Wollen, pp. 136–37.

3. Ibid., p. 139. Wollen states: "Semiologists have been surprisingly silent on the subject of iconic signs. They suffer from two prejudices: firstly, in favour of the arbitrary and the symbolic, secondly in favour of the spoken and the acoustic. Both these prejudices are to be found in the work of Saussure, to whom language was a symbolic system which operated in one privileged sensory band." Umberto Eco critiques what he regards as "naive notions" of iconicity in *A Theory of Semiotics* (Bloomington: Indiana University Press, 1979), pp. 192–217.

4. Wollen, pp. 149–53.

5. Charles S. Peirce, *Collected Papers of C. S. Peirce*, 8 vols., ed. Charles Hartshorne and Paul Weiss (vols. 1–6, 1931–38), A. W. Burks (vols. 7–8, 1958) (Cambridge: Harvard University Press, 1931–58), 2:228 (hereafter cited as *CP*).

6. Ibid., 2:276.

7. Ibid.

8. Ibid., 1:23–25.

9. Ibid., 1:123.

10. Ibid., 2:322.

11. Ibid., 2:281. Peirce acknowledged the conventional aspects of the iconic sign, noting that the image "is largely conventional in its mode of representation," and he remarked on the existence of "icons in which the likeness is aided by conventional rules" (2:279). For a discussion of Peirce's view of iconic signs see Eco, pp. 192–200. See Thomas A. Sebeok, "Iconicity," *Modern Language Notes* 91 (1971): 1435–36, for a discussion of Peirce's and Eco's views on the cultural codings of signs. For yet another

viewpoint on iconic signs and culture see Hubert Damish, "Semiotics and Iconography," in *The Tell-Tale Sign*, ed. Thomas A. Sebeok (Lisse, Netherlands: Peter de Ridder Press, 1975), p. 30.

12. Charles Morris, *Writings on the General Theory of Signs* (The Hague: Mouton, 1971), p. 273.

13. Alan Williams, "Circles of Desire: Narration and Repetition in *La Ronde*," *Film Quarterly* 27 (1971): 40–41; Wollen, pp. 138–39.

14. *CP* 7:445–46.

15. Ibid., 2:278.

16. Teresa DeLauretis's reliance on Peirce in *Alice Doesn't* (Bloomington: Indiana University Press, 1984), is mediated through the semiotics of Eco. DeLauretis persuasively argues for a semiosis that will articulate the female as a subject within a self-analyzing critical practice addressing the reality of women's social experience.

17. André Bazin, *What Is Cinema?*, trans. Hugh Gray, 2 vols. (Berkeley: University of California Press, 1967), 1:13.

18. Ibid., 1:15.

19. Ibid., 1:39; see also pp. 25–26, 46–47. Bazin passionately rebuked montage: "Montage, which we are constantly being told is the essence of cinema . . . is the literary and anticinematic process *par excellence*. Essential cinema, seen for once in its pure state, on the contrary, is to be found in straightforward photographic respect for the unity of space" (p. 46).

20. Ibid., 1:29.

21. Ibid., 1:35–36. Bazin appeared to equate the ambiguity of deep focus with the spectator's freedom to explore the framed image, but he also ignores the filmmaker's control of the spectatorial gaze through lighting, composition, and the flow of the mise-en-scène. It might be argued that Welles's *Citizen Kane*, elevated by Bazin as a milestone in restoring ambiguity to film, ultimately manipulates the audience as thoroughly as does montage cinema. Certainly it is no less concerned with artistic control.

22. Ibid., 1:47.

23. Sergei Eisenstein, "The Cinematographic Principle and the Ideogram," in *Film Form*, trans. Jay Leyda (New York: Meridian Books, 1957), p. 242. Eisenstein maintained that only the artist's perception of reality and the urge to manipulate observed events in changing them into art was natural.

24. Ibid., p. 239. Like Bazin, Eisenstein's aesthetic discounted certain film styles as unacceptable. In Eisenstein's view, American filmmaking employed montage in a technically proficient manner, but mere comparison of images was ideologically insufficient. What was required was a qualitative leap: "The leap proved beyond the *limits of the possibilities* of the stage—a leap beyond the *limits* of situation: a leap into the field of montage *image*, montage *understanding*, montage as a means before all else of revealing the *ideological conception*" (p. 239).

25. Sergei Eisenstein, "A Dialectical Approach to Film Form," in Leyda (ed.),

p. 60; Eisenstein, "Dickens, Griffith, and the Film Today," in Leyda (ed.), p. 251.

26. Von Sternberg, pp. 315–16, 318.
27. Bogdanovich, p. 23.
28. Wood, pp. 58–63. For a different opinion consult Kaplan, *Women and Film*, pp. 49–60.
29. Von Sternberg, p. 314.
30. Deleuze, p. 29.
31. Ibid., p. 61.
32. Lewis Jacobs, *The Rise of the American Film: A Critical History* (New York: Teachers College Press, 1968), p. 468.
33. Deleuze, p. 33.
34. Von Sternberg, p. 321.
35. Deleuze, p. 33.
36. Harry Berger, Jr., "Conspicuous Exclusion in Vermeer: An Essay in Renaissance Pastoral," *Yale French Studies* 47 (1971): 262.
37. Quoted in Kevin Brownlow, *The Parade's Gone By* (Berkeley: University of California Press, 1968), p. 202.
38. Recently, Raymond Durgnat voiced an opinion that in some ways resembles mine. He referred to illusionism as a demonstration of virtuosity that is "almost always used for purposes of self-reflexivity (as is the conjuring trick) and formalism." Durgnat, "Mind's Eye, Eye's Mind: Transformation by Context," *Quarterly Review of Film Studies* 9 (Spring 1984): 89–100. The political inferences of certain types of reflexivity are examined by Dana Polan in "A Brechtian Cinema? Towards a Politics of Self-Reflexive Film," in *Movies and Methods II*, ed. Bill Nichols (Berkeley: University of California Press, 1985), pp. 661–72.
39. H. Berger, p. 261.
40. Sarris, *The Films of Josef von Sternberg*, pp. 29–30.
41. Deleuze, pp. 109–10.
42. H. Berger, p. 262.
43. Smirnoff, p. 668.
44. Von Sternberg's ill-fated production of *I, Claudius* for Alexander Korda almost allowed the director to bring his conceptualization of the original Messalina to the screen. Surviving footage from the film was featured in the BBC documentary *The Epic That Never Was*.
45. Quoted in Sarris, *The Films of Josef von Sternberg*, p. 30.
46. Sarris speculates on the influence of censorship on von Sternberg's films. This leads him to a curious value judgment: "Sternberg seems to have been driven, perhaps partly by the censors, to retreat into the exotic past. Up to now, Sternberg has confined himself for the most part into a world encompassed within his own lifetime, and there is something to be said for an artist who imposes his personal vision on the present. Though Sternberg continues to comment on the present in *The Scarlet Empress*, his meaning is somewhat obscured by the massive detail of period recreation" (ibid., p. 39).

47. Mario Praz, *The Romantic Agony*, trans. Angus Davidson, 3d ed. (London: Oxford University Press, 1956), p. 197.
48. Nichols, *Ideology and the Image*, p. 125.
49. Bateson, pp. 180, 182.
50. Ibid., pp. 189–90.
51. Reik, p. 310; see also Deleuze, pp. 145, 163.
52. Ibid., p. 313.
53. H. Berger, p. 262. Berger writes: ". . . the imaginary world is tonally presented in an attitude of serious playing; *sèrio ludere* meaning playing seriously with full knowledge, however seriously you play, that you are only playing. It is 'only a game,' but a game which (like all games) is to be played or taken with dead seriousness while it is going on."
54. Von Sternberg, p. 265.
55. Quoted in Michael O'Pray, "On Adrian Stokes and Film Aesthetics," *Screen* 21 (Winter 1980/81): 93.
56. Peirce, *CP* 4:531.
57. Nichols, *Ideology and the Image*, pp. 125–26.
58. Ibid., p. 111.
59. See Morris Weitz, *The Opening Mind* (Chicago: University of Chicago Press, 1977).
60. Jurij Lotman, *Semiotics of Cinema*, trans. Mark E. Suino (Ann Arbor: University of Michigan Press, 1976), p. 4.
61. Leopold von Sacher-Masoch, "The Adventure of Ludwig II, Appendix III," in Deleuze, p. 238.
62. A. Williams, p. 40.
63. Zucker, p. 17.
64. Freud, "The Unconscious" (1915), *SE* 14:187. Condensation refers to the unification of elements into a collective figure. Displacement is a process by which charged material (latent meaning) is transferred to some other aspect of the dream that is superficially unimportant (not laden with psychic intensity). Concrete representation ensures the presentation of ideas through "immediately intelligible" forms. See Freud, "On Dreams" (1901), *SE* 5:683. The thought achieves a concrete being through dream figuration. Overdetermination presupposes multiple sources that account for the dream thought's meaning. Symbolization in dreams was "a characteristic of the unconscious thinking which provides the dream-work with the material for condensation, displacement and dramatization" (ibid., p. 685). Freud also discussed identification in dreamwork as a process of unification in which persons "linked by a common element" are represented in the dream by one, "while the second or remaining persons seem to be suppressed. . . ." Freud, "The Interpretation of Dreams" (1900), *SE* 4/5:320.
65. Victor Burgin, "Photography, Fantasy, Fiction," *Screen* 21 (Spring 1980): 60.
66. Silverman, *The Subject of Semiotics*, p. 55.
67. J. Allan Hobson, "Dreaming Sleep: The Brain as Camera-Projector,"

Dreamworks 1 (Spring 1980): 86. See also Marsha Kinder, "Narrative," *Dreamworks* 2 (Spring 1982): 216–25.

68. For an example of this kind of division see Peter Baxter, "On the Naked Thighs of Miss Dietrich," *Wide Angle* 2 (1978): 18–25.

69. Gaston Bachelard, *The Psychoanalysis of Fire*, trans. Alan C. M. Ross (Boston: Beacon Press, 1964), p. 49.

70. Nichols expresses a somewhat similar view in *Ideology and the Image*, p. 101.

71. Bateson, pp. 137–38.

72. Metz, pp. 229–30.

73. Ibid., p. 124.

74. Ibid., pp. 229–30. In *Ideology and the Image,* Nichols wisely suggests that film's similarities to dreamwork constitute stylistic resemblances that are not well explained by reliance on a linguistic model.

75. Jonathan Culler, *Structuralist Poetics* (London: Routledge & Kegan Paul, 1973), pp. 16–17.

76. Silverman lucidly explains the Lacanian view of subject formation in *The Subject of Semiotics,* pp. 126–93.

77. Mardi Jon Horowitz, *Image Formation and Cognition*, 2d ed. (New York: Appleton-Century-Crofts, 1978), p. 78; M. Vernon, *The Psychology of Perception* (Boston: Penquin Books, 1962); Heinz Werner, *Comparative Psychology of Mental Development* (New York: International Universities Press, 1957); N. Lukianowicz, "Visual Thinking and Similar Phenomena," *Journal of Mental Science* 106 (1960): 979–1002; Ralph Berger, *Psyclosis: The Circularity of Experience* (San Francisco: W. H. Freeman, 1977).

78. Decio Pignatari, "The Contiguity Illusion," in *Sight, Sound, and Sense,* ed. Thomas A. Sebeok (Bloomington: Indiana University Press, 1978), p. 94.

79. Freud, "The Ego and the Id" (1923), *SE* 19:21.

80. M. Vernon, "Relationship of Language to the Thinking Process," *Archives of General Psychiatry* 16 (1969): 225.

81. Pignatari, p. 90.

82. Bateson, pp. 139–40.

83. Freud, "The Unconscious," pp. 190–91. See also Meredith Anne Skura, *The Literary Use of the Psychoanalytic Process* (New Haven: Yale University Press, 1981), p. 10.

84. Pignatari, pp. 88–89.

85. Ibid., pp. 93–94.

86. Sarris, *The Films of Josef von Sternberg,* p. 35; Zucker, p. 19.

87. Metz, p. 18.

88. Ibid., p. 230; Lacan, *Écrits,* p. 163.

89. Peirce, *CP* 4:242.

90. John K. Sheriff, "Charles S. Peirce and the Semiotics of Literature," in *Semiotic Themes,* ed. Richard T. De George (Lawrence: University of Kansas, 1981), p. 68.

91. For a discussion of Roland Barthes's view on the "process of nomination" that eliminates the possibility of transverbal interpretants see Seymour Chatman, *Story and Discourse: Narrative Structures in Fiction and Film* (Ithaca: Cornell University Press, 1978), p. 111. However, Barthes appears to embrace the idea that there are meanings evoked by film that are beyond the grip of a verbal signified; see Barthes, "The Third Meaning," *Artforum* 16 (January 1973): 46–50.
92. Eugene Ferguson, "The Mind's Eye," *Science* 197 (1977): 827–36; Robert Ornstein, *The Psychology of Consciousness* (San Francisco: W. H. Freeman, 1972); Horowitz, *Image Formation and Cognition*.
93. Horowitz, p. 78. See also Peirce, *CP* 2:276–79, 2:302.
94. Peirce, *CP* 1:23.
95. Ibid., 7:364; see also 1:306.
96. Ibid., 1:377.
97. Pignatari, p. 88.
98. Ibid., pp. 88–89.

Chapter Five: Stories of Suffering, Paradoxes of Fixation

1. Deleuze, p. 112.
2. Barthes, *The Pleasure of the Text,* p. 10: "The pleasure of the text is not the pleasure of the corporeal striptease or of narrative suspense. In these cases, there is no tear, no edges: a gradual unveiling: the entire excitation takes refuge in the *hope* of seeing the sexual organ (schoolboy's dream) or in knowing the end of the story (novelistic satisfaction). Paradoxically (since it is mass-consumed), this is a far more intellectual pleasure than the other: an Oedipal pleasure (to denude, to know, to learn the origin and the end), if it is true that every narrative (every unveiling of the truth) is a staging of the (absent, hidden, or hypostatized) father—which would explain the solidarity of narrative forms, of family structures, and of prohibitions of nudity, all collected in our culture in the myth of Noah's son covering his nakedness." Raymond Bellour, in particular, has been associated with the theoretical view that Oedipalizes all of classical narrative cinema, often in a very programmatic fashion. See his analysis of *North by Northwest* in "Le blocage symbolique," *Communications* 23 (1978): 235–50.
3. Mulvey, "Visual Pleasure and Narrative Cinema," p. 14.
4. DeLauretis, p. 109.
5. Ibid., p. 134.
6. Rapaport, "Psychoanalysis as a Developmental Psychology," pp. 209–253; Wolff, "Cognitive Considerations," p. 310.
7. Naomi Schor offers an interesting discussion of the role of detail in the so-called decadent literary text, in "Details and Decadence: End-Troping in *Madame Bovary*," *Sub-stance* 26 (1980): 27–35.
8. Griffith, pp. 8–9.
9. Brownlow, p. 194.

10. Nichols, *Ideology and the Image*, p. 110.
11. Ibid., p. 115. Nichols attributes this disinterest in narrative to von Sternberg's greater interest in eroticism.
12. Robin Wood, "The Play of Light and Shade," *Personal Views* (London: Gordon Fraser, 1976), p. 98.
13. Brownlow, p. 194.
14. Von Sternberg, p. 301.
15. Wood, "The Play of Light and Shade," p. 98.
16. Von Sternberg, p. 295.
17. Deleuze, p. 33.
18. Nichols, *Ideology and the Image*, p. 112.
19. Deleuze, p. 58.
20. Patricia Mellencamp, "Spectacle and Spectator: Looking through the American Musical Comedy," *Cine-Tracts* 1 (Summer 1977): 29.
21. Freud, *Beyond the Pleasure Principle*, p. 14.
22. Mellencamp, "Spectacle and Spectator," pp. 28–29.
23. Ibid.
24. Kaplan, *Women and Film*, p. 56.
25. Ibid., p. 56.
26. Patricia Mellencamp, "Made in the Fade," *Cine-Tracts* 3 (Winter 1981): 13.
27. Mulvey, "Visual Pleasure and Narrative Cinema," pp. 11, 14.
28. Mellencamp, "Made in the Fade," p. 13.
29. Wood, "Venus de Marlene," p. 63. Wood examines the ambivalence of the ending of *The Scarlet Empress* in "The Play of Light and Shade," pp. 112–13. See also Durgnat, "Six Films of Josef von Sternberg," pp. 26–31.
30. Mellencamp, "Spectacle and Spectator," p. 28.
31. Mircea Eliade, *Myth and Reality*, trans. Willard Trask (New York: Harper & Row, 1963), p. 102.
32. Reik, p. 323.
33. Deleuze, pp. 23–24.
34. Linda Williams interprets the interchangeability of the two women portraying Concha in *That Obscure Object of Desire* (Luis Bunuel's version of *Woman and Puppet*) as a projection of the subject's divided self and the structural oppositions inherent in desire. Yet the doubling might also demonstrate the female's masquerade of identity in a protective iconic strategy against male desire. Williams, *Figures of Desire* (Urbana: University of Illinois Press, 1981), pp. 198–205.
35. Reik, pp. 421–22.
36. The contractual nature of the masochistic alliance functions as an indicator of the paradoxical male position in Sacher-Masoch's novels. In von Sternberg's films, the contract appears in Don Pasquale's obsessive attempt to buy Concha's agreement with the cabaret *(The Devil Is a Woman)* and also in Nick Townsend's effort to end Helen's nightclub stint *(Blonde Venus)*.

37. Sacher-Masoch, *Venus in Furs*, p. 135.

38. Durgnat, "Six Films of Josef von Sternberg," p. 31.

39. Brownlow, p. 203. Brownlow quotes von Sternberg: "Everyone in my films is like me . . . spiritually." See also Sarris, *The Films of Josef von Sternberg*, p. 54.

40. Rene Girard, *Deceit, Desire, and the Novel: Self and Other in Literary Structure*, trans. Yvonne Freccero (Baltimore: Johns Hopkins University Press, 1965), p. 15.

41. Reik, p. 304. Reik notes that the masochist can always rationalize suffering as the result of external events rather than as self-generated occurrences.

42. Sarris, *The Films of Josef von Sternberg*, p. 23.

43. Deleuze, pp. 62–63.

44. It might be argued that the dream sequence in *The Scarlet Empress* is typical of Slavko Vorkapitch–style Hollywood montage sequences, but the formal characteristics of the sequence, such as the spatial wipes, and other visual motifs are uncannily repeated later in the film.

45. Sacher-Masoch, *The Aesthetics of Ugliness*, quoted in Deleuze, p. 45.

46. Sacher-Masoch, *Venus in Furs*, pp. 153, 151.

47. Deleuze, pp. 50–51.

48. Freud, "The Theme of the Three Caskets," p. 299. "Choice stands in the place of necessity, of destiny. In this way man overcomes death. . . . No greater triumph of wishfulfillment is conceivable. A choice is made where in reality there is obedience to a compulsion."

49. Laplanche, p. 107.

50. Barthes, *The Pleasure of the Text*, pp. 47–48.

51. Smirnoff, p. 668.

52. Bersani, *A Future for Astyanax*, p. 160.

53. Deleuze, p. 31.

54. Ibid.

55. Silverman discusses the *fort/da* game as a ritual of loss rather than mastery (as Freud theorized), in "Masochism and Subjectivity" (p. 2). One might also read *fort/da* as a demonstration of the symbolic transitional object which registers ambivalence toward the mother's mobility. The game signifies her absence as a painful experience, but it also suggests the possibility of freedom (into individuation). The *fort/da* game is approached by Peter Brooks in "Freud's Masterplot," *Yale French Studies*, nos. 55–56 (1977): 280–99. According to Brooks, the game's compulsion to repeat overrides the pleasure principle and suspends temporal progress. Consequently, he concludes, Freud's "masterplot" reveals the operation of the death instinct in the text.

56. Sade, *Juliette*, quoted in Deleuze, p. 61.

57. Deleuze, p. 31.

58. Ibid.

59. *Blonde Venus*, script, n.d., Script Collection, Theatre Arts Library, Uni-

versity of California, Los Angeles, California. This undated script accounts for many of the film's events through a much more conventional strategy than the final film: Helen never hits bottom; Nick has her followed and anonymously assisted as she flees from Ned; and in the final scene, Nick and Helen take Johnny away from Ned, who has compromised his custody of the boy by his relationship with his maid. In *Ideology and the Image,* Nichols stated that von Sternberg wished to end the film with the backstage Paris scene (p. 132). Although the absence of a transition between the Paris scene/New York reunion might be used as the perfect example of lack of cause/effect structuring by von Sternberg, the obvious practical difficulties in assigning "authorial" control over the film's ending, disputed by Paramount and von Sternberg, make such a judgment unwise.

60. Maurice Merleau-Ponty, *The Primacy of Perception* (Evanston: Northwestern University Press, 1964), p. 420.

61. Ornstein, *The Psychology of Consciousness,* pp. 76–79; Bateson; Lawrence Marks, *The Unity of the Senses* (New York: Academic Press, 1978).

62. Jacqueline Rose, "Paranoia and the Film System" *Screen* 17 (Winter 1976/77): 102.

63. Tania Modleski, "Time and Desire in the Woman's Film," *Cinema Journal* 23 (Spring 1984): 23–24. Modleski writes: "Unlike most Hollywood narratives, which give the impression of a progressive movement toward an end that is significantly different from the beginning, much melodrama gives the impression of a ceaseless returning to a prior state" (p. 24). The link between masochism and melodrama is one that deserves further attention at all levels of textual and spectatorial analysis. Deleuze explains masochistic time as a temporality in which there are two streams of time, one that focuses on suspense and the other on expectation (p. 63).

64. Wood takes exception to Mulvey regarding this issue in reference to *Blonde Venus.* It is true, as he asserts, that the division Mulvey sets up between the narrative being propelled by the male and a female-centered visual pleasure "simply won't do for Sternberg" because Dietrich initiates narrative action. But it is also true (as Mulvey maintains) that Dietrich is the centerpoint of the film's erotic vision. See Wood, "Venus de Marlene," p. 63; see also Mulvey, "Visual Pleasure and Narrative Cinema," pp. 14–15.

65. "Morocco," in Baxter (ed.), p. 86.

66. Jean Rousset, "Madame Bovary ou le livre sur rien," *Forme et Signification* (Paris: J. Copin, 1962), p. 133, quoted in Girard Genette, *Figures of Literary Discourse,* trans. Alan Sheridan (New York: Columbia University Press, 1981), p. 123.

67. Rosamund Tuve, *Allegorical Imagery* (Princeton: Princeton University Press, 1966), p. 364.

68. Barthes, "The Third Meaning," pp. 46–47, 50.

69. Ibid., p. 50.
70. Lea Jacobs and Richard de Cordova, "Spectacle and Narrative Theory," *Quarterly Review of Film Studies* 7 (Fall 1982): 295.
71. Christian Metz, *Film Language*, trans. Michael Taylor (New York: Oxford University Press, 1974), p. 46.
72. Raymond Durgnat, "Film Theory: From Narrative to Description," *Quarterly Review of Film Studies* 7 (Spring 1982): 122.
73. Durgnat comments: "Almost every detail in the shot must be omitted from such 'telescopic' synopses. The result must be to make a shot look more like a broadly stated event than a description—i.e., to retain the narrative function and dispense with the rest. No doubt every shot includes a certain amount of roughage—circumstantial detail which isn't read. . . . But many details are very relevant to the narrative, and indeed part of it" (ibid., p. 113). Pignatari argues that a *narrative syntagm* is not "a common syntagm at all, but rather a paradigm, an icon—or at least, a paradigmatic syntagm." According to Pignatari, a plot should not really be considered a concept, but a nonverbal model, "an icon . . . of life." Pignatari, pp. 86–88.
74. V. F. Perkins, *Film as Film* (Harmondsworth, England: Penguin Books, 1972), p. 23.
75. Roman Jakobson, "Closing Statement: Linguistics and Poetics," *Style in Language*, ed. Thomas A. Sebeok (Cambridge: M.I.T. Press, 1960), p. 358.
76. Roland Barthes, *A Lover's Discourse: Fragments*, trans. Richard Howard (New York: Hill and Wang, 1978), p. 243. Betty R. McGraw suggests that Barthes's comment refers to the primal scene, in "Semiotics, Erotographics and Barthes's Visual Concerns," *Sub-Stance* 26 (1980): 71.
77. Mulvey, "Visual Pleasure and Narrative Cinema," pp. 11–12.
78. Nichols, *Ideology and the Image*, p. 112.
79. Louis Audibert, "The Flash of the Look," in Baxter (ed.), p. 100.
80. Laplanche, p. 102.
81. Jonathan Culler, *Flaubert: The Uses of Uncertainty* (Ithaca: Cornell University Press, 1974) p. 231.
82. Jacobs and Cordova, pp. 295–96.
83. Deleuze, p. 33. In *The Pleasure of the Text*, Barthes says that "the word can be erotic" if it is "extravagantly repeated" (p. 42).

Chapter Six: Mechanisms of Masochistic Narrativity

1. Jean Mitry, *Esthétique et psychologie du cinéma*, 2 vols. (Paris: Editions Universitaires, 1963), 1:120–22. See Dudley Andrew's discussion of Mitry in *The Major Film Theories: An Introduction* (New York: Oxford University Press, 1976), pp. 185–211. See also Marie-Claire Ropars, "The Function of Metaphor in Eisenstein's *October*," *Film Criticism* 2 (Winter–Spring 1978): 10–34; Metz, "Metaphor/Metonymy, or the Imaginary Referent" *The Imaginary Signifier*, pp. 149–298; and Williams, *Figures of Desire*.

2. Williams, *Figures of Desire,* p. 59.
3. Zucker, p. 18.
4. Ibid.
5. Marks, p. 222.
6. Williams, *Figures of Desire,* pp. 70, 72.
7. Metz, *The Imaginary Signifier,* pp. 184–85.
8. Williams, *Figures of Desire,* p. 72.
9. Ibid., p. 71.
10. Paul Ricoeur, "Metaphor and the Main Problem of Hermeneutics," *New Literary History* 6 (1974): 109–10.
11. Marks, p. 98.
12. Ibid., p. 253.
13. Jean Piaget, *Plays, Dreams, and Imitation in Childhood* (New York: W. W. Norton, 1951). See also Wolff, pp. 300–43; H. Werner and B. Kaplan, *Symbol Formation* (New York: Wiley, 1963). Wolff interprets and expands Piaget's developmental analysis of language acquisition. Of particular importance is the child's initial use of language without the recognition of discrete classes of objects.
14. Wolff, pp. 342–43.
15. Marks, pp. 102, 254.
16. Sarris, *The Films of Josef von Sternberg,* pp. 23, 25.
17. Marks, p. 103: "Metaphoric expressions of the unity of the senses evolved in art from fundamental synesthetic relationships, but owe their creative impulse to the mind's ability to transcend these intrinsic correspondences and force new multi-sensory meanings."
18. Zucker remarks: "The literature concerning the films of Josef von Sternberg invariably contains the word 'mysterious.' The task of a further discussion of Sternberg is not an attempt to answer or resolve the mystery nor to search for a key to a system of codes that will unlock the films. In Sternberg's films the mysteriousness is an absolute, unsusceptible to clarification and thus, destruction" (p. 17).
19. Max Black, cited in Andrew Ortony, "Beyond Literal Similarity," *Psychological Review* 86 (May 1979): 177.
20. Peirce, *CP* 2:277.
21. Pignatari, p. 93.
22. Ibid. Pignatari refers to paronomasia as iconic likeness in language. Onomatopoeia is the most obvious form of iconicizing the signifier. Sound paramorphism (paronomasia) also occurs in the form of alliteration, colliteration, rhyme, and rhythm, which push symbolic language toward primary process.
23. Peirce, *CP* 2:277.
24. Marks, p. 254.
25. Mitry argues that there are no pure metaphors, that the cinema does not have an equivalent to literary metaphor since cinematic metaphors must be created through juxtaposition rather than by substitution (1:120–22). Williams discusses Mitry and cinematic metaphors in *Figures of Desire,*

p. 50. A primary source from which to begin a discussion of metaphor and film is Roman Jakobson, "The Metaphoric and Metonymic Poles," *Fundamentals of Language,* 2d ed., rev. (The Hague: Mouton, 1971), pp. 90–96.

26. Sarris, *The Films of Josef von Sternberg,* p. 18.

27. Genette, *Figures of Literary Discourse,* p. 204.

28. Allan Paivio, "Imagery and Synchronic Thinking," *Canadian Psychological Review* 16 (1975): 147–63; Durgnat, "Film Theory: From Narrative to Description," pp. 110–11.

29. Paivio, pp. 149, 12.

30. Ibid., p. 161.

31. Ernst Kris, *Psychoanalytic Explorations in Art* (New York: International Universities Press, 1952), p. 258. Merton Gill suggests that primary process mechanisms are not the product of censorship but of a paradoxical imposition *and* release of censorship. Gill, "The Primary Process," in *Motives and Thought,* pp. 285–87.

32. Jean-François Lyotard, "The Unconscious as Mise-en-scène," in *Performance in Postmodern Culture,* ed. Michel Benamour and Charles Caramello (Milwaukee: University of Wisconsin Press, 1977), p. 94. Bateson considers metaphor to be the essence of primary process (*Steps to an Ecology of Mind,* p. 139).

33. Metz, pp. 193–94.

34. Ibid., pp. 77–78.

35. Durgnat, "Six Films of Josef von Sternberg," p. 30; Wood, "The Play of Light and Shade," p. 101.

36. Durgnat, p. 30.

37. Wood, p. 101.

38. Kris, p. 247. Irony is a crucial element of von Sternberg's films and has been neglected as an area of inquiry in his films (and film in general). Dudley Andrew has suggested that irony functions to shock the audience out of the filmic illusion. This certainly seems to hold true of *The Scarlet Empress.* See Andrew, *Concepts in Film Theory* (New York: Oxford University Press, 1984), p. 151.

39. Kris, p. 258.

40. Ibid., p. 250.

41. From the viewpoint of Freudian psychology, Damish remarks on the transverbal nature of dream imagery: ". . . Freud's notion of regression also registers the questions of the relation between visual and verbalized thought within the dependence of desire: the (dream) image is not the mirrored double, the perceptible manifestation of thought as constituted in the element of language; it is both the locus and the product of an activity which allows impulses originating in the unconscious, and which have been refused all possibility of verbalization, to find expression through figurative means and to move at ease (in Freud's terms) on a stage *other* than that of language" (pp. 34–35).

42. Kristeva, quoted in Jenny Laurent, "The Strategy of Form," in *French Literary Theory Today*, ed. Tzvetan Todorov (Cambridge: Harvard University Press, 1982), p. 39.

43. Erwin Panofsky, *Studies in Iconography* (New York: Harper & Row, 1939), p. 3.

44. Culler, *Structuralist Poetics*, pp. 388–89.

45. Theodore Thass-Thienemann, *Symbolic Behavior* (New York: Washington Square Press, 1968), pp. 16–17.

46. Carl Jung, "Symbols of Transformation," in *The Collected Works of C. G. Jung*, trans. R. F. C. Hull, 17 vols. (Princeton: Princeton University Press), 5:140.

47. William Luhr and Peter Lehman, "'Crazy World Full of Crazy Contradictions': Blake Edwards' *Victor/Victoria*," *Wide Angle* 5 (1983): 11–12. The von Sternberg system counters the classical norm Luhr and Lehman describe: "The classical Hollywood style constructs sexual difference through strict codes of camera positioning, cutting, lighting, casting, costuming, etc. A stable, predictable sexual surface is always maintained and desire is never misplaced. There is nothing natural in the codes that guarantee this; to the contrary, they constitute a strict system which prevents the ideologically undesirable from occurring" (p. 13).

48. Wood, "Venus de Marlene," p. 62.

49. Bateson, pp. 140–41.

50. Burgin, p. 66.

51. Thass-Thienemann, p. 55.

52. The presence of puppets, mechanical carousels, and dolls are found in all the films and are often associated with the male, as in *Dishonored* (the head of the Secret Service) and *The Scarlet Empress* (the Grand Duke). The male, like the puppet, does not master but is mastered; his actions are controlled.

53. Deleuze, p. 62.

54. Sacher-Masoch, *Venus in Furs*, p. 144. Smirnoff comments on the relationship of masochism to martyrdom: "As the writings and the iconography concerning martyrdom so clearly show, there is always a basic component of ecstasy: the mystical trance, the tortured and languid body exposed to blows, the exquisite agonies, the often orgasmic quality of posture and facial expression. And those same elements are to be encountered in all erotic literature and pictorial representations of masochism" (p. 667). In light of these remarks, masochism can be said to provide an alternative to Stephen Heath's discussion of sexual difference and Lacan's concept of *jouissance*. Lacan's remarks on Bernini's statue of St. Teresa might usefully be read through a theory of masochism. St. Teresa's experience, which Lacan uses to illustrate the *jouissance* of woman, is less evidence of woman's pleasure than a very obvious example of masochistic pleasure. St. Teresa's own words reveal the connection: "the pain was so great that I cried out, but at the same time,

the sweetness which the violent pain gave me was so excessive that I could not wish to be rid of it." See Heath, "Difference," *Screen* 19 (1978): 50–112.

Jean-François Lyotard discusses the "power of the dependence" that Freud's patient, Schreber, sought in his delusionary role as "the prostitute of God." Lyotard, "Use Me," trans. Michel Feher and Tom Gora, *Semio-texte* 4 (1981): 82–85. See also Freud, "Psycho-Analytic Notes on an Autobiographical Account of a Case of Paranoia" (1911), *SE* 23:1–84. Lyotard compares the prostitute to the martyr because they both testify through humiliation that they want their position of extreme dependence. Similarly, Jesus' request for dependence ("Thy will be done") proves the "strength of powerlessness" (p. 83). Lyotard insists, however, that this "demand for dependence" does not entail the wish to be dominated or to participate in the "dialectic of the slave" (p. 84). Neither is he willing to associate it with a sexual politics of a sadistic or a masochistic position. Instead, he considers "use me" to be "an enunciation of vertiginous simplicity . . ." characterized by the wish, "I'll be your sacrifice and your tissues. You be my orifices, my palms and my membranes. Let's get lost and let's leave the power and the abject justifications of the redemption dialectic behind" (p. 84). Nevertheless, the fundamental masochistic wish for a symbiosis that would remove the barriers of separation/difference does resemble Lyotard's description of the desire to become the other's "sacrifice" and "tissues." While Lyotard says that the masochist wants to die by the partner's hand, Smirnoff claims that this is not the purpose behind the alliance; rather, the masochist wishes "to be branded" (Smirnoff, p. 668).

55. Deleuze, pp. 84, 163.
56. Sacher-Masoch, *Venus in Furs*, p. 145.
57. Joanna Hubbs, "The Worship of Mother Earth in Russian Culture," in *Mother Worship: Theme and Variations*, ed. James J. Preston (Chapel Hill: University of North Carolina Press, 1982), p. 131. Hubbs writes: "But that control and submission [are] rooted in the mythological structure I have been describing, that of the Mother Goddess and her son and consort, the dying god—a structure that infuses the whole culture and imposes itself on the entire course of Russian history" (p. 132).
58. Deleuze, p. 84. Deleuze also argues that "the cross represents the maternal image of death, the mirror in which the narcissistic self of Christ (Cain) apprehends his ideal self (Christ resurrected)" (p. 84).
59. Ibid., p. 62.
60. Ibid., p. 61.
61. Metz, *The Imaginary Signifier*, p. 193. In silent films dissolves were not always syntagmatically coded as punctuation marks.
62. Wood, "The Play of Light and Shade," p. 112.
63. Max Black, *Models and Metaphors: Studies in Language and Philosophy* (Ithaca: Cornell University Press, 1962), pp. 236–37.

Chapter Seven: Iconic Play and Masochistic Performance

1. Sarris, *The Films of Josef von Sternberg*, p. 19. In addition to Sarris, Zucker addresses the ambiguity of von Sternberg's characters in "Some Observations on Sternberg and Dietrich," pp. 17–24, as does Wood in "Venus de Marlene," p. 61.

2. Sebeok, "Iconicity," pp. 1439–42. See also Gregory Bateson, "Redundancy and Coding," in *Animal Communication*, ed. Thomas A. Sebeok (Bloomington: Indiana University Press, 1968), pp. 614–26.

3. Bateson, *Steps to an Ecology of the Mind*, pp. 140, 180–85. Nichols discusses paradox and filmic narrative structure in *Ideology and the Image*, pp. 93–103.

4. Bateson, *Steps to an Ecology of the Mind*, pp. 140–41.

5. Sacher-Masoch, *Venus in Furs*, p. 143.

6. Deleuze, p. 31. Lily is both "imperious and coquettish," a phrase Sacher-Masoch used to describe a female character in his novel *The Siren*.

7. Sarris, *The Films of Josef von Sternberg*, p. 35.

8. Von Sternberg, pp. 311–12.

9. Edgar Wind, *Pagan Mysteries of the Renaissance*, new and enlarged ed. (New York: Barnes & Noble, 1968) p. 204.

10. Von Sternberg, p. 323.

11. Wind, p. 165.

12. Zucker, p. 19.

13. Ibid., pp. 18–19.

14. Sacher-Masoch, p. 220.

15. Ibid., p. 223. Wanda arrives, skips "gleefully across the room," and wonders out loud if she will "still be able" to perform her task: bind Severin for whipping. Once he is tied, Wanda calls for her new lover to whip Severin, who is promptly "dephantasized": "I suddenly saw with alarming clarity how blind passion and lust have always led men, from the time of Holofernes and Agamemnon, into the net of woman's treachery, into poverty, slavery and death. It was as though I were awakening from a long dream" (p. 226).

    Concha's changes of mind in *The Devil Is a Woman* are as numerous as Wanda's. Von Sternberg wanted the film to bear the title *Capriccio Espagnol*. According to his autobiography, Paramount changed the title in hopes of boosting anticipated lackluster response to the film (p. 267). As a musical form, the capriccio is a development of the early *ricercare*, which literally means "pursuit" and is characterized by the repetition of overlapping themes. During the nineteenth century the capriccio became virtually synonymous with a musical showpiece, often a virtuosic display for violin. The musical form's illusion of caprice, of apparent improvisatory flights of fancy, actually masks a structure of unrelenting determinism—not unlike von Sternberg's films.

16. Williams, *Figures of Desire*, p. 199.

17. Marcel Oms attributes Concha's return to Don Pasquale to their inescapable shared past and "perhaps also by her remorse, certainly by gratitude in the conviction of having been made by him" (p. 72). Oms, "Josef von Sternberg," *Anthologie du Cinéma* 60, a supplement to *L'Avant-scene du Cinéma*, no. 109 (December 1970), rpt. in Baxter (ed.), pp. 59–80. Durgnat attributes Concha's deathly return to a vampish sadism that "springs from class vindictiveness." Durgnat, "Six Films of Josef von Sternberg," p. 30. Sarris lends Concha's association with death the romantic poeticism of his own prose: "Black quite simply means death, and Marlene may be one of many deaths for both Atwill and Sternberg, the death of art, of poise, of poetry, of inspiration, of the will to continue" (*The Films of Josef von Sternberg*, p. 42).
18. Genette (ed.), *Figures of Literary Discourse*, p. 216.
19. Von Sternberg, p. 56.
20. Sacher-Masoch, *Venus in Furs*, pp. 223–24.
21. Mulvey, "Visual Pleasure and Narrative Cinema," pp. 11–12.
22. Sacher-Masoch, *Venus in Furs*, p. 194.
23. John Baxter calls attention to the stork/fish motif in *The Cinema of Josef von Sternberg* (New York: A. A. Barnes, 1971), p. 124.
24. Thomas Mann, *Confessions of Felix Krull, Confidence Man* (New York: Random House, 1955), p. 79.
25. Sacher-Masoch, *Venus in Furs*, p. 160.
26. Ibid., p. 179.
27. Durgnat, "Six Films of Josef von Sternberg," p. 31. Concha's costuming is all that is left of Conchita's stay in a convent in the original source material. See Pierre Louys, *Woman and Puppet*, trans. G. F. Monkshood (London: Greening, 1908).
28. Pignatari, p. 93.
29. Zucker, p. 18.
30. Maurice Blanchot, *L'entretien infini*, quoted in Regis Durand, "The Disposition of the Voice," in *Performance in Postmodern Culture*, ed. Michel Benamou and Charles Caramello (Milwaukee: Coda Press and The Center for 20th-Century Studies, 1977), p. 110.
31. The iconic sign always contains the possibility of foregrounding its participation in performance; it is a sign that inherently displays, poses, and playacts.
32. Von Sternberg, p. 322.
33. Loewald, p. 203; see also Marks, pp. 102–3. Loewald remarks: "In the course of the development of civilization, of the variegated ways in which language becomes both reduced and elevated to a vehicle for civilized human communication and expression of thought and feelings and for abstract thought, the primordial power and concrete impact of language become attenuated and relatively neutralized, as the density of the primary process gives way to the discursiveness and articulation of secondary process. In most creative forms of language such as . . .

poetry, and dramatic art, the primordial power of language comes again to the fore" (p. 203–4).

34. Loewald, p. 187.
35. Pignatari, pp. 94–95.
36. Loewald, pp. 202–3.
37. John Kobal, *Marlene Dietrich* (London: Studio Vista, 1968), p. 59.
38. Burgin, p. 62.
39. Sarris, *The Films of Josef von Sternberg*, p. 8.
40. Sacher-Masoch, *Venus in Furs*, p. 145.
41. Von Sternberg, pp. 219, 321.
42. Sarris, *The Films of Josef von Sternberg*, p. 23.
43. Audibert, p. 96.
44. Wood, "The Play of Light and Shade," p. 99.
45. Von Sternberg, p. 219.

Chapter Eight: Masochism and the Perverse
Pleasures of the Cinematic Apparatus

1. Jean-Louis Baudry, "The Apparatus," *Camera Obscura*, no. 1 (Fall 1976): 119.
2. Ibid.
3. Ibid., pp. 116–18. Bertram Lewin, to whom Baudry refers, commented: "That the ego boundaries are lost in sleep and dreams we know . . . the dreamer, or sleeper, remains in unified contact with the breast. . . . The sleeper has identified himself with the breast . . . and become divested of his body—which is then lost, merged in its identification with the vastly enlarged and flattened breast, the dream screen. In short, the sleeper has lost his ego boundaries because when he went to sleep he became united with the breast." Lewin, "Sleep, the Mouth, and the Dream Screen," *Psychoanalytic Quarterly* 15 (1946): 427. See also Lewin, *The Psychoanalysis of Elation* (New York: W. W. Norton, 1961), pp. 146–74; and Lewin, "Inferences from the Dream Screen," *International Journal of Psycho-Analysis* 29 (1948): 224–31.
4. Baudry believes that the dream screen and the cinema have a privileged relationship to orality as a governing metaphor and as a modality of reception: "It may seem peculiar that desire which constituted the cine-effect is rooted in the oral structure of the subject. The conditions of projection do evoke the dialectics internal/external, swallowing/swallowed, eating/being eaten, which is characteristic of what is being structured during the oral phase. But, in the case of the cinematographic situation, the visual orifice has replaced the buccal orifice: the absorption of images is at the same time the absorption of the subject in the image, prepared, predigested by his very entering the dark theater. The relationship visual orifice/buccal orifice acts at the same time as analogy and differentiation, but also points to the relation of consecution be-

tween oral satisfaction, sleep, white screen of the dream on which dream images will be projected, beginning of the dream" (p. 125). For a psychoanalytic view of the association between orality, a regressive perceptual modality, and "screen" images see Frank, pp. 48–77. See also Stoller, *Perversion*, p. 148; and Kubie, p. 216.

5. Eberwein, pp. 48–53; and Eberwein, *Film and the Dream Screen* (Princeton: Princeton University Press, 1984).

6. Lewin, "Sleep, the Mouth, and the Dream Screen," pp. 420–21.

7. Baudry, p. 117.

8. Ibid., p. 118.

9. Eberwein, "Reflections on the Breast," p. 53.

10. Eberwein, *Film and the Dream Screen*, pp. 34–40.

11. In classical Freudian theory, the female is theorized as experiencing a negative castration complex resulting from the trauma of coping with her lack of a penis. See Freud, "Female Sexuality," pp. 234–35. In Lacanian theory, the female's negative entry into the symbolic is stressed.

12. Keiser, "Body Ego during Orgasm," p. 163.

13. M. Masud Khan, "The Function of Intimacy and Acting Out in Perversion," *Sexual Behavior and the Law*, ed. Ralph Slovenko (Springfield, Ill.: Charles C. Thomas, 1965), pp. 402–3.

14. Ibid., p. 400. Khan observes that perversions are much more on the order of dreaming and acting out through dreams than are neuroses.

15. Deleuze, p. 17.

16. Loewald, pp. 160–63. Loewald maintains that the loss of the love object is the strongest stimulant to memorial activity.

17. Ibid., p. 165.

18. Ibid., p. 400.

19. Mastery was never defined by Freud as an instinctual drive, although he considered the Death Instinct (Thanatos) as a primal drive toward a return to nothingness, to stasis. The compelling link between compulsion and masochism is pursued briefly by Silverman in "Masochism and Subjectivity." Although he never uses the word masochism, Brooks also considers compulsion and the repetition of unpleasurable experience from a point of view that could well encompass a theory of masochism (operating within Freud's notion of the Death Instinct; pp. 280–300).

20. Silverman, "Masochism and Subjectivity," pp. 2–3. Silverman's characterization of the *fort/da* game as affording the pleasure of "false recovery" and loss is persuasive, but she sustains the misleading principle that masochism can be unproblematically equated with passivity (p. 3). While Silverman pursues the issue on the basis of instinct theory, it is more logical to approach masochism as an ego function (object relations or "social" defense) than as an instinct, especially from a feminist perspective. See Esther Menaker, "Masochism—a Defense Reaction of the Ego," *Psychoanalytic Quarterly* 22 (1953): 205–9.

21. Loewald, p. 67.

22. Ibid., pp. 67–68.

23. Laplanche and Pontalis, pp. 482–83.
24. Horowitz, pp. 139–50. Horowitz refers to "unbidden images," that is, intrusions into perceptions that "enter awareness under their own autonomy" and signal the perceiver's loss of ego autonomy over image formation—a situation not unlike the cinema. See also D. Galin, "Hemispheric Specialization: Implications for Psychiatry," in *Biological Foundations of Psychiatry*, ed. Robert Grenell and Sabit Gabay (New York: Raven Press, 1976), pp. 132–58.
25. Kris, *Psychoanalytic Explorations in Art*, p. 54.
26. Keiser, "Body Ego during Orgasm," p. 164.
27. Winnicott, p. 9. The dream screen might be considered the child's first "not-me" possession, the magically introjected breast that serves as the precursor to the child's first fetishistic transitional objects.
28. Judith S. Kestenberg and Joan Weinstein, "Transitional Objects and Body-Image Formation," in Grolnick et al. (ed.), p. 82. Kestenberg and Weinstock comment on the dream screen's function: "A good dream screen is like a good blanket; it shields one from distraction and maintains one's identity as a requisite for undisturbed drive satisfaction. By providing a framework for memory and imagery, it ensures a harmonious integration between external and internal reality. By reuniting the dreamer with the original drive object, it facilitates continuity and yet gives free rein to illusory play with space, weight, and time." Film, like dream, promises a perceptual unity (with the dream screen) which—paradoxically—forms the basis of the pleasures of the fragmented self and multiple, shifting identifications.
29. David Rapaport, "Conclusion: Toward a Theory of Thinking," in Rapaport (ed.), p. 696.
30. Laplanche and Pontalis, pp. 482–83.
31. Keiser, "Body Ego during Orgasm," p. 163.
32. Doane, "Misrecognition and Identity," p. 28. The theoretical application of Lacan's theory of mirror misrecognition to film ignores the significant fact that the film images cannot be controlled by the subject, nor do they offer mirror-likeness except in the very broadest sense of represented bodies to spectatorial body. Mastery over the signifier seems the most tenuous rather than the most obvious of filmic pleasures.
33. Ibid.
34. Mahler et al., p. 8; M. Mahler and B. Gosliner, "On Symbiotic Child Psychosis: Genetic, Dynamic and Restitutive Aspects," *The Psychoanalytic Study of the Child* 10 (1955): 198. For a lucid overview of Mahler's position on the narcissism of the undifferentiated self/object see Jay R. Greenberg and Stephen A. Mitchell, *Object Relations in Psychoanalytic Theory* (Cambridge: Harvard University Press, 1983), pp. 287–90.
35. Mahler, *On Human Symbiosis*, I:216.
36. Freud, "The Ego and the Id," p. 27.
37. Chodorow, p. 64; Edith Jacobson, *The Self and the Object World* (New York: International Universities Press, 1964), pp. 35–36.

38. Jacobson, pp. 35–36.
39. Freud, "Female Sexuality," p. 236.
40. Spitz, pp. 72–78.
41. Ibid., pp. 114–15.
42. Keiser, "Body Ego during Orgasm," p. 161. According to Keiser, if the body ego is insufficiently established, the wish to be loved becomes equated with annihilation (p. 166).
43. Mahler et al., p. 45.
44. Kestenberg and Weinstein, p. 82; Joseph Kepecs, "A Waking Screen Analogous to the Dream Screen," *Psychoanalytic Quarterly* 21 (1952): 167–71.
45. Winnicott, pp. 111–12.
46. Dickes, "Parents, Transitional Objects, and Childhood Fetishes," pp. 304–7.
47. Bak, "Fetishism," p. 292. Although Bak affirms the importance of identification with the mother in the formation of fetishism, he adheres to the view that castration fear and the fantasy of the maternal phallus are of central importance to all perversions. In a later article, he denounces theories that argue for an infantile fetishism independent of castration fear. Bak is adamant that true fetishism must function to bring about orgasm. Pre-Oedipal fetishes and transitional objects, he maintains, have a different sexual function related to separation anxiety and identification with the penisless mother. However, he admits that castration anxiety can be exacerbated by early object loss (abandonment) trauma. Bak does not believe fetishism depends upon a defensive ego splitting but upon the "uncertainty [that] helps maintain oscillatory identification with either parent, prevents the clear demarcation of the two sexes that would lead to certainty of sexual identity, and sustains a bisexual position, by fused self-representations." Bak, "Distortions in the Concept of Fetishism," *The Psychoanalytic Study of the Child* 29 (1974): 205. See also Bak, "The Phallic Woman," p. 16. Imre Hermann associates the desire to cling to the mother's body with masochism as a reaction formula to anxiety. See Hermann, "Clinging and Going in Search: The Relationship to Sadism and Masochism," *Psychoanalytic Quarterly* 45 (1976): 5–36. P. J. Van der Leeuw theorizes that masochism results from the child's wish to escape feelings of helplessness. Relief is found in "masochism or in clinging to the primary identification" (p. 369).
48. Metz, *The Imaginary Signifier*, pp. 48, 53.
49. Chodorow, p. 68.
50. Winnicott, p. 111. Freud regarded the child's later rejection of the mother as partially (and very strongly) founded on the disappointment of weaning: "A second reproach, which does not reach quite so far back, is a rather surprising one. It is that her mother did not give her enough milk, did not suckle her long enough. . . . It would seem rather that this accusation gives expression to the general dissatisfaction of children, who, in our monogamous civilization, are weaned from the breast after

six or nine months, whereas the primitive mother devotes herself exclusively to her child for two or three years. It is as though our children had remained forever unsated, as though they had never sucked long enough at their mother's breast." Freud, "Female Sexuality," p. 234.

51. Chodorow, p. 60.
52. Mahler, "On the First Three Subphases," p. 338.
53. Loewald, p. 47. Loewald refers to this fantasized state of ego perfection as one attained in the undifferentiation of self from environment: the ego and ego-ideal in fantasized merger. It is properly only within the context of this merger that infantile omnipotence should be discussed (p. 19).
54. Frank, p. 56.
55. Freud, "Civilization and Its Discontents," p. 68.
56. Ibid., p. 68.
57. Loewald, p. 11.
58. Ibid., pp. 16–17.
59. Freud, "Female Sexuality," p. 235.
60. W. Gillespie, "Notes on an Analysis of Sexual Perversion," *International Journal of Psycho-Analysis* 33 (1952): 397.
61. Chodorow, p. 60. Chodorow continues: "Orality and the oral attitude of incorporation (the fantasy of taking in the mother or her breast) as a primary infantile mode, for instance, is not an inevitable extrapolation from nursing. It is one defensive technique for retaining primary identification (a sense of oneness) when this is being eroded—when the mother is beginning to be experienced as a separate person. Or, for instance, the infant's internalization of aspects of its relationship to its mother which are experienced as bad often results in splitting off and repression of that part of the ego involved in this bad relationship. This internalization avoids reacting to these bad aspects in the outside world and possibly driving the infant's mother away. Separateness during this early period threatens not only anxiety at possible loss, but the infant's very sense of existence."
62. Loewald, p. 17.
63. Ibid.
64. Chodorow, p. 79.
65. Ibid.
66. Coppelia Kahn makes this point in "The Hand That Rocks the Cradle: Recent Gender Theories and Their Implications," in *Mother Tongue,* eds. Shirley Nelson Garner, Claire Kahane, and Madelon Sprengnether (Ithaca: Cornell University Press, 1985), p. 88. Freud discusses identification in "Mourning and Melancholia" (1917), *SE* 14:237–58.
67. Jim Swan, "*Mater* and Nannie: Freud's Two Mothers and the Discovery of the Oedipus Complex," *American Imago* 31 (1974): 9–10. See also Chasseguet-Smirgel, "Freud and Female Sexuality," p. 283.
68. Laplanche, p. 103.

Index

A Note on the Author

Gaylyn Studlar is currently an assistant professor of film studies at Emory University. She also has taught at North Texas State University and the University of California at Santa Barbara. Studlar earned her Ph.D. in cinema studies from the University of Southern California and has previously published in *Film Quarterly*, *Frauen und Film*, and the *Quarterly Review of Film Studies*, among other journals. In addition to her work in film, she is a cellist, earning the Master of Music degree from the University of Southern California.